Social Work with the Aged
and Their Families

MODERN APPLICATIONS OF SOCIAL WORK

Edited by JAMES K. WHITTAKER

James Garbarino and Patrick Brookhauser, **Safe Environments for Handicapped Children: Dealing with the Abuse and Neglect of Special Children.** 1987.

Roberta R. Greene, **Social Work with the Aged and Their Families.** 1986.

Francine Jacobs and Heather B. Weiss, **Evaluating Family Programs.** 1987.

Harry H. Vorrath and Larry K. Brendtro, **Positive Peer Culture.** Second Edition 1985.

Ralph E. Anderson and Irl Carter, **Human Behavior in the Social Environment.** Third Edition 1984.

Anthony M. Graziano and Kevin C. Mooney, **Children and Behavior Therapy.** 1984.

Larry K. Brendtro and Arlin E. Ness, **Re-Educating Troubled Youth.** 1983.

James K. Whittaker and James Garbarino, **Social Support Networks.** 1983.

James Garbarino, **Children and Families in the Social Environment.** 1982.

Norman A. Polansky, **Integrated Ego Psychology.** 1982.

George Thorman, **Helping Troubled Families.** 1982.

Steven P. Schinke (ed.), **Behavioral Methods in Social Welfare.** 1981.

Social Work with the Aged
and Their Families

Roberta R. Greene

ALDINE DE GRUYTER
New York

About the Author

Roberta Rubin Greene is a Senior Staff Associate for Family Practice Advancement, National Association of Social Workers, Inc., Silver Spring, Maryland. She is a major contributor to various professional journals and is the author of *Continuing Education for Gerontological Careers*.

Aldine de Gruyter (Formerly Aldine Publishing Company)
Division of Walter de Gruyter, Inc.
200 Saw Mill River Road
Hawthorne, New York 10532

Library of Congress Cataloging-in-Publication Data

Greene, Roberta, 1940–
    Social work with the aged and their families.

    Bibliography: p.
    Includes index.
    1. Social work with the aged. 2. Aged—Family relationships. 3. Family social work. 4. Intergenerational relations. I. Title.
HV1451.G74   1986   362.6′042   86-4483
ISBN 0-202-36043-1 (lib. bdg.)
ISBN 0-202-36044-X (pbk.)

Printed in the United States
10 9 8 7 6 5 4 3 2 1

Contents

PREFACE

The major objective of this book is to develop the social worker's capacity for direct practice with the aged, their families, and with societal agents with whom he/she interact. It provides a framework for implementing comprehensive psychosocial diagnosis within a family context and social work intervention based on a clinical understanding of the aged persons, the family, the community, and institutional environments.

This work is an outgrowth of the demand and need for geriatric services in the United States, which have grown dramatically in recent years—a phenomenon that in large measure is a response to the increases in the number and proportion of aged individuals in our population.

While most persons over 65 years of age are relatively well-functioning individuals, a sizable minority is likely to experience various forms of economic, social, and emotional distress.

Over the years, and despite federal funding, there has been a critical shortage of qualified personnel in all allied health professions that serve the aged (Federal Council on Aging, 1978). Moreover, if present trends continue, about 80% of the elderly who need assistance for emotional and mental problems will never be served (Butler, 1978). By providing a framework for specialized social work practice with the aged and their families, it is hoped that a contribution will be made to meet that need.

Most elderly Americans, four-fifths of all people over 65 years of age, have living children. Psychological distress in the aging needs to be addressed within the context of these family relationships.

Social and demographic changes over the last several decades have had a dramatic effect on family structure. As a result of these demographic changes and demand for services, schools of social work are experiencing widening interest in the field of aging. There is an ever-increasing need for educational materials that can address the distinct forms of up-to-date knowledge, attitudes, and skills for competent social work practice with the aged and their families.

The purpose of this text, which introduces the Functional-Age Model of Intergenerational Therapy, is to provide social workers, as well as other direct service practitioners, with a systematic family approach to this topic. It is an innovative view of treatment that can be used wherever an older adult is part of the family constellation and is designed to provide a method for assessment and treatment within a family context. As an intergenerational treatment model, it is concerned with both the elderly person's functioning and the family system in which it takes place. By offering a holistic and systematic way of looking at biopsychosocial problems related to the aging process, it provides a framework to be used in gathering and integrating information about the client system.

The text is organized into two major sections. Part I provides information needed to formulate a psychosocial assessment of the older adult's functional age within his/her family system. It will enable the student to clearly understand and define the problems within the family system by providing an understanding of the aging process. Part II deals with the selection and implementation of a range of intervention strategies. In short, this text will enable the selection and application of appropriate therapeutic modalities based on clinical understanding of the behaviors of the aged person and his/her family systems.

The author would like to thank her family and friends for all their support while she was writing this book; their encouragement never went unnoticed. I would also like to thank a number of people who contributed to the preparation of the manuscript. I am most grateful to Margaret Rafner who edited the book and commented on the contents from a practice perspective. To Inge Engel who typed this manuscript my special gratitude. A note of thanks to my colleagues who contributed case examples—Paulette Nehama of the Jewish Social Service of Greater Washington, Geraldine Brittain and Rachael Roberts of the Family and Child Services of Washington, D.C., and Edith Fleshner and her staff at the Hebrew Home of Greater Washington.

A special word of thanks to Dr. Jirina Polivka for her contributions to this book and her help in conceptualizing the model. Finally, I would particularly like to acknowledge the Council on Social Work Education for allowing me to use some of the materials I developed for their national curriculum project funded by a grant from the U.S. Department of Health and Human Services, Administration on Aging, #90AT0120 entitled *Continuing Education for Gerontological Careers*.

Roberta R. Greene

IN REMINISCENCE

Nancy Alison Greene

In Memory of Sadie Rubin—
My Mother and Nancy's Grandmother,
Roberta R. Greene

She wore a stunning gold locket around her graceful neck and had a fourteen-carat gold heart to go with it. When she spoke there was an unmistakable southern twang in her voice and she had all the southern hospitality to accompany it. She didn't live a charmed life but was willing to give you her all—if that's what it took.

I was young and didn't understand when she told me, "do this," "try not to do that," and "it's for your own good." Now, I know, it was caring—caring *about* me and caring *for* me. Very few people take the time to do that for anyone but she cared for everyone. She cared for you if you were the queen of England or a black person in the 1950s who needed a seat on the bus after a long day's work.

I remember nonsignificant things: who polished my nails first, taught me to click my tongue, and bought clothes at her favorite shop. Things only I should remember. When I got older she was my "Ann Landers" and I wrote her every few weeks. One week I got a package in the mail. It was the locket I admired. A few weeks later she died. Farewell, Grandma.

CHAPTER

1

A New Practice Model for Intergenerational
Family Treatment

Within the past several decades, theoreticians, researchers, and practitioners have become increasingly interested in the aged and the aging process. The last 20 years have seen a burgeoning of information related to the scientific and systematic study of aging known as gerontology. As a result, gerontologists have been able to draw from many related disciplines in order to better understand the biological, psychological, and social aspects of aging.

With each theoretical advance and the expansion of the knowledge base came information pertinent to professional social work as practiced with older adults and their families. This text provides an integrative theoretical framework for social workers interested in mental health practice with this segment of the population. The framework is based upon a philosophy that maximizes self-actualization for all family members, supports both interdependence and autonomy within the family system, and enhances the quality of life across the generations. Concepts selected represent the major converging conceptual trends that form a practice and knowledge base for intergenerational family therapy. While many of these ideas have been conceived independently, the purpose of this text is to provide the theoretical linkages between ideas and concepts. The text not only utilizes some of the existing theoretical ideas about therapy with the aged, it also introduces and expands new areas for practice consistent with effective social casework with the elderly and their families.

Over the last two decades, geriatric social workers in agencies across the country have experimented with established social work techniques in an attempt to find more appropriate ways of working with their elderly clients. The challenge of devising holistic yet specialized services has had mixed results and has given birth to many diverse services and programs. Some have centered around the delivery of concrete services, which meet the physical needs of the elderly, such as Meals-on-Wheels or home health care. Others (such as stroke rehabilitation groups or nursing home preadmission counseling) involve modified casework techniques to provide supportive services to elderly clients and their adult children.

The pressure to develop new treatment modes in geriatric social work has come from a variety of sources. As the numbers and proportion of elderly persons in the United States population rapidly increased, so, too, did the demand for geriatric services. In 1900, those age 65 and over, three million people, represented only 3% of the total population. As of 1980, there were more than 25 million people 65 or older, a figure representing 11% of the population. By the year 2000, close to 32 million Americans will enter these ranks. In addition, the percentage of elderly people in the population, compared to the number of persons under 18, is expected to continue to rise well into the next century (American Assoc. of Retired Persons, 1984).

While most persons over 65 are relatively well-functioning individuals, a sizable minority is likely to experience various forms of emotional, social, and/or economic distress. According to the 1981 White House Conference on Aging, it is estimated that 15–25% of Americans over 65 will experience significant symptoms of mental illness. These demographic changes, along with related sociocultural trends and problems, have given impetus to social work agencies to find additional ways of working with this growing clientele. National policy and legislative initiatives, such as Title XIX and XX, Medicare and the Older Americans Act, have also contributed to service development.

Despite the recognition of need and advances in social service programs for elderly clients, very few (family) practice models have appeared in the literature (see Eyde and Rich, 1983; Silverstone and Burack-Weiss, 1983). It should be acknowledged, however, that the goal of closing the gap between social work theory and social work practice is difficult to achieve. It involves the integration of the most current knowledge of human behavior and the adaptation of existing methods and techniques.

One might rightly ask if the existing methods used to assist other client groups are not also suitable for helping the elderly. While there are those who would agree that following established methods can achieve positive results, there are practitioners who believe that new treatment models are needed as well. This point of view grew out of general frustration with the methods and delivery systems used with other client populations, which were all too often found to be inappropriate for older clients, and was supported as work in the field clearly began to demonstrate the necessity for additional knowledge and skills to provide optimum help to the elderly and their families.

Dissatisfaction with existing practice techniques on the part of caseworkers serving the elderly has brought about modifications in the more traditional treatment skills and techniques. New knowledge about human behavior and the aging process has also contributed to changes in treatment. Stereotypes and attitudes toward aging and the aged were examined, too, as geriatric practitioners recognized their critical role in service delivery. Gradually, as a result of these multiple factors, new treatment ideas have been developed. While many geriatric caseworkers have been using new methods and techniques for a number of years, not enough has been done to conceptualize and bring together this information in a form that could be used by other professionals. This text, which describes the functional-age model for intergenerational therapy, is such a synthesis.

This chapter discusses the evolution of the model as an outgrowth of the psychosocial method. It also describes how the delivery of services in the field led to modifications in that method in order to better serve the elderly client. In addition, it defines and presents the rationale for the inclusion of the model's various components. Chapters 3 through 12 describe the content of the model as it relates to assessment and treatment, and provide suggestions for the model's application.

THE HISTORICAL DEVELOPMENT OF THE PSYCHOSOCIAL METHOD: ITS CONTRIBUTIONS TO THE MODEL

The functional-age model of intergenerational therapy is derived from the casework approach most often associated with social work—the psychosocial treatment method. The first caseworkers in the field of geriatric social work were often trained in this eclectic form of practice, which seeks to enhance personal and social functioning. It is a process used in defining the client's problem and determining casework interventions; it focuses on the client's inner psychological issues and the social context in which they take place. Casework from the psychosocial perspective rests on individualized treatment and aims to provide optimum conditions for human growth and development.

Psychosocial therapy encompasses both the general and unique tradition of social work by striking a middle ground between intra- and interpersonal relationships. This means that the caseworker who employs this treatment method is interested in the client's psychological development as well as his/her social and environmental situation. A psychosocial assessment is employed as a tool to study the strengths of the client's personality and to mobilize the resources of the environment needed to improve interpersonal functioning (Hamilton, 1951; Hollis, 1977). In brief, the caseworker works with the client to achieve an understanding of the problem (assessment) in order to work toward the resolution or alleviation of his/her difficulties (treatment).

The psychosocial approach, ideally suited for understanding elderly clients and their families in a variety of life circumstances, is "based on an open theoretical system" (Hollis, 1977, p. 130). As a problem-solving method it has a rich historical base, and its current practice, which reflects this multifaceted theoretical heritage, is quite diverse. In fact, the psychosocial method has been influenced by such a wide range of thought systems that it becomes difficult to establish precise boundaries for the term. This text presents those assessment and treatment components of the method thought to be most pertinent to social work with the aged and their families. Together they constitute the major building blocks of the functional-age model of intergenerational treatment (see Table 1.1).

Throughout its history, the psychosocial approach has drawn from many sources, augmenting its knowledge base and adopting innovative and diverse interventive strategies. The addition of new theoretical stances has resulted in an even wider range of treatment modalities that provide a broad foundation for today's practitioner. The roots of the psychosocial method can be traced to the Charity Organization Society movement and its concern with the alleviation of poverty (Garrett, 1950). During those beginning years, caseworkers supplied their clients with material services and tried to help them deal with economic, social, and health problems. Stressful social issues were a concern, and interventions centered on encouraging individual responsibility and improving coping skills. Subsequently, greater interest developed in internal or personality factors.

The works of Richmond (1917, 1922) best reflect social work's early interest in improving socioeconomic conditions through individual adjustment. She defines casework as "those processes which develop personality through adjustments consciously effected, individual by individual between men and their environment" (Richmond, 1922, p. 98).

The early definition of casework as a psychosocial method of intervention led to an interest in how clients' adjustment is affected by their cultural milieu and set the stage for including both personality issues and environmental factors in assessment. It also heightened the recognition of the need for an orderly and logical method for assembling information about these matters. As a result, a study-diagnosis-treatment format emerged as a medium for clarifying client needs and problems, and the aim of the practitioner became one of effecting change in the person, the environment and/or both (Hamilton, 1951; Janchill, 1969). This holistic view is clearly reflected in the functional-age model. Historically, the psychosocial method has maintained its concern with the individual *and* his/her environment; however, it has not always placed equal emphasis on both factors. During the 1930's, the Great Depression kept alive the need for direct environmental intervention. At the same time, however, Freudian theory brought about a major change in casework practice, shifting the focus from *problem* to *person* (Janchill, 1969). Caseworkers gave increasing attention to pathological behaviors and unconscious personality issues. Concepts such as relationship, transference, and resistance were incorporated into social work practice and emotional difficulties thought to produce social maladjustment were of major concern. Psychoanalytic theory became the primary resource for understanding human behavior and for diagnosing clients. Caseworkers turned to studying an individual's *current* behaviors in the light of his/her *past* experiences. Thus, history-taking came to be a central component in the psychosocial treatment method.

The id–ego–superego triad, used as a means for examining personality structure and the ego's effectiveness in promoting well-being, was another Freudian concept that influenced psychosocial casework practice. This approach to studying personality was modified as well as strengthened by neo-Freudians and continues to be part of the treatment method employed by many caseworkers today. Its usefulness has been in providing an understanding of ego functioning, in evaluating ego strengths and in providing techniques for ego support (Anderson and Carter, 1978; Perlman, 1957). Both Freudian and neo-Freudian thought have had a major impact on casework and other therapies with the aged. In general, Freudians have held a negative view of the capacity of the elderly to engage in insight-oriented treatment, often leading to discrimination in service delivery (see chapter XIII). However, some geriatric caseworkers have employed selected psychoanalytic concepts in their therapy with older adults. The functional-age model incorporates the psychodynamic approach to personality and the concept of transference as it applies to the therapeutic relationship.

While initially classical Freudian theory may be said to have had a negative effect on the field of gerontology, neo-Freudian views, as represented by Erikson (1950), have given new direction to clinical practice with the aged. With their emphasis on introspection, self-concept and adjustment to loss, they have provided practitioners with a psychiatry of the life cycle. Erikson's contributions to the functional-age model are reflected throughout the text, particularly in the discussion of life review.

While psychosocial casework reflects the influence of Freudian and neo-Freudian thought, it has also utilized psychological and sociological theories in developing its knowledge and practice base. Throughout the 1940's and 1950's, the behavioral sciences supplied many useful ideas for social work practice. Some, such as role theory, have added a whole new dimension to psychosocial practice by providing a

TABLE 1.1. Theoretical Foundations of the Functional-Age Intergenerational Treatment Model

Time frame[a]	Major theorist(s)	Theory	Major theme	Concepts adopted for the model
1915–1920 Classic 1940, 1951 1964, 1952	Mary Richmond Gordon Hamilton Florence Hollis	Social diagnosis	Improving economic and social conditions through personality adjustment	1. The importance of socioeconomic conditions to personal well-being 2. The need for a psychosocial study format
1930's Classic 1940–1950	Sigmund Freud Lucille Austin	Psychoanalytic theory	Understanding emotional difficulties that produce social maladjustments	1. The role of the client-worker relationship in therapy 2. The historical view of personality assessment 3. The place of unconscious motivations in daily functioning
1950 Classic 1963, 1968	Erik Erikson Robert Butler	Ego psychology	Promoting the ego's effectiveness in enhancing psychosocial well-being	1. The integrity of ego-functions throughout the life cycle 2. The place of reminiscence in adaptation
1934 1936, 1945 1951 1959 1968	George Herbert Mead Ralph Linton Talcott Parsons Ervin Goffman Helen Harris Perlman	Role theory	Studying social functioning as an interactional process	1. Patterns of behavior as they relate to social position(s) 2. The link between personal identity and social (family) identity

6

Date[a]	Theorist	Theory	Focus	Key concepts
1950, 1968 1968	Ludwig von Bertalanffy Walter Buckley	Systems theory	Observing behaviors and effecting change at a multidimensional/interactional level	1. The family as a dynamic system 2. The relevance of all levels of societal systems
1954 1963 1973 1971	Nathan Ackerman Virginia Satir Ivan Boszormeny-Nagy Murray Bowen	Family therapy	Viewing the family as treatment unit	1. The family as a focus for assessment and change 2. The dynamics of change in a family system
1961 1961 1963	Jurgen Ruesch Don Jackson Virginia Satir	Communications theory	Linking family problems to communication and organization	1. Family patterns of communication as a means to organization 2. Organization as a means to meeting needs
1950	Erik Erikson	Developmental family theory	Understanding the family as a developing unit with phase-specific tasks	1. The historical development of the family as an assessment tool 2. Family development tasks as "normal" crises

[a]Refers to publication dates.

conceptual bridge between psychological and sociological processes (Ackerman, 1957). With role theory as an assessment and treatment tool, caseworkers have been better able to give ample attention to the social and cultural influences on behavior. Problems have been addressed in *interactional* as well as *intrapsychic* terms. As caseworkers began to take a greater interest in patterns of communication and interaction, particularly among family members, they found that role theory was an important vehicle for maintaining the person-in-the-situation stance. Inasmuch as role theory helps the practitioner understand the continuous interplay between the person and his/her social experience, it is given major emphasis in the functional-age model. As seen in chapter 8, understanding the family as an interactional unit permits the caseworker to assess individual identity as expressed in the family group. Role theory also allows the practitioner to evaluate reciprocal or complementary family role behaviors (Ackerman, 1957; Perlman, 1968). Role analysis not only provides an efficient means of understanding the individual and his/her family situation, it can also lend itself to an appreciation of the biological aspects of role performance. Each role is composed of a number of activities that include psychological, physical, and social considerations, all of which are essential to satisfactory task performance. Since a biopsychosocial approach is particularly essential to social work with the aged and their families, the role concept makes a substantial contribution to the functional-age model presented in the text.

If role analysis can be viewed as an effective vehicle for defining and clarifying many aspects of biopsychosocial functioning, then systems theory can be considered the very essence of the psychosocial method (Hollis, 1970). Systems theory sees the human personality in constant interplay with the surroundings, with each adjusting to changes in the other. It is therefore ideally suited to offer "a framework in which social interaction can be objectively and comprehensively understood without jeopardy to the work of individualization" (Janchill, p. 148).

Systems theory, with its inherently multidimensional and multidisciplinary nature, has had a major impact on social work thought. It permits the caseworker to understand and treat a client without dichotomizing internal and external factors.

The value of the systems approach to the geriatric caseworker is best expressed by Berger and Federico (1982):

> Systems theory is helpful to the social worker in the struggle to incorporate information from multiple sources into a coherent whole. A systems approach is inherently multidisciplinary and calls upon the practitioner to draw from many social, behavioral, and biological disciplines rather than having an allegiance to any one discipline. Viewing the individual in interaction with environmental forces sharpens our focus for both assess-

ment and intervention purposes and supports a process view of life consistent with professional purpose (Berger and Federico, p. 40).

The area of social work practice most influenced by general systems theory has been family therapy. While family interviews have long been a part of casework practice, it was not until the mid-1950's that this method of treatment came to the fore. Caseworkers came to see that whenever one member of a family is in trouble, all are in trouble, and that as practitioners they must be prepared to turn to family-centered interventive methodologies. As a result, family therapy was readily adopted into the psychosocial method, thus providing a greater opportunity to view the person as both an individual and as a member of the family.

The recognition of the family as a system and treatment unit of choice is central to the functional-age model. The model emphasizes the interdependence among family members as well as the dynamics of change. It necessitates that the caseworker evaluate and treat the family as an organizational structure that is a functioning whole, and suggests that systems theory be seen as the integrating tool to accomplish this end.

As therapists utilized several of the theoretical facets of role, system, and small group theories in their orientation to treatment, they began to employ communications theory to analyze casework as a helping process (Strean, 1971). Communication, the transfer of information within and between systems, was observed to be closely related to organization. This realization led to a concern about how family problems could be addressed through an alteration in the forms of communication among its members. The therapist's task from this point of view is that of studying interactional patterns and helping families to employ clear or functional modes of communication. The functional-age model makes particular use of these concepts in chapter 10.

Family developmental theory, the newest concept to be included in the psychosocial method, is an outgrowth of family systems thinking. The interplay between individual and family development was the next logical step in the search for a holistic approach to evaluation and treatment. Just as therapists came to realize that the family group is more than a number of individual personalities, so, too, did family developmentalists come to accept that family development is more than "a collection of individual life cycles" (Carter and McGoldrick, 1980). Rather, family development focuses on the interweaving of historical and biological time. It suggests that different tasks take center stage at various phases of family development, and the family's adaptational capacity is challenged at each stage. This concept has had a major impact on the functional-age model, which examines and offers treatment techniques appropriate to families with members who may be in various stages of the life cycle.

In summary, the psychosocial method has evolved from a number of different theories. This text has adopted those that offer a psychodynamic approach to intergenerational treatment spanning intrapsychic, interpersonal, and developmental dimensions. The aim is to provide the practitioner with a comprehensive framework that will enable him/her to assess and treat the older adult within a family context. (It should be stated that while the model places an emphasis on working with the family, it does provide sufficient information and techniques for practice with the older adult whose family is not available.)

THE FUNCTIONAL-AGE MODEL

Change of Emphasis in the Psychosocial Treatment Method

Despite its rich and diverse assessment and treatment base, the psychosocial casework method has fallen short of meeting the needs of certain client groups, one of which is the elderly. Clinical experience has led the author to believe that an intergenerational casework approach requires certain changes in emphasis in the psychosocial treatment method. In the following section, these factors and the reasons they have been given special attention in the functional-age model are discussed. The two major changes in perspective are: the importance of sufficiently addressing the biological aspects of the aging process; and the need for encouraging family participation in treatment.

Assessment of an elderly client needs to take into consideration the complex interplay of sociocultural, psychological, and biological factors. The social, psychological, and physical aspects of the person's functional capacity are so intimately related that all demand attention in order to understand the presenting problem and to arrive at an appropriate treatment plan. The ideal method for achieving this goal is to call upon a multidisciplinary assessment team (Gaitz and Baer, 1970). However, this is a luxury few social workers have; consequently, the geriatric practitioner must be knowledgeable in all the areas related to the client's functioning.

Geriatric social workers need to talk with clients about health-related issues, such as the number and types of medication currently being taken, as well as their side effects, and be cognizant of the ways in which various drugs impact upon mental functioning (Lowy, 1979). Body changes make the elderly particularly sensitive to drugs which can have profound effects on personality and behavior. Of particular importance are disorders that cause impairment in brain functioning. Decrements in memory, cognition, judgment, and orientation, as well as changes in affect, may be related to these organic brain disorders. Symptoms may be brought about by multi-infarct (stroke), infection, thyroid deficiencies, tumors, malnutrition, and other illnesses such as diabetes. The way in which geriatric social workers can become knowledgeable in these areas and be prepared to work with physicians and other professionals appropriately is discussed in chapter 3.

In addition to the biological aspects of the aging process, there are certain aspects of psychological functioning that have particular relevance for geriatric social work practice (Butler and Lewis, 1982; Lowy, 1979). In this regard, it is essential for the caseworker to take a complete history. Without it, the affective or emotional aspects of an elderly client's functioning cannot be fully understood. Caseworkers who actively encourage reminiscences will find that their clients often recall meaningful events in their lives. They may want to discuss their thoughts about their own aging and about their impending death. The geriatric caseworker must be open and available to listen to these issues, which are often at the core of the therapeutic process in working with the older adult. The professional can apply his/her comprehensive attention to the client only if he/she has examined his/her own attitudes about these issues (see chapters 13 and 14) and believes that older people have the potential for growth and change.

Another reason for taking an adequate history is the importance of the sociocultural factors that influence the aging process and impact upon the client's functional capacity. Just as with other client groups, each elderly person must be viewed as an individual within a social context. Despite the fact that the aged often tend to be seen as one homogeneous group, there is a wide variation among them in their norms, values, etc., relative to ethnic, religious, and cultural milieus, communities or groups. A client's position or role in a given social structure is an important variable to include in assessing and planning with and for the client. For example, social workers have been increasingly involved with older adults engaged in the retirement process. As professionals, social workers should recognize that each person has a particular view of retirement based, in large part, upon the meaning of work in that individual's culture. For instance, American society values involvement in work and devalues leisure time (Lowy, 1979). Therefore, it can be expected that retirement from work may pose emotional conflicts for many Americans. Even so, there is a wide variation among clients that requires investigation.

Perhaps what is most challenging about working with elderly clients is their position in society and the accompanying political implications. Questions related to an older person's access to public services and the general societal status of the aged are of almost daily concern to caseworkers. The extent to which practitioners engage in hearings, lobby for legislation, and participate in conferences is an individual matter. However, it is important for caseworker and client alike to understand that the ability to meet the need for services, their funding, and the general availability of programs relates, in part, to the political process. A substantial number of the problems for which services are sought must be addressed politically as well as clinically. One example is the increased number of families that have "become available" to help older members as states have developed programs to provide financial assistance to supplement family care at home. The change in policy came about through the joint lobbying efforts of caseworkers in direct practice, social planners, politicians, clients, and their families.

In summary, the geriatric social worker must develop expertise in the biological, psychological, and sociocultural aspects of aging, all of which impact upon the client's functional capacity. An understanding of these factors allows the caseworker to come to a biopsychosocial diagnosis or evaluation of the client and to establish a holistic individualized treatment plan.

An intergenerational casework approach, however, requires more than a biopsychosocial understanding of the older adult. It also demands active concern with and, wherever possible, participation by family members. Achieving a family perspective in social work with the aged and their families has been difficult at best. On the other hand, the child guidance movement and family counseling fields have long looked at the idea of the designated or identified patient with a jaundiced eye. In the 1950's these pioneers in family treatment, recognizing the need for a family perspective in both the evaluation and treatment phases of therapy, began looking at the whole family. On the other hand, intergenerational forms of family treatment involving an older adult are just in their infancy. Throughout the 1960's and 1970's, geriatric caseworkers were still urging their colleagues to use family-centered approaches in casework (Blenkner, 1965; Freed, 1975; Greene, 1977, 1978; Spark, 1974).

The tardy development of a conceptual base for this type of treatment can be traced to a number of different factors. One is the myth of alienation of older family members. Gerontologists have long been interested in the quality of relationships between the elderly and their adult children (Brody, 1966; Shanas, 1960; Sussman and Burchinal, 1962; Troll, 1971). In large measure, they have attempted to refute the myth of family alienation of the elderly, and to counter the stereotypic belief that older people are abandoned by their families and left to be cared for in institutions (Shanas, 1979). Interest has also focused on the interrelationship of demographic factors, family structure, and interactional patterns (Shanas, 1979; Treas, 1977). Issues of geographic proximity versus distance, emotional bonds, and family cohesiveness have often been the focus of research (Brody, 1984; Sussman, 1965; Sussman and Burchinal, 1962).

At the same time, the myth of family alienation has persisted within the social work community despite increasing evidence to the contrary, and many geriatric caseworkers have continued to focus on the individual client. Shanas believes that this myth of alienation actually has been created and perpetuated by professional workers in the field of aging and childless older people. Unfortunately, many social workers who see a disproportionate number of older people with little family or informal supports persist in identifying family breakdowns as alienation (Butler and Lewis, 1982; Freed, 1975).

It should be noted, however, that four fifths of all older people have living children. Most of these elderly persons, while able to live fairly independently, prefer to receive assistance where necessary from family members rather than from social service agencies. In fact, the family has been and continues to be the major source of social support for the impaired elderly (Brody 1981, 1984; Brody, Poulshock and Masciocchi, 1978). Butler and Lewis (1982) have pointed out that it is rare to find an older person who really has no family, whether it be a brother, sister, or "adopted" kin. They go on to say that, as families come in increasingly multiple forms (single-parent, two-paycheck couples, blended, etc.), they provide additional kin potential that should not be overlooked.

Yet, many social workers and the general public continue to romanticize the past and look back with nostalgia to the "cohesive" three-generation family of earlier times. There is increasing evidence that this so-called extended family of the past, where all lived under one roof, probably never existed to any great degree (Butler and Lewis, 1982; Nydegger, 1983). Recent historical studies have documented that the "typical" multigenerational household was, in fact, unusual in the English and American past. Those few people who survived to old age did not prefer to live with their children. While coresidence might have been more common, it existed mainly because of economic necessity. These households "often consisted of conglomerations of nuclear family members, unmarried siblings of the nuclear couple, lodgers, hired hands, slaves, indentured servants, apprentices. . . . " (Butler and Lewis, 1982, p. 149). Actually, it is only in modernized nations, with increased longevity, that the multigenerational family occurs with any real frequency (Brody, 1979, 1985).

Romanticized, idealized, and/or stereotypic notions of the family can stand in the way of understanding family dynamics and profoundly affect social work practice. In every society, family position or status imposes certain obligations and confers particular rights on family members (Nydegger, 1983). While these dynamics may vary widely from society to society and from one "American" family to another, they need to be understood in order to assess and treat the multigenerational family. Social workers must be careful not to over-emphasize the "ideal family" or view the elderly as passive victims of family conflict or breakdown. This approach prevents each family from being understood in its own right and can lead to the avoidance of family forms of treatment (Greene, 1978).

Another practice impeding the development of intergenerational forms of family treatment is the concentration on the dynamics of the "isolated nuclear family" rather than on the kinship system (Freed, p. 579). Research in gerontology has indicated that most older people with adult children actually live in close proximity to them, sharing mutual activities and exchanging goods and services. While studies have confirmed that there are sustained emotional bonds and respon-sible intergenerational behavior, many practitioners do not accept and integrate this fact in their current practice (Freed, 1975; Greene, 1978).

Theorists who focus on intergenerational family dynamics have pointed out that there is a major connecting link between the genera-tions based on loyalty, reciprocity, and indebtedness, which can be found to some degree in all families (Bowen, 1971; Erikson, 1950; Boszormenyi-Nagy and Spark, 1973). Erikson, one of the few life-cycle personality theorists, was among the first to stress the intergenerational nature of family dynamics; Bowen has stressed that people in each generation are healthier and more productive when viable emotional contact between generations is maintained; Nagy and Spark have discussed how each family has developed its unique code and system of exchange that must be explored in therapy. The geriatric caseworker must keep these underlying principles in mind and become more knowledgeable about intergenerational family dynamics if a family-centered casework approach is to be achieved.

A review of the practice of intergenerational forms of casework suggests still another reason for its delayed development. While the family systems approach has been adopted by caseworkers in many fields of practice, geriatric practitioners have been more reluctant to embrace it. This reluctance continues despite the large numbers of adult children calling social service agencies about their elderly parents (Greene, 1978).

All too often the family reaching out for help for an older member in crisis is not involved in the assessment and treatment process. In most instances, the presenting problem is seen as resting with the older relative who is designated as "the identified patient." The family usually comes to the agency with a specific complaint involving the older relative. "Our mother seems to forget so much lately . . . and she does some pretty strange things, too. . . . We are all pretty shaken up about it." The specificity of such a complaint makes it far too easy to identify the mother as the patient.

The conception of casework with the older adult in crisis presented in this text is different. The author suggests that the social worker reach out to the family and that the family group be viewed as the client system. The picture of the intergenerational network as the client system is rather inclusive. It may involve more than one generation or family unit. In the case of the older mother who "needs help with her forgetfulness," the families of her children and grandchildren may all conceivably be involved. The social worker needs not only to explore the circumstances around the forgetfulness of the mother, but also to discover the meaning of this behavior within the family system.

The author believes that, during a crisis, the older adult becomes central to the event taking place within the family network; the social worker can expect the sudden changes in the older person's functioning to have an effect on other family members. By taking this theoretical position, the caseworker can come to understand the presenting problem in family systems terms. The concern then becomes how the mother's forgetfulness affects all the members of the family.

Figure 1.1 illustrates this viewpoint. In part (A), the identified client, the older mother, is part of the family system, but on the periphery. The members of the family all point to the mother as *the* problem. If the caseworker does not redefine the problem in family terms, the older person is treated as an individual apart from the rest of the individuals in the system. In part (B), the mother is central to all family happenings just as the spokes of a wheel are to the axis. Here the family is helped to understand the crisis within a family context. In this way, the mother's forgetfulness is everybody's personal concern and the family system is considered the "client." The social worker can expect changes in the older person's functioning to have an effect on other family members. To underscore the fact that all members of the family are to be viewed as the client, this text refers to the crisis-connected older member as *the pivotal client* rather than as the identified patient.

Most elderly clients come to the attention of an agency at a time of crisis. At that time, the question, "Who is the client?" must be asked. The crisis involves the entire family. Consequently, assessment and treatment must take into account both the elderly person's biopsychosocial needs and the family's adapting and coping capacity. Unfortunately, geriatric caseworkers have neither had a philosophy of nor have

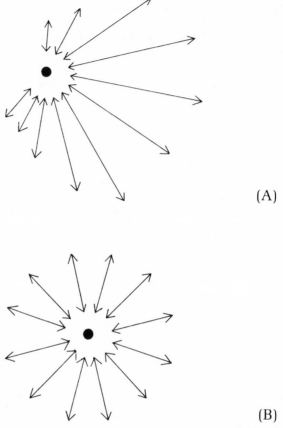

(A)

(B)

FIGURE 1.1.   The functional-age model: identified versus pivotal client. (A) Identified client; (B) Pivotal client. Diagram developed with Dr. J. Polivka, George Mason University, Fairfax, VA.

they practiced vigorous outreach to families. In fact, they have often been more caught up in the vulnerability of the older person, and unintentionally, in some cases unnecessarily, become surrogate family members (Freed, 1975; Greene, 1977). Chapter 2 suggests ways of reaching out to families during the intake process. Those caseworkers who have pursued a family-centered approach to casework with older adults have been flexible and have modified techniques to fit the client system. For example, they may decide to interview the elderly person alone and/or with his/her family in the home as well as in the office. It is essential, however, that the caseworker perceive the older person's problem(s) in *family* terms.

Thinking in intergenerational family terms means that the therapist has considered the family, among other things, as a source of information about the pattern of change that has occurred in their older member:

> Families are the silent, unknowing biographers, indirectly recording life events, successful adaptation, and failures of all family members. Their shared experiences provide them the ability to view complementary quirks and habits of older members with a tolerance and humor unmatched by professional outsiders. Their intense motivation, love, and concern fuels their help seeking and advocacy when others are giving up. With this sense of continuity, families become the most knowledgeable observers of change. Complex and subtle changes associated with normal or pathological aging are sensed by observant family members. Families also sense an older member's resonse to change that may be healthy or unhealthy. They are aware of past response patterns as well as past and present tolerance levels. They know how the older member perceives change and what meaning the change has to the older person. Families sense the mood and humor of the older person. Families know the past, observe the changes, watch the response to change, and interpret its meaning. They provide the context of change and psychological distress (Eyde and Rich, 1983, p. 45).

Thinking in intergenerational terms also means that the caseworker has considered the family group as a care-giving resource. Family members are often available and can be called upon to work with the caseworker on behalf of the older person. A family member may be able to care for an older relative at home with the assistance of support services such as a homemaker, Meals-on-Wheels or respite care. In those situations where this is not possible or necessary, a family member may act as case manager by planning, arranging and/or maintaining services for the elderly relative. In the process of working out these arrangements, the caseworker becomes aware of the unique dynamics that characterize that client system. This information about the family can then be used in selecting appropriate interventive techniques.

The family, however, is more than a source of information or a care-giving resource. It is an important treatment unit. Geriatric social workers have a major responsibility for assessing and treating the older person's family group and addressing family needs. They need to be professionally prepared to understand the complexity of biopsychosocial functioning of the aged person as well as its impact on family functioning. As family therapists, they should be well equipped to understand intergenerational relationships and the structural changes brought about by a biopsychosocial crisis in any one of its members.

A major obstacle to easing such a crisis is often the family's lack of familiarity with the various aspects of the aging process and their reluctance to accept the functional changes in their older member. The family group seeking help is usually bewildered by the often sudden turn of events in their lives due to the physical, psychological, and/or social changes that have occurred. They are often confused and frustrated with their own inability to understand, accept, and deal with the problem. The geriatric caseworker can play a critical role in the resolution of these family difficulties. The functional-age model provides the caseworker with a framework for dealing with such issues. It suggests, as is discussed in the next section, innovative diagnostic and treatment modalities for problem-solving in crisis situations arising around family adjustment to the changing needs of its aging members.

THE COMPONENTS OF THE FUNCTIONAL-AGE MODEL OF INTERGENERATIONAL FAMILY TREATMENT

The functional-age model of intergenerational family treatment is an innovative approach that can be used wherever an older adult is part of the family constellation. It is designed to provide a method for assessing and treating an older adult within a family context. As an intergenerational model, it is concerned with both the elderly person's functioning and the family system in which it takes place. The interdependence among family members and the dynamic nature of family structure and organization are concepts that provide its philosophical and conceptual base. This multifaceted approach requires that the social worker play a central role in processing and integrating evaluative information in order to arrive at family-centered interventions.

The model contains several elements, that together provide a systematic way of looking at problems and clarifying them. It is a framework used in gathering and integrating information about the client system. The comprehensive assessment thus obtained can then be employed to establish realistic treatment goals involving the family as a unit.

The assessment should address the multicausal nature of human problems, centering around a systematic appraisal of the functional capacities of the older person as the pivotal client. In determining the level of functioning, the geriatric social worker is expected to obtain a full picture of the complex interaction among biological, psychological, and social variables. At the same time, he/she will assess the structural and organizational properties of the family. In this way, the impact of the older adult's functional skills upon the coping or adaptational capacities of the family will be revealed. In short, the functional-age model offers an approach for evaluating the client system that is a composite of one particular member's biopsychosocial functioning within a family context. This allows for adaptive and maladaptive patterns to be identified and appropriate interventions to be made.

The core of the treatment construct, as depicted in Table 1.1, is the functional age of the older member. As can be seen, functional age is

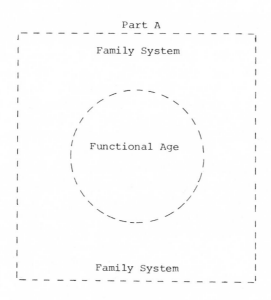

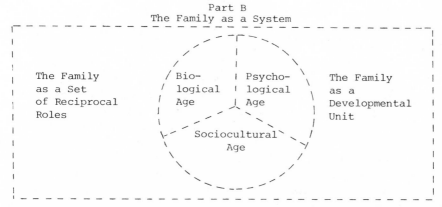

FIGURE 1.2   The functional-age model of intergenerational family treatment.
Model developed by Greene and Polivka.

comprised of three basic spheres related to adaptational capacity: the
biological, the psychological, and the sociocultural (Fig. 1.1). Functional skills are those attributes that are instrumental in meeting
environmental demands. An assessment of the individual from this
perspective allows the caseworker and family alike to understand the
structure of life and daily living habits of the older adult. (A complete
description of this process can be found in chapters 3–5.) Those factors
found to interfere most with activities of daily living are the ones most
likely to have brought the older adult to the attention of the social

service agency. It is not the particular diseases of old age but the *effects* of these conditions upon mental and physical functioning that can affect the ability of older adults to perform certain daily tasks.

The family is distinguished by a high level of interdependence and interrelatedness; when there is a change in the competencies of the older member, one should expect to see some degree of change throughout the family system. Therefore, when changes in the older adult's functional capacities reach crisis proportions, noticeable changes in family functioning can also be anticipated. As can be seen in Table 1.1, the functional age of the older person becomes the central focus of concern when families in crisis seek help. However, the functional-age model of intergenerational treatment underscores the idea that the social worker cannot address the older person's problems without also addressing the issues that affect the whole family system.

Figure 1.2 spells out those properties of the family group that are to be evaluated in order to arrive at a family-centered treatment plan. As can be seen, the family unit is to be understood as a social system, a set of reciprocal roles and a developmental unit. A system has been defined as a set of components interacting with each other within a certain boundary. A social system is a grouping of persons in a definite sphere who interact and influence each other. All social systems have their own particular order, structure or organization. The caseworker who recognizes the family as a social system acknowledges this and keeps in mind the systems properties of the family unit. Of particular importance to the model is the concept that the family consists of individual members who together form a group. However, the group is more than just a summation of the individual lives of its members. As these individual members interact, they create an additional entity— the life of the group. The perspective of the family as a system necessitates that the caseworker assess the life of the group and treat the family as an organizational structure that is a functioning whole (see chapters 6 and 10).

A role in the social structure carries with it expectations of behaviors that are defined and sanctioned by the society. Translating the concept of role into family terms would mean that there is a division of labor within the family group and that each member would be expected to behave in a prescribed pattern in a given situation. Family roles also define certain rights and obligations for the members. Role changes and transitions in old age are considered by some to be inevitable (Bengston and Treas, 1980). Some of these may create alterations in feelings of self-worth and well-being for the older adult. As a result, there can be changes throughout the family system. The functional-age model of intergenerational therapy suggests that role expectations are an important element in defining interaction between generations. The social worker who understands how these expectations enter into family functioning is better equipped to be of help to the client system in meeting these life transitions.

Family functioning is not static. It changes as a "result of significant changes in formal family organization and changes in the number, age and composition of the generations" (Eyde and Rich, 1983, p. 11). The dynamic nature of the family life cycle is an important element included in the model. Family developmental theory offers the case-worker perspective relative to how each family member is influenced by, and in turn shapes, other members' development. It addresses how the family changes over time and is concerned with the effects of shifting membership and the changing status of all members in *relationship to one another* (Carter and McGoldrick, 1980).

Erikson (1964) was one of the first major theorists to point out that the family, along with its members, faces developmental issues throughout the life cycle—"living together means that the individual life stages are intertwined" (Erikson, 1964, p. 14). The adoption of this perspective allows the caseworker to place the older person's developmental history in a family context. This may require that he/she act as negotiator in helping the family cope with conflict resulting from change. In short, the use of the family developmental history permits the social worker to understand the course of family life over time in order to assist with the developmental issues of the present.

In summary, the functional-age model for intergenerational treatment offers a framework for assessment and treatment of the older adult within a family context. It provides a tool for the *simultaneous* assessment of the biopsychosocial functioning of an older adult and the life of the family group. The model offers the practitioner the means of bridging the gap between an adequate understanding of the older person and a sufficient knowledge of the family as a unit. This integrated assessment process directs the caseworker in engaging the family and in selecting family-focused treatment modalities.

CHAPTER

2

Special Issues of the Entry Phase

INTAKE

The interview(s) initiating the therapeutic process constitute a critical time for setting the tone of the helping relationship and establishing the boundaries of treatment. It is then that the caseworker and client begin to establish a professional relationship, define the problem, become oriented to the treatment process, and determine whether the service required is within the parameters of the agency's functions. In short, it is the time for the practitioner to provide the client with information on how the helping process is carried out and on the relevance of particular procedures and practices. While casework is an interactional process, it is the therapist who takes the lead in arriving at casework goals within a framework that begins here.

A prospective client enters the service system through some form of intake. Intake has been defined as an application or request for service. "It is a process in which a request is made by or in behalf of a person, family, or group and a decision is made about the disposition of the application" (Northen, 1982, p. 168). During the intake process, worker and client explore "the potential areas of work upon which the helping process may focus" (Shulman, 1979, p. 5). In clarifying this purpose, the worker does not merely engage in a fact-finding exercise; rather, he/she concentrates on obtaining a dynamic picture of the client in interaction with others. The social worker should also be prepared to clarify his/her role and be able to indicate how and in what ways the practitioner and agency may be helpful.

While intake procedures with the aged and their families are in some respects similar to those employed with other client groups, there are important differences. This chapter focuses on some of the special considerations related to the initial contacts with the elderly and their families. It also provides specific suggestions for using the functional-age model of intergenerational treatment as a framework at this critical stage of casework.

THE FUNCTIONAL-AGE MODEL AT INTAKE

Practitioners and students alike are often puzzled by what questions to ask during the first interviews: Should I encourage the client to talk? Should I interrupt with a question? Is some information more relevant than other information? What do I need to know about the client to properly understand the problem? Questions such as these can be answered more easily if the caseworker comes to the initial contact with sufficient guidelines for assessment and treatment. General social work principles and practice methods are not enough; they must be well integrated and form a satisfactory framework for practice.

Having an assessment and treatment orientation is one of the most critical aspects of the professional use of self and is first put into action at intake. Such a frame of reference provides the caseworker with a theoretical foundation that shapes the direction of his/her therapeutic activity. Having such a model and a working knowledge of its assumptions offers those much needed guidelines about not only whom to include in the interview, but how to conduct it. For example, if the functional-age model suggests that a family operates as a social system, then the practitioner must retain that mind-set *throughout the casework process.* Questions at intake should be focused upon determining who the key persons in the family system are, how they all perceive the problem, how they interact as a unit, and so on. In a situation in which a daughter requests Meals-on-Wheels for her father, both family members would be considered part of the client system. In some situations, other siblings and/or members of the daughter's family, perhaps even a close neighbor, would be included. The request would be explored from both the father's and daughter's perspective in order to understand the presenting problem as it affects the family. Casework goals would be mutually agreed upon, with the older person, as pivotal client, taking as active a role as he/she can.

With a theoretical practice model the caseworker has a guide to the intake procedure. Professional decisions about questions to be asked, persons to be requested to attend an interview, and location of the interview all stem from the theoretical framework. The practitioner who believes in family-focused casework strives to promote the inter-dependence of the family group and seeks to reinforce reciprocity among its members. The caseworker's activities, interventions, and use of resources will be linked to these principles and will build upon the strengths of the group and its coping capacity.

It should be clearly stated that a practice model offers more than just a philosophical stance. A practice model is a point of departure in problem-solving and suggests alternative *actions* for treatment. Appraisal of a problem rests upon what *"the client and caseworker both hold in the center of focus"* (Perlman, 1957, p. 119). Maintaining that focus is the responsibility of the caseworker who needs an assessment format to understand the problem within an organizational framework. Throughout the intake and evaluative process, data or "facts" about the nature of the problem are collected. The questions of how data are selected and how they are related to the problem are determined by the model, which provides the method of looking at the data (assessment) and arriving at possible treatment resolutions.

From the initial contact, case information is perceived and used differently, depending on the caseworker's treatment orientation. He/she is continually developing "hypotheses" about the nature of the problem as it relates to the client [system]. There is an *ongoing ordering* and *interpretation* of the information gathered as it relates to both the problem(s) and the course of treatment. "The problems identified in the assessment should be justified by the data collected. At the same time, it is open to amendment as new information is uncovered and as circumstances change" (Silverstone and Burack-Weiss, 1983, p. 47).

The data are collected with a concern for accuracy with the practice model shaping the process. This allows the caseworker to select which facts are important from the many he/she knows about the client(s) and suggests what additional information must be gathered to complete the evaluations in an *integrated* form (see chapters 3 through 8). Assessment begins with the first intake interview, whether it takes place by phone or in person. At that time, the caseworker needs to know what it is he/she hopes to accomplish, what information (data, facts) he/she needs to obtain, and what plan for successive interviews he/she might care to put into action.

Parameters for this casework activity can be derived from the functional-age model, which suggests that family crisis situations arising out of the changing biopsychosocial needs of an aging family member can best be resolved through family-focused assessment and treatment modalities. The major concern is understanding the older adult's functional capacity and the family system in which it takes place in order to arrive at appropriate interventions. The model presupposes that a change in the functional competencies of an [older] member brings about change throughout the family system. Thus the caseworker must be prepared *at intake* to begin gathering and evaluating pertinent data about the older adult *and* the developmental and systems properties of the family.

The following case illustrates how the functional-age model can serve as a problem-solving interview format and provide the caseworker with an intake focus:

Mrs. G. called the intake worker of an Atlanta family service agency and requested a list of senior citizen apartments for her 85-year-old mother, Mrs. S., who lived in New York. The daughter sounded upset, and indicated that she had just received a phone call from her mother's neighbor who said, "Mrs. S. is always wandering around 'lost.' You are her daughter. Why don't you come up here and get her!"

The caseworker suggested that Mrs. G. might want to come into the agency to get the housing information and to discuss her concerns. She focused her intake interview so as to obtain the following information: Mrs. S., the oldest of ten children, was the only member of her extended family to migrate to the United States from Italy. She raised Mrs. G., an only child, "single-handedly," as she was widowed when Mrs. G. was only 3 years old. Mrs. G. described her mother as "fiercely independent and hard-working," struggling as a laundress and taking in extra ironing in order to save for Mrs. G.'s college education. Having retired only 6 years ago, she still lived in the same apartment in the old neighborhood. There were several friends who "looked in" on her, and she knew most of the neighborhood shopkeepers.

Mrs. G. was very concerned about "what to do with her mother." She said that she visited her several times a year, and, within the next few weeks, was going to New York to bring her mother to Atlanta for her usual summer visit. She was thinking of "just packing up the apartment and bringing Mother to Atlanta permanently." The caseworker suggested that Mrs. G. not "hurry things along," and offered to meet with them both before any action was taken. The caseworker also explained some of the dynamics of uprooting an [older] person, especially if he/she had not participated in the decision. The possibility of establishing a more structured helping network in New York comprised of neighbors and friends was also suggested.

When Mrs. G. returned with her mother from New York, she called to request an appointment "only for herself." "You won't believe what my mother's apartment was like. Even worse than last time." Assuring Mrs. G. that "it would be okay to discuss this with her mother present," the caseworker requested that Mrs. G. ask her mother to join them.

As they entered the office, Mrs. G. said, "Mother came with me today, but I doubt if it will do much good. She insists that she can only speak and understand Italian." Turning her head toward Mrs. S., the caseworker said she knew only a little Italian and raised her eyebrows as if to say, "What do we do now?" Mrs. S. replied, "That's all right, dear. I'll speak English for you." The caseworker used that opportunity to ask Mrs. S. if she would be willing to explain what it was like to live in the "old neighborhood."

Mrs. S. went into detail about each of her neighbors, explaining how they had seen Mrs. G. grow up to be a college-educated woman with children of her own. Mrs. S. said that "there was no way she could imagine life without them; nor could she live in an area where she could not buy 'real' Italian vegetables and meats."

With some prompting by the caseworker, Mrs. G. said she felt she could not let her mother go back to her apartment in New York. "Mama, you've let it get so run-down! I would be worried about you."

The caseworker acknowledged their feelings and asked if there might be a resolution that would satisfy them both. She encouraged mother and daughter to discuss solutions with each other and make suggestions, describing programs such as homemaker services, community helping networks and friendly visiting. She also stressed the importance of Mrs. S.'s receiving a medical examination.

Mrs. S. was persuaded to follow up and received a complete physical. The doctor concluded that Mrs. S. had not been receiving a proper diet and could benefit from a more structured meal plan. The caseworker was given permission to talk with the physician and then met with the family twice more. Using the information she had collected about the family, the caseworker was able to help them arrive at a plan: Mrs. S. would return to New York where one of her Italian neighbors would "share" the cooking responsibilities with her. Mrs. S. also agreed to obtain homemaker services once every 2 weeks so that "her daughter would not worry."

Satisfactory and speedy resolution of this case was possible because the caseworker was able to use her diagnostic skills to facilitate timely decision making. She initiated and maintained a family-centered approach and quickly moved to engage both mother and daughter in the casework process. This interview focus permitted her to define the problem in family terms. She also obtained a brief developmental history in order to better understand how past events affected present-day functioning of the family system. Biological, sociocultural, and psychological variables were all taken into account. Treatment goals were established by the family, with the pivotal client taking the lead and the caseworker making suggestions.

Intake and assessment are not clearly delineated phases. Despite this fact, which was well illustrated by the above case, there are questions that need to be answered as early as possible in the helping process: (1) What was the precipitating *event* that brought the client(s) to the attention of the agency? (2) How does the request for service reflect the problem? (3) How can the precipitating event and/or presenting problem be understood from a historical and family perspective? (How had the balance within the family system been upset?) (4) Who are the persons who comprise the client [family] system? The support network?

As the casework activity moves into the assessment and treatment phases, the caseworker should be able to interpret and organize this information, arriving at a family-focused biopsychosocial assessment. The evaluation needs to contain a definition of the presenting problem from a family and developmental point of view, and to describe how the change(s) in the functional capacities of the older adult have altered the balance within the family system. In this way, interventions and services that help restore individual and/or family functioning can be introduced.

EXPECTATIONS CONCERNING THE HELPING PROCESS

As has already been stated, the opening phase of therapy is that critical period wherein the therapeutic relationship is being established and the presenting problem is being defined. This process actually is set in motion before the caseworker and client(s) see each other for the first time. It begins with the client(s)' expectations about the helping process and with the professional skills, values, and attitudes the caseworker brings to assessment and treatment.

> The interview begins before it starts. It begins before the two participants meet, in their thoughts and feelings as they move toward the actual encounter. The client's decision to contact the agency for an interview is often the result of a series of complex, interrelated decisions. The residuals of these decisions may affect the client's initial behavior in the interview (Kadushin, 1972, p. 106).

The client family that comes to a social service agency already has some idea of what they want, "a conception of a better tomorrow" (Perlman, 1957). They bring with them expectations concerning the nature of the agency and the role of the helping professional, and often make concrete requests that reflect their thought about a solution to the problem.

> "Is my mother eligible for a day-care center with Spanish-speaking staff?"
>
> "Can you refer my father to a senior housing project in his old neighborhood?"
>
> "Can your agency provide my grandmother with a kosher Meals-on-Wheels program?"

Problems brought to social services agencies are complex and multifaceted. At the same time, they are often described in a specific manner, reflecting the client's general expectations of the agency and already tried but failed solutions. Paying sufficient attention to the request while exploring the full ramifications of the situation is critical. Upon assessment, the overt request, often for a concrete service, may or may not be appropriate. However, clients anticipate and often presume that the practitioner will provide a specific service or help them make particular arrangements.

Creating a distinction between requests for concrete versus therapeutic services establishes a false dichotomy. It is important for the caseworker to look beyond the concrete request in order to understand how a particular service is perceived by the client. The caseworker must have an appreciation for individual and family dynamics in order to select services appropriate to client needs. In most instances, geriatric casework involves a complex interweaving of what Mary Richmond (1922) termed "direct counseling" and "indirect action."

The principle of "starting where the client is" suggests that the caseworker assess why a family has arrived at a particular solution for their relative. Including specific questions in early interviews can often provide needed information for the caseworker and at the same time lessen anxiety for the family. The following are examples of such questions directed toward a mother and daughter concerning a home-maker request:

> (*For the daughter who has initiated contact*): What makes you feel your mother needs a homemaker? Have you tried other ways of helping her, such as other services? Can you tell me what she is not able to do now that she was able to do previously? How would a homemaker help you as her daughter? Does your mother know of your concern and thoughts about obtaining a homemaker?

> (*For the mother*): Do you know that your daughter is concerned about how you are managing? How did you feel about your daughter calling us? How do you think you are managing here in your apartment? (Are there any difficulties?) Do you know about our agency and what we do? Are there ways you think the agency could help you?

The way a family tackles a problem reflects the nature of their interpersonal relationships and their developmental history. These relationships have often been taxed by the task of care-giving over an extended period of time, and maladaptive patterns may be brought to the surface during crisis situations. During the intake process, many unresolved issues may come to the fore and can either be couched in polite or hostile terms. The caseworker should listen carefully for clues to the nature of such family relationships as they affect the family's views of the agency, their expectations of the worker, and their potential for involvement in treatment:

> "My mother always has been demanding."

> "Dad and I never were really close."

> "My brother and I never have seen eye-to-eye about our mother."

> "You know, I really never liked my mother, nor she me. My sister is going to have to take care of her now."

Expectations about the caseworker and the agency are also shaped by cultural norms. As will be seen in chapters 5 and 12, ethnic and minority group membership can affect the client's perception of the problem and outlook about treatment. Unfortunately, many programs and services for the elderly are designed primarily to meet the needs of the majority of society rather than to take into account the heteroge-neous nature of the older population (Green, 1982; Moriwaki and Kobata, 1975). This becomes an obstacle to treatment when inappro-priate and/or unacceptable services and programs are not utilized by minority elderly. The individual caseworker can sometimes ameliorate such problems at intake by making a special effort to understand and assess the presenting problem in culturally relevant terms.

The expectations that clients have about the agency and the helping process are usually best dealt with in a straightforward manner. Clients should be encouraged to express their concerns, doubts and fears about treatment and agency services. This is not easily accomplished, as clients may be reluctant to share information, particularly if the caseworker is seen as an authority figure. However, the casework process rests on the ability of the worker to "hear" the client's problem and to demonstrate that she/he has sufficient interest and professional competence to deal with it.

While the establishment of a helping relationship at intake is strongly influenced by the client's preconceived ideas about the treatment process, the caseworker's professional skills, values, and attitudes are equally important. As was discussed earlier in this chapter, the worker is formulating a biopsychosocial assessment throughout the intake process, which is an outgrowth of the framework or treatment model brought to the assessment procedure. The study is also influenced by the caseworker's views about "how best" to help the aged and their families.

Caseworkers' ideas and values about themselves as helping professionals are a product of their individual and professional socialization. These values set the stage for practice and

> affect the people toward whom practice is directed, as well as the quality of social work. . . . Throughout social work's history in North America two values have dominated its practice: the worth, dignity and uniqueness of the individual and the right to self-determination by individuals, groups or constituents in a community (Lowy, 1979, p. 53).

The predominance of these values can at times present issues for the practitioner. For example, the belief in self-determination implies that the client has the right to make his/her own decisions and choose among alternatives. Putting this into practice can present difficulties when the values of the caseworker and the perceptions of the client are not in agreement, as in the following case:

> Mrs. C., an "eccentric" 88-year-old woman, lived alone in a two-bedroom house with an estimated 35 cats. She had been known for many years to the family service agency and the department of human services. Periodically, these agencies would receive complaints from her neighbors about her "deplorable living conditions."
> Mrs. C. came to know one of the "young sweet social workers" whom she would allow, on occasion, to enter her home. While the caseworker considered the house to be in "a most unsatisfactory condition" from her own point of view, she nonetheless observed that Mrs. C. was able to take care of her personal needs, including hygiene and meal management. Mrs. C. also indicated that she would resist any efforts to "make her go to one of those old age homes." Attempts by the neighbors to have Mrs. C. declared a protective service case were not followed through, as it became evident that Mrs. C. was capable of making her own decisions.
> This stance was severely tested one very cold winter, when neighbors

learned that the heat had been turned off because Mrs. C. had forgotten to pay the bill. Once the bill was paid, the gas company refused to reenter the home to turn the heat back on unless it was cleaned first. The social worker who was concerned because of the below-freezing temperatures made a home visit. She brought several blankets with her, knowing she might fail to convince Mrs. C. to stay at a hotel or shelter until the heat could be turned back on.

At first, Mrs. C. refused to leave the house or even to allow a cleaning service to come in. However, the caseworker was able to draw upon her previous experiences and positive relationship with this client. She outlined the alternatives to Mrs. C. in an honest, direct fashion, making it clear that there was "no way we would just walk away and allow Mrs. C. to freeze." ("What should *we* do?") Mrs. C. decided to allow the cleaning crew in the next day, but said she "would only pay for 3 hours of service." She thanked the worker for the blankets, which she used that night.

Cases such as these test the caseworker's ability to walk that fine line between allowing the client the right to self-determination and making decisions that are consistent with the safety and welfare of the client. Very often there are no clear-cut right or wrong answers in such situations. Peer supervision and support can be critical in resolving such cases.

Another potentially thorny intake issue involves the development of treatment goals and objectives. This major step in establishing a working alliance is affected by the practitioner's values and ideas about "what is best for the client." Difficulties are more likely to occur in this area when goals are not established mutually.

There is a growing body of literature indicating that the elderly respond positively to interventions that call upon them to play an active role in decision-making (Lowy, 1979; Silverstone and Burack-Weiss, 1983). Most elderly clients, while frightened by illness or advancing frailty, prefer that the least restrictive measures be taken to assure their safety. However, this should be assessed on a case-by-case basis with an ear to the pivotal client's needs and desire. If this is not done and goals solely reflect the family's and/or caseworker's point of view, excluding those of the older person, then treatment can be adversely affected. The following case illustrates what happened when the caseworker responded to a son's specific intake request for service without paying sufficient attention to the mother's perception and feelings about the situation:

Mrs. B. was brought to the attention of a family service agency by her son, who was concerned about her recently diagnosed "heart problem." Mrs. B. was vague about her condition but said it meant she "could no longer be on her own." Upon hearing her medical diagnosis, Mrs. B. gave up her apartment in Florida, where she had retired, and shipped all her belongings to her son's home.

Mrs. B. lived with her son for a short time, but problems with her daughter-in-law led the son to contact the agency for "help in locating an apartment for his mother."

During the time that housing was being sought, there were reportedly many disagreements and difficulties between the son's mother and wife. The son, who called the agency daily, was sure everything would be okay as soon as "mother had a place of her own." The caseworker also assumed that Mrs. B. wanted to have her own apartment when Mrs. B. said she "only wanted to be out of her daughter-in-law's kitchen." The worker proceeded to help Mrs. B. find "suitable housing."

In the next 2 years, Mrs. B. tried several different living arrangements, moving from her own private apartment to a shared duplex, and finally to sheltered housing that provided meals and a daytime nurse on staff. Each move followed a series of "attacks" for which "no physical cause" could be found. Mrs. B. would call her son in the middle of the night, describing a "pounding of her heart." He would meet her in the emergency room of the hospital where the doctors would reassure him and Mrs. B. that she had not suffered a heart attack. The son finally became desperate when the housing manager, troubled by the repeated appearance of rescue vehicles and personnel, asked Mrs. B. to move.

The caseworker decided to have a family meeting to deal with the crisis. She encouraged everyone to openly express what they thought would best solve the problem. She herself admitted that she was "at a loss as to how Mrs. B. could continue in her own place." The son pointed out that he too "felt like a failure in trying to help preserve his mother's sense of independence." The caseworker then asked Mrs. B. what she felt was the best solution based upon her life's experience. Mrs. B. said that one of her best memories was when she "had tuberculosis at the age of 12." She described how she was nursed back to health by her mother, who allowed her to "sit under a tree in summer and sip lemonade and eat cake." The caseworker asked what the equivalent would be for Mrs. B. at age 75. She replied, "Sitting in the beautiful lobby of the [nursing] 'home'."

Once the caseworker and family were able to hear Mrs. B., they were prepared to help her in a way that was congruent with her needs. When she knew she could not be cared for in her son's home, she set her own alternative goal—moving to a community-sponsored nursing home, which she perceived as nurturing, safe, and secure. The caseworker's strong preference for independent living biased the intake and assessment process. She realized that she had impeded earlier resolution of the problem by arriving at interventions based upon her own values rather than those of the client.

Casework is an interactional process. Client values, expectations, and concerns can only be understood if the caseworker first understands what she/he also brings to the helping relationship.

BEGINNING THE HELPING PROCESS

The manner in which the elderly person comes to the attention of an agency is one of the first considerations in intake. Agencies serving the aged are usually approached in a variety of indirect processes rather than through direct application by the older person (Greene, 1977; Lowy, 1979; Silverstone and Burack-Weiss, 1983).

Despite their growing number and their increased risk of mental disorder and social dysfunction, the elderly continue to be underserved by mental health workers. While 15–25% of the elderly in the community have significant symptoms of mental illness, the older population uses mental health services at only half the rate of the general population (Taeuber, 1983; White House Conference on Aging, 1981).

Many elderly people are reluctant to use a social work agency, which they associate with "the poor" or "those unable to cope with adversity." The initial contact with an agency may come about only after many unsuccessful attempts to handle a problem independently (Silverstone and Burack-Weiss, 1983). The request for help may be initiated through a referral by another agency or program (nutrition site, golden age club or hospital), through calls by a concerned friend or relative, or through an outreach program of a community agency.

A major goal during intake, whether the request for service be by or in behalf of an elderly person, is to establish a working relationship with the older person and, wherever possible, within a family context.

When a family member calls about his/her older relative, the functional-age model suggests that the caseworker view the family group as the client. Family-focused casework can often be achieved by involving both the concerned relative and the older person in the intake process. This means that intake questions should focus on both the older adult's functional capacities and the family's adaptive response, as seen in the following case:

> An adult daughter called a social service agency to request "Meals-on-Wheels" for her recently widowed, 65-year-old father. The caseworker, keeping in mind the seemingly young age of the father and the possible effects of loss on the family system, directed her questions accordingly. She explored the appropriateness of the request by inquiring about the father's ability to shop for himself, drive or walk to the grocery, and prepare meals, taking into consideration his cultural attitudes about this role.
>
> The caseworker also inquired about the daughter's concerns. Did she take her father shopping or prepare his meals? How would she describe their relationship, and how had it changed following the death of her mother? The caseworker also wanted to find out if the father knew of the daughter's call to the agency. Her aim was to hold a joint interview with them, at which time she could further explore the father's situation, observe the interaction between father and daughter, and explain the functions of the agency.
>
> The caseworker arranged to meet the daughter at the father's apartment in order to better assess his activities of daily living within the home environment. She learned that the father was agile and alert and was

"keeping up" the apartment to his own satisfaction. He enjoyed shopping for groceries weekly with his daughter, but seemed to call almost daily about a "forgotten item." He would keep the daughter on the phone for "long periods of time" about "small, unimportant matters."

As the family talked with the caseworker, it became clear that the father felt lonely and depressed following the death of his wife. His calls to the daughter about meal preparation were an attempt to seek her attention and companionship. Once the problem was more clearly defined, the case-worker was able to offer appropriate services, identify the father's actual needs, clarify the daughter's role, provide a friendly visitor, and provide grief-work counseling.

When an older person is referred by another family member or agency, care must be given not to designate the elderly person as "a case." One should assume that the older person is competent to describe his/her own situation as well as to understand the functions of the agency. The caseworker may wish to obtain additional information from the other agency after gaining permission from the elderly person. However, the older person is usually best able to relate his/her experiences and to provide information and access to his/her family members and/or significant others. The following case illustrates how an older woman, who had initially been referred for nursing home placement, was able to remain in her own apartment:

The resident manager of a senior citizens housing project, Mrs. T., called the intake service of a sectarian family service agency. She requested help in "getting Mrs. L. out of the project, where she was a danger to herself and others," and into the religious community's nursing home facility. Mrs. T. said that Mrs. L. often sat in the lobby with a dazed look. That morning, Mrs. L. had left a pot on the stove too long and "had almost burned down the building." The manager stressed that Mrs. L. did not belong in the project "as she was no longer able to take care of herself."

The caseworker indicated that she would need to talk with Mrs. L. before any plans could be made. She asked the manager to inform Mrs. L. that the agency had been contacted and that a social worker wanted to visit with her. The caseworker followed up with a phone call to offer an appointment time and to assure Mrs. L. that she "wanted to hear her point of view."

When the caseworker arrived, Mrs. L. seemed somewhat confused and disoriented. However, Mrs. L. was able to describe her situation to the caseworker, who adjusted her interviewing pace to meet the client's needs. Mrs. L., a childless widow, had worked for the government for 40 years until her retirement. She had moved into the building 5 years ago to be near her only relative, a niece, who had recently had cancer surgery. Mrs. L. "absolutely did not want to bother her with any problems." When the caseworker asked what these problems might be, suggesting she might be able to help, Mrs. L. seemed relieved and anxious to talk. She said she had been very worried lately, and wondered why she was always so tired. She also explained that she usually read the paper daily, paid her own bills, and generally took care of her own affairs. For the last several months, she had noticed troubling changes. She fell asleep in the lobby, was thirsty, and had to urinate frequently. She repeated that she "did not want to trouble her niece."

The caseworker, noting the changes in physical as well as psychological functioning, suggested a medical examination. Mrs. L. was willing to make an appointment with her family physician if someone could provide transportation. The caseworker made the necessary arrangements for a volunteer driver, and also encouraged Mrs. L. to talk with her niece about recent developments.

During the medical exam, lab tests indicated that Mrs. L. had diabetes, which quickly responded to a change in diet and proper medication. Mrs. L.'s mental functioning dramatically improved. The caseworker then followed up with the resident manager, acting as an advocate for Mrs. L., who wished to remain in the building.

In situations where the older person has been referred by the staff of another agency, it is important to respect the older person's right to privacy, confidentiality, and selection or rejection of service. The older person may also refuse to involve his/her family. This, too, should be respected. In addition, not all family members may wish to be involved in planning for a relative. Accustomed roles, old alliances, and communication patterns should be taken into account. Quick assessment of the nature of long-standing relationships can provide needed direction for the caseworker in such circumstances. Inquiries about the client's expectations of the agency can also offer guidelines.

INTERVIEWING INDIVIDUALS AND/OR FAMILIES

While there are no sure-fire lists of rules for [first] interviews, their most crucial characteristic, and that of successive interviews, "is that the interaction is designed to achieve a consciously selected purpose" (Kadushin, 1972, p. 8). The content of the interview should be chosen to facilitate that purpose, and the caseworker's activities must be consciously planned.

The theoretical orientation in family systems therapy tends toward interviewing the whole family group (Group for the Advancement of Psychiatry, 1970). In practice, however, while some family therapists confine themselves exclusively to interviews with the entire family, others may work with one person, emphasizing a family focus, and still others with various combinations of selected family members. This decision has to be handled flexibly in social work with the aged and their families. Sometimes the older person may have no immediate family; in other situations the family may be estranged or physically unavailable. There are also times when diagnostic considerations dictate working with the individual alone (maintaining the goal of understanding the elderly client within a family perspective).

Such [seemingly] procedural questions are often decided by the caseworker's bias for or against family therapy. Clients rarely experience their problems as located within the total family. It is the therapist who communicates this orientation and helps each family member see "the problem" as a "family problem." By asking to meet with the whole family, the practitioner creates the opportunity for members to communicate and listen to each other, and challenges the family's capacities for decision-making and change (Stamm, 1972). However, the caseworker first must be convinced of the value of this approach and impart it to the family. Some possible ways of accomplishing this are:

"Please join us at our first meeting. We'd like your point of view."

"Your input will be valuable to the family."

"I'd like to hear from everyone in the family."

"In my experience, I have found it most helpful to hear from everyone."

"Can you meet with us at least one time to give us your ideas?"

There are many benefits to be gained from conducting a family group interview. It can help the worker not only understand each family member in terms of his/her own personality, but also in terms of his/her relationship to other family members. Family transactions and alignments among members can be observed in the "here and now." Family interviews can also assist the family in learning about their patterns of communication and interaction, and give them the chance to direct their energies to a combined resolution of the problem (Wynne, 1971).

This process is best set into motion at intake, when the family is most mobilized to deal with the crisis at hand. The caseworker who first establishes a relationship with the elderly person and offers him or her concrete services may find the family available later. If it happens that despite the caseworker's efforts the family does not wish to participate, care should be taken to understand the older person's role in the family from that person's perspective.

The impression should not be conveyed that older adults do not request counseling or other services for themselves. They do. When an older adult requests personal counseling or therapy, it is equally important for the caseworker to understand both the individual and the systems with which he/she interacts (Shulman, 1979). The assessment focus is the client as he/she is affected by others.

Mrs. C. called a family service agency requesting an appointment to talk with a social worker. She explained that while her husband had died over 2 years ago, she recently felt very depressed, and found herself "crying at the drop of a hat." Mrs. C. said that she had managed to get through the first few months after Mr. C.'s death by just functioning day to day. Gradually, she returned to her usual activities and routine, but had recently found she did not want to go anywhere.

Several family members had encouraged Mrs. C. to seek help. Her adult daughter, who lived locally, insisted that she had "to get out and do things" and could not understand why her mother was so upset. When her son came to town on a business trip, he noticed her depression and suggested she go to the United Way Agency. Mrs. C.'s sister-in-law also came to visit and was concerned. During their conversations, Mrs. C. said she came to realize that she still did not believe her husband was dead. It was as if he "might still walk through the door." "When I spoke of my husband, I never said 'Harold is dead' or 'My husband died,' but rather 'My darling left me' or 'My sweetheart is gone'." These realizations, recalled at the initial interview, led Mrs. C. to seek counseling.

Other pertinent information was elicited during the intake interviews: Mrs. C. was one of four siblings. Following her marriage to Mr. C., she moved away from her hometown. She was the only family member to do so, and her parents were very reluctant to see her go. Mrs. C. tried to get her parents to visit her, but they never did. Two years after Mrs. C. and her husband moved to the Midwest, Mrs. C.'s father died. She "confessed" to the caseworker that she "still felt guilty about leaving home, and knew her father's health began to deteriorate soon after she left."

Mrs. C.'s most pressing present concern was her relationship with her daughter, Joan. What had been described as a "close model mother-daughter relationship" had changed since Mr. C.'s death. Joan was "not very patient and easily aggravated." While her son often talked about Mr. C. and how much he had loved his father, Joan had never discussed the loss. Mrs. C. was sure her daughter "was just not dealing with her father's death."

While Mrs. C. was seen for individual counseling, the caseworker obtained a picture of her past and present relationships. This information provided both the therapist and client with an awareness of family patterns in dealing with death. This, in turn, led to an understanding of the dynamics of Mrs. C.'s depression and allowed for the selection of appropriate interventions. In effect, the caseworker was able to conduct family-focused interviews without other family members being physically present.

For the older adult who has no significant others, has never married and/or had children, information regarding his/her family of origin is a vital part of the biopsychosocial assessment. The caseworker should also obtain a history of relationships at work and in neighborhood settings. The older client who is truly an isolate is rare. That client often comes to see the social worker as a surrogate family member. Treatment plans can sometimes include providing a friendly visitor and/or creating a neighborhood-family network (Ross, 1978).

Whether an interview be with an individual or a family group, there are some special considerations in interviewing the frail and/or ill elderly. Geriatric social workers often find themselves in a variety of nontraditional interview settings with older adults who may have limiting, and sometimes multiple, impairments. This requires special sensitivity, flexibility, and skill on the part of the interviewer. Of particular importance is the payment of sufficient and caring attention to the older adult, who should always be an integral part of decision-making and case-planning. Even in the most complex of situations with multiple problems, it is usually possible to elicit needed information from the older client in a manner that respects his/her dignity.

FORMING A PROFESSIONAL RELATIONSHIP

While the concept of the therapist–client relationship has always been central to the various casework methods, family therapists have not given it major emphasis. Family therapists, who are primarily concerned with educating the family group about its dysfunctions and improving communication among family members, often see them-selves as consultants, facilitators, and/or coaches. The efforts of the therapist are directed toward observing patterns of behavior and confronting members in the "here-and-now" in order to help the group deal with underlying problems. Care is given not to "favor" one family member over another in the form of a special relationship unless that is part of a planned therapeutic technique.

The functional-age model of intergenerational family treatment has a different treatment perspective. While the caseworker often employs particular family therapy techniques, the therapist–client relationship, particularly with the pivotal client, plays a key role. The model, as an outgrowth of the psychosocial method, relies heavily upon the case-work relationship and its emphasis on acceptance and support as a means of reaching out to the oftentimes reticent elderly client.

Relationship is a generic term referring to the dynamic interactions and psychological connections between people (Northen, 1982). In therapy, it is the interactional and emotional bond between the client and the therapist (Northen, 1982; Perlman, 1957). Relationship is an integral part of a communication network and has been considered "the soul of social casework" (Biestek, 1957). In fact, many treatment models, including the one presented in this text, suggest that the relationship is the basis for therapeutic growth and change (Northen, 1982).

There has been much written about the positive use of the relation-ship in the interview process (Fischer, 1978). The early social work theorist viewed the relationship as the keystone of the casework process and basic to all treatment (Hollis, 1972; Perlman, 1957). Perlman (1957) saw relationship as a catalyst and as an enabling dynamic in the problem-solving method. She defined the therapeutic relationship as an emotional state in which client and therapist, having some common interest and goal, interact with feeling. Relationship in this sense grows out of shared emotionally charged situations and contributes to positive intercommunication. When used by a practitioner in a disciplined, professional way, the relationship becomes the glue, so the client knows that he/she is working with someone who is concerned about his/her problem. Nowhere is this more so than in casework with the elderly.

In brief, it can be said that almost all forms of therapy begin with the planned and disciplined use of the relationship. It is through the establishment of this helping relationship that the client who is experiencing discomfort and/or pain comes to view the therapist as someone who can provide help. It is through this process that the practitioner establishes a therapeutic atmosphere and a working alliance.

The Rogerian (Rogers, 1957, 1967) approach to therapy is the one most often associated with the importance of the relationship to constructive personality growth, change, and/or development. Rogers proposed that the attitudes and feelings of the therapist, which facilitate a democratic environment, trust and independence, are at the core of the treatment process. He asserts that if the client is able to experience the practitioner as a person who communicates a sense of caring and a sense of the client's worth, positive change in personal and social functioning is likely to occur.

According to Rogers, this change will occur because all individuals have an innate tendency to develop all of their capacities in ways that serve to maintain or enhance themselves. These capabilities are nurtured by the accepting therapist who communicates to the client feelings of the client's worth. This point of view has considerable applicability for the geriatric specialist who has been trained to appreciate that elderly clients need to be given the opportunity for growth *and renewal*. This means that the older client is perceived as being able to continue to discover and to utilize innate potential (Butler and Lewis, 1982). The practitioner needs to bring to the therapeutic encounter with the elderly client both interpersonal communication skills and professional values and attitudes that reflect the social work philosophy of respecting the client's abilities and potential for growth.

Contemporary social work theorists (Fischer, 1978; Kadushin, 1972) share Rogers's optimistic view that

> in a wide variety of professional work involving relationships with people—whether as a psychotherapist, teacher, religious worker, guidance counselor, social worker, clinical psychologist—it is the *quality* of the interpersonal encounter with the client which is the most significant element in determining effectiveness (Rogers and Stevens, 1967, p. 85).

Constructive personal growth is believed to be closely associated with the practitioner's sensitivity and genuineness in communication.

Rogers cautioned that many professional training programs "make it more difficult for the individual to be himself and more likely that he will play a [strictly] professional role" (Rogers and Stevens, p. 100). As a result, some practitioners become so overburdened with "theoretical and diagnostic baggage" that they are less able to understand the client's world as it appears to the client. An example of this phenomenon is the caseworker who is reluctant to make a home visit because "it is not the way therapy is conducted." Such an attitude denies the practitioner the opportunity of observing elderly clients in their own environment where activities of daily living can be assessed firsthand. The recent social work literature continues to suggest that the casework relationship requires the capacity for feeling emotion and, at the same time, remaining separate enough to maintain a proper perspective. This stance contributes to both an accurate professional assessment of the client and to an understanding of the person in his/her situation.

In order for a relationship to be helpful and growth-producing, it must contain certain basic elements that cut across many theoretical orientations. Those most often discussed include empathy/understanding, warmth/acceptance, and genuineness (Fischer, 1978; Hollis, 1964; Northen, 1982; Perlman, 1957). Interviews that include these characteristics contribute to an atmosphere which reduces anxiety and can produce a favorable context for growth and/or change. Such an atmosphere provides the bedrock for clinical communication within the functional-age model.

Empathy, the first of these relational characteristics, is the ability or capacity of the caseworker to deal sensitively and accurately with the client's feelings and/or experiences. Empathy is the capacity to feel *with* the client and the ability to communicate this understanding. The therapist who understands the client's world view and perception(s) focuses on both verbal and nonverbal clues, which enable the caseworker to better understand both manifest and latent content and to respond appropriately to the client's meanings.

Empathy enables the practitioner to enter into the client's world through his/her own imagination while retaining the capacity to maintain an objective perspective. The ability to perceive clients accurately and realistically in the ongoing helping process is critical to the integrity of the therapeutic relationship.

A second major characteristic of the helping relationship is "nonpossessive warmth" (Rogers, 1967), which refers to the practitioner's acceptance of the client as an individual. The worker who demonstrates such warmth accepts and cares about the client in a nurturing but nonpatronizing and nondominating way. While this calls for a nonblaming, nonjudgmental attitude on the part of the worker, it does not condone antisocial or self-destructive acts. Such an approach allows the client to feel respected and to experience him/herself as a person of worth. The caseworker involved in decision-making situations with the elderly client may find it difficult to strike a balance between his/her wish to ensure that the client live in a safe environment and the right of the client to self-determination, as was illustrated earlier in the case of Mrs. C.

The caseworker's respect for the client as an adult is as crucial as his/her capacity to accurately evaluate the problem. Perceiving and treating the aging client as a responsible adult is difficult for some caseworkers, who assume they know what is best and, in the guise of being helpful, take over for the client. This phenomenon must be addressed effectively in the supervisory conference if the client's needs are to be served.

The third component of the helping relationship is genuineness or authenticity. Genuineness refers to the worker's capacity to be open or real with the client. The worker who demonstrates genuineness is able and willing to acknowledge and address his/her own feelings about the client.

While being genuine infers that workers be themselves, it does not mean they should disclose their total selves to the client. Nor does it mean that the therapist loses his/her sense of objectivity. What is involved is the development of sufficient self-awareness on the part of therapists to employ their own genuine responses constructively. The need for achieving professional objectivity through self-management is essential: If the caseworker is too involved with his/her own feelings, he/she will not be in a position to perceive the client with clarity and objectivity. In short, the worker needs to continually make a conscious self-assessment of his/her feelings while remaining genuine and empathetic toward the client.

It should be pointed out that there are those who do not subscribe to the Rogerian approach to the therapeutic relationship, particularly with elderly clients (Goldfarb and Sheps, 1954; Turner, 1961). Goldfarb, a pioneer in geriatric psychiatry, and his social work colleague, Turner, proposed that the therapeutic interview with older clients needed to be structured differently from those with younger, relatively healthier clients. They contended that the therapist is best able to help the older patient by assuming a parental, authoritarian role. Their assumptions were that the aged client feels helpless and wishes to be dependent, and thereby presses the therapist into a powerful parental position. Utilizing the helping role to the fullest means the therapist fosters dependency as well as the illusion of his/her power.

This philosophy of the treatment relationship, which suggests that it is a mistake for the caseworker to confront a client's sense of helplessness, grew out of Goldfarb and Turner's experience working in a home for the aged in which less than 10 hours of psychiatric care per week was available for 925 residents. Treatment sessions consisted of 5- to 15-minute structured interviews spaced as widely apart as possible. Despite the large size of the caseload and the small number of staff, the rate of success was considered high and was attributed to their approach to relationship.

It seems reasonable to conclude that caseworkers should be open to different concepts of relationship, making adjustments in their individualized style where appropriate to fit the setting and the needs of the client. In any case, the importance of the *planned, professional* relationship cannot be overemphasized. Far too often, the inexperienced worker who may feel awkward or uncomfortable attempts to relate to the older client as an older family member or as a friend. While the practitioner wants to be accepting, the professional nature of the relationship must always be kept in mind. The goal of every such relationship is to bring about change in the life of the client, and this can only be accomplished through the disciplined use of the professional self.

CHAPTER

3

Aspects of Functional Age

This chapter is divided into two parts. The first presents a general introduction to assessment and functional age. The second describes the biological aspects of functional age.

INTRODUCTION TO ASSESSMENT

Casework is a unique social work procedure for helping individuals, families, and/or groups to cope more effectively with problems in psychosocial functioning. It rests on a body of specialized knowledge, technical expertise, and humanistic values; it generally includes intake, assessment/diagnosis, and treatment elements. This division, while artificial in that all aspects of casework are intertwined, is a necessary one as it allows for a description of the social worker's role throughout the casework process. In chapter 2, the various tasks of the practitioner during intake were discussed, and the concept that assessment as well as treatment begin with the first worker and client contact was emphasized. This chapter is the first of six to specifically address assessment procedures and techniques; however, it is well to bear in mind that assessment, which begins at intake, is also part of the treatment process.

At the heart of the casework method is the psychosocial study or assessment. Assessment is a social work procedure used to examine the client's problem for purposes of selecting interventions or treatment modalities. Any assessment aims to identify and explain the nature of a problem, to appraise it within a framework of specific elements, and to use that appraisal as a guide to action (Perlman, 1957). Its purpose, whether the problem rests with an individual, family, group or community, is to bring together the various facets of the client's situation in an orderly, economical manner.

Diagnostic assessment of an individual involves *getting to know the person*—his/her motivations, strengths, weaknesses, and capacity to change. Assessment is not only a cross-sectional study of the client's situation and his/her traditional mode of behavior, but an ascertainment of what psychological, biological, and sociocultural factors can contribute to effecting change. A diagnostic evaluation of an older adult, as with other age groups, is a method of looking at the presenting problem(s), determining what the dynamic issues are, and selecting possible corrective measures to alleviate or eliminate the problem (Butler and Lewis, 1982).

Assessment of a *family* involves viewing it as a *system* or group in which *development* and *role allocation* take place. Structure, communication patterns, and cultural milieu are among the many factors that vary from one family to the next and that need to be evaluated. Understanding the interactional patterns within the family is the major goal of the assessment. This allows the caseworker to work toward modifying those elements of family relationships which interfere with the management of life tasks. It also provides a picture of the way in which "individual symptoms" are intertwined with family functioning.

The functional-age model of intergenerational therapy offers particular diagnostic tools for the geriatric social worker. First, it employs and expands upon the concept of functional age as a means of evaluating the complex interaction among the older client's biological, psychological, and sociocultural processes. Second, it provides the knowledge and techniques needed to accomplish that evaluation within a family context. In the following chapters, the rationale and treatment techniques for viewing the functional capacities of the older adult as they relate to and have reciprocal effects within the family are presented. They require that the caseworker simultaneously evaluate the older adult and his/her family in order to arrive at a family-focused treatment plan. In their entirety, the following chapters on assessment aim to offer the practitioner the means for understanding the individual as a biopsychosocial being as he/she interacts within his/her family network and with other social systems.

WHAT IS AGING?

Aging refers to the regular [behavioral] changes that occur in mature genetically representative organisms living under representative environmental conditions as they advance in chronological age. When evaluating the relative abilities and disabilities of the older adult, the geriatric social worker is most interested in knowing to what extent and in what ways *aging* has affected the individual's capacity for going about his/her activities of daily living. This task is made difficult by virtue of the fact that gerontologists are just beginning to provide adequate information concerning the complex question(s) about how people age. In addition, some of the basic terms of this relatively new and rapidly growing field, such as aging itself, have yet to be appropriately defined. As a result, there are several definitions to consider.

The most common definition continues to be that of chronological age. Chronological age is simply based on the passage of time or the number of years that have passed since the person's birth. "Some feel that people become old at age 65." Inasmuch as it is only a measure of calendar years, it is not a reliable index of an individual's bodily changes or of his/her abilities or limitations; nor does this measure address the important differences between individuals in their patterns of aging (Kastenbaum, 1979). While the validity of this definition of aging has been questioned, it continues to be used as a criterion for determining the time for retirement and for receiving age-related benefits and services such as social security and medicare.

When scientists study the process of aging, they are usually interested in the dimensions or the phenomena most related to their own discipline. Therefore, many definitions of old age are limited by the perspective of a professional group: Biologists tend to study and define age in terms of organic or bodily functioning; psychologists in terms of mental functioning; and social psychologists and sociologists in terms of social functioning (Brink, 1979). Inasmuch as aging is a complex biopsychosocial process, these unidimensional approaches to it fail to provide a comprehensive picture of the older adult.

Still another approach to aging is to examine the individual's relative performance capacities. As a researcher, Birren (1969) was one of the first gerontologists to address the issue of how to appraise an individual's level of functioning in a given environment relative to others his/her age. His interest in age-associated changes and their effect on the person's capacity to deal with his/her living conditions led to his description of "three kinds of aging": *biological, psychological,* and *social.* Biological age refers to physiological age-related changes and the functional capacities of vital organ systems that contribute to life expectancy; psychological age refers to the adaptive capacities of the individual and his/her ability to adjust to environmental demands; social age refers to the roles and social habits of an individual with respect to other members of a society.

Birren's conceptualization provides a biopsychosocial life-cycle perspective on the processes of aging and contributes to an understanding of the funtional capacities and treatability of the older client. As a result, the concept has great applicability for geriatric social work practice and therefore was adopted as the theoretical underpinning for the assessment framework presented in this text.

BIOPSYCHOSOCIAL ASSESSMENT OF FUNCTIONAL AGE

The question of how to evaluate and what to include in a bio-psychosocial assessment of an older adult remains complex and difficult at best. Social workers are faced with a multitude of factors that can possibly influence the aged client's circumstances encompassing, among other things, the person's past experiences and family history as well as current medical problems and housing arrangements. Nonetheless, on the basis of this evaluation the caseworker is expected to arrive at "reasonable, reachable treatment goals," including an understanding of whether the problem(s) can be "reversed or ameliorated" and a picture of what kind of services and supports are needed (Butler and Lewis, 1982).

This section provides a perspective on some of the assessment methods currently used by gerontologists to measure various aspects of functional capacity. It also suggests how geriatric social workers can achieve clinical effectiveness in using the psychosocial method in multidimensional geriatric assessment by employing the functional-age model as a framework.

Both the scientific and service communities have long been concerned with the issue of defining and studying the aging process, and with devising a method(s) to obtain a comprehensive diagnostic picture of the functional capacities of the older adult. The goal of determining how functional abilities vary from individual to individual and the need to measure these differences, while well recognized, has not been easy to attain.

As early as the late 1800's and the early 1900's, there was an interest in measuring health status as it relates to activities of daily living. At that time, information was obtained through health interview surveys, and questions generally dealt with the number of persons who were sick and unable to work on a given day. This information represented the first approach to concepts of disability or dysfunction. As the concept of disability was refined, questions about the duration of an illness and issues relevant to the classification of types of dysfunction emerged.

Early longitudinal studies of functional capacity focused on differences in scores on a single trait, such as cardiovascular disease or intelligence. However, gerontologists called for the development of a composite or global indicator of overall functioning. The goal was the development of an index that would classify large amounts of information about interrelated changes associated with aging. It was hoped that this index of what is often referred to as functional age (Birren, 1959) could be used to predict such things as employment capabilities, the likelihood of survival, or the capability of independent living.

In the last three decades the range of available measures of biological, mental, and social functioning has been greatly expanded (Katz, 1983). The current literature reveals that we now have fairly sophisticated assessment instruments and measurement procedures with which to evaluate the aged (Granick, 1983). Although it is not feasible or necessary to describe the total array of tests here, geriatric caseworkers should familiarize themselves with the better known and more widely used ones, particularly those that are multidimensional and that may be appropriate for their client population and agency setting.

Multidimensional assessment procedures are those that combine within a single instrument the major domains of a comprehensive evaluation. There is an attempt to reliably quantify all relevant medical, functional, and psychosocial attributes and deficits in order to achieve a rational basis for therapy and resource planning. Multidisciplinary assessment has also been found useful in determining optimal use of nursing homes and establishing baseline data for documenting change over time (Rubenstein, 1983). While approaches to assessment vary between programs, depending upon goals and setting, most include information on physical health, functional abilities, psychological health and social networks. A recent book by Kane and Kane (1981) provides an analysis of existing geriatric assessment instruments and describes in detail which are best for a particular population and setting.

Three instruments, each of which contains mental health and cognitive status subtests and is pertinent to geriatric social work, are briefly described here. The Multidimensional Functional Assessment Questionnaire, better known as OARS, was the first integrated system for evaluating the older adult and has become a model for other scales. Developed initially in response to a request by the Administration on Aging to examine alternatives to institutionalization, OARS (Older American's Resources and Services) provides a comprehensive means of assessing individual functioning as it relates to service utilization. It is currently being used in over a hundred research and clinical settings as an empirical and decision-making tool. In addition, it has been employed by individuals evaluating the effects of specific service packages and in policy development and implementation.

CARE, the Comprehensive Assessment and Referral Evaluation, was originally devised as part of a cross-national geriatric home-based study involving over 850 community residents (over age 65) from the New York and London metropolitan areas. It comprises three sections—psychiatric, medical, and social—and requires an average of 90 minutes to complete.

The Multilevel Assessment Instrument (MAI) was recently developed at the Philadelphia Geriatric Center. It was designed to measure the well-being of the aged in the areas of physical health, cognition, activities of daily living, time use, social interaction, personal adjustment, and perceived environment. It contains a total of 216 items and takes less than an hour to administer.

Multidimensional geriatric assessment, which can be achieved by the instruments described, has been found to have several benefits. For instance, follow-up studies suggest that accuracy of diagnosis of functional, psychological, and/or social problems tends to improve when special systematic attention is paid to the elderly patient. In turn, improvement in diagnostic accuracy contributes to improved treatment. In addition, preliminary data suggest that careful assessment can help to alleviate the problem of inappropriate drug regimens and iatrogenic illness. There is also suggestive evidence that proper assessment can decrease unnecessary nursing home placements and reduce rehospitalization rates (Rubenstein, 1983).

Despite the obvious benefits derived from multidimensional assessment instruments, it is important to realize that they cannot replace other professional forms of clinical assessment. While some social workers may find that such instruments provide a useful adjunct to their own professional judgment, others may find them too time-consuming or awkward to administer in their particular milieu. More importantly, such scales do not utilize the information-processing skills usually associated with the psychosocial casework method; nor do they recognize the interactional role of the practitioner in shaping the assessment process. In addition, these standardized assessment instruments are often used after the older person has been removed from his/her natural home environment and family system, and without reference to earlier life experiences (Eyde & Rich, 1983).

Despite the difficulties in multidisciplinary assessment, an evaluation of the older adult's functional capacities is a necessary and central component of the holistic view of assessment presented in this text. Observing and assessing the client in his/her environment and coming to an understanding of his/her level of functional skills provides critical diagnostic information. By evaluating the individual's relative competence in meeting environmental demands, the caseworker begins to get at the heart of the problem(s) that have brought the pivotal client and his/her family to seek help.

Needless to say, a social work approach to the assessment of functional age is different from that of other disciplines. While it encompasses an understanding of the three dimensions of aging (biological, social, and psychological) as defined by Birren (1959), a social work assessment of an older adult begins with the specialized knowledge, skills, and professional values inherent in the psychosocial casework method. This approach is *dynamic* and views the needs of the elderly client as a product of *complex interaction* among biological, psychological, and social variables. In order to understand and assess the client's level of functioning, pertinent information about these variables along with an individual and family history must be obtained. The goal is a *process-oriented* biopsychosocial study or diagnosis rather than a numerical index or indicator.

Essential to all casework practice is an evaluation of the client's problem and the many factors that affect its existence, nature, and solution. A dynamic diagnosis may be understood as an evaluation of the "factors at play in the person-problem-situation complex":

> The dynamic diagnosis is a kind of cross-sectional view of the forces interacting in the client's problem situation. These forces are currently operating within the client himself, within his social situation, and between him and his situation. The dynamic diagnosis seeks to establish what the trouble is, what psychological, physical, or social factors contribute to (or cause) it, what effect it has on the individual's well-being (and that of others), what solution is sought, and what means exist within the client, his situation, and organized services and resources by which the problem may be affected. The formulation of a dynamic diagnosis would in effect be a judgment based on a *configuration* of the data [in these areas] (Perlman, 1957, p. 171).

As suggested by Perlman, the challenge to the geriatric social worker, as to all caseworkers, is to integrate all necessary information about the client in interaction with his/her relevant social systems so as to meet his/her practical needs.

Clearly, a dynamic view of functional age is distinguished by its problem focus. Activities of daily living, such as the ability to use the telephone, shop, prepare meals, do housekeeping, use a car or public transportation, handle one's own finances or dress and feed oneself, are of interest as they relate to the older person's capacity to live as independently and as fruitfully as possible. A dynamic approach to assessing functional age is not an automatic "formula-ridden method of age classification" to be used solely as an experimental and/or research tool. Rather, it provides a concept for appraising an individual's level of functioning in a given environment relative to others of his/her age (Birren and Renner, 1977, pp. 4–5). In this way a clear distinction can be made between an individual's chronological age and the person's actual physical, mental, and social situation.

In summary, the functional-age model is concerned with the functional capacities of the older adult as he or she advances in chronological age. It recognizes that while aging has both normal and disease properties associated with it, it is a process of change that occurs in individuals after maturity, or full bodily growth (Birren and Renner, 1980, p. 4). This view allows for both the expansion and the decline in capacity in any of the biological, psychological, and/or social areas of functioning, and requires a *comprehensive assessment* of each within a family context. *In this sense, biopsychosocial assessment of an older adult is inherently a dynamic evaluation of the person's functional age.*

BIOLOGICAL ASPECTS OF FUNCTIONAL AGE

Introduction

Of all the areas of information in which the geriatric social worker must be knowledgeable, the biological aspects of aging seem the most forbidding or out-of-reach. Many caseworkers feel that this information is difficult to learn and requires special abilities. Many erroneously believe that the biophysiological problems of aging are entirely out of their area of professional expertise, and "abandon" these issues to other allied health professionals. Yet caseworkers who are not familiar with the basic biological factors associated with aging are at a decided disadvantage, because they are not properly prepared to assess their elderly clients nor to work effectively with other professionals.

Aging is a normal biopsychosocial process of change that occurs in all organisms over their life spans. The three areas of aging (biological, psychological, sociological) interact with each other in a complex way that is just beginning to be understood. This makes many symptoms difficult to evaluate as they can be the result of multiple determining factors. The caseworker who is able to raise assessment questions about these interrelationships is more likely to arrive at a realistic and accurate appraisal of the client's problem.

Because caseworkers often make home visits and develop a long-term therapeutic relationship with their clients, they are in an ideal position to obtain information about the client's *total* situation. Assessment relevant to biological functioning should not be overlooked, and information about factors such as nutritional habits, ease of mobility, availability and use of medication, and understanding of and compliance with medical/health regimes should be obtained.

Clearly the geriatric caseworker cannot become an expert on biomedical problems, nor is this desirable. However, it is important to be well-informed. This chapter suggests some of the key biological issues in aging of which the caseworker should be aware. It is recognized that this is a rapidly growing field of study and information can soon become outdated. For this reason, a list of assessment questions is provided at the end of the chapter. The questions are intended as a guide for the caseworker who can then ascertain the most recent information on that particular topic.

Biological Age

Biological aging refers to those changes in the structure and functions of body organs and systems that occur over time (Zarit, 1980). As one of the three kinds of aging discussed earlier, it is the process most closely associated with the individual's capacity for survival or position along his/her life span.

Biological age, in the strictest sense, is a measure of the functional capacity of the vital life-limiting organ systems (see Zarit, p. 85). Such an assessment leads to a prediction as to whether the individual is "older" or "younger" than other persons of the same chronological age; this, in turn, permits an understanding of whether the individual has a longer or shorter life expectancy than other persons of his/her average age (Birren and Renner, 1977):

> "He has the heart of a 40-year-old."
> "She has the stamina of a woman half her age."

Physiological changes play a primary but *not* exclusive role in determining biological age. Physiological aging includes all time-dependent changes in structure and function of the organism, eventually contributing to diminished efficiency (of organ systems) and increased vulnerability to disease and death (Weg, 1975).

Physiological changes associated with advancing age should be differentiated from pathological changes. Normal aging is characterized by the *general* progressive loss of physiological capacities. These include, among other things, a reduction in lung capacity, a slowing in the speed of response and reaction time, a reduction in the margin for stress, and an increase in healing time. However, there is a difference between these age-related biological changes and those related to a specific disease. For example, calcification of the arterial system is a progressive process associated with age. At the same time, it has been shown that cerebral blood flow and oxygen consumption do not decline *simply* as a function of aging, but in proportion to the degree of actual vascular *disease* (Finkel et al., 1982).

Clearly, physiological functioning and health status are important factors in how a person functions in old age. However, given the complexity and lack of homogeneity of the geriatric population, it is well to keep in mind that there are marked individual differences in the onset and rate of physical change with age. In addition, organs and subsystems within the individual age differently (Keller and Hughston, 1981). So, while chronological age and health status are correlated to some extent with chronic ailments and physical disabilities occurring more frequently in the old, it is necessary to remember that there are always variations and exceptions to this general pattern (Zarit, 1980). Therefore, the caseworker should not conclude that physical change(s) in an elderly client are "simply a result of age." All conditions require a multifaceted assessment, with consideration given to biological, psychological, and sociocultural factors. There are many instances where other professionals are needed to accomplish this task. The social worker can play a crucial role in alerting the client family and/or physician to a perceived difficulty that requires further exploration.

Assessing Biological Age

It has already been stated that biological age is, to a large degree, a reflection of changes in various bodily systems and that these changes can affect the physical and psychological functioning of the older adult. During assessment, the social worker focuses on how these biological and physiological processes interact with and influence personality and social behavior. In order to complete this evaluation, the practitioner must first be aware of how the basic physiological systems function and how they may change with age. In addition, he/she must be prepared to consult with the client's physician where appropriate. This section highlights the major characteristics of the eight organ systems, with special emphasis on those issues of greatest concern to social work practice.

The Reproductive System and Human Sexuality. Because society has been willing to accept the myth that older people are feeble, unproductive, and asexual, and researchers have generally been reticent to investigate sexuality among older adults, stereotyping and folklore have obscured our understanding of this activity in later life. It is often *erroneously* assumed that older people do not have sexual desires or are too frail or sick to engage in this activity. However, from the studies that have been conducted on sexuality and aging, one fact has clearly emerged: Most older people continue to have sexual needs and interests on into their 80's and possibly beyond, and those healthy older persons who want to maintain their sexual activity are able to do so (Butler and Lewis, 1976; Comfort, 1980; Zarit, 1980).

As with other physiological systems, there are a number of age-related changes in human sexual physiology and performance. While these changes are usually minimal and a natural part of the aging process, they can have a major effect upon the older client who may not understand their implications. The geriatric caseworker can play a significant role by correcting misconceptions and providing information.

Older Men. The older man may experience a slower physiological response to sexual stimuli and take longer to obtain an erection. While these changes occur after a young man reaches the height of his sexuality, they are more pronounced and identifiable in those over 50. For most older men, the refractory period (the capacity for erection following ejaculation) cannot be regained as quickly as for younger men. On the plus side, however, there is generally greater control of ejaculatory demand, which means that "the older man can remain erect and make love longer before coming to orgasm" (Butler and Lewis, 1982, p. 142; Comfort, 1980).

The most important point is that the older man does not lose his facility for erection as he ages unless there are other physical or emotional problems. In other words, impotence is never a consequence of chronological age alone (Comfort, 1980). If older men lose interest or become impotent, a number of factors could be involved and should be assessed including: (1) general ill health and disease (e.g., diabetes); (2) vascular insufficiency; (3) hypertension; (4) prostate enlargement and other genitourinary problems; (5) neurological disorders; (6) excessive drinking and/or alcoholism; (7) drugs, and prescribed medication (e.g., major and minor tranquilizers, antidepressants, and antihypertension medications);* (8) depression; (9) fatigue; (10) long periods of abstinence; (11) social expectation of impotence in age.

Older Women. While sexual function in women has been less fully researched, evidence suggests that older women experience fewer changes than do men. The capacity for orgasm continues on into old age, and, if in reasonable health, the older woman can expect to continue sexual activities until late in life. Unfortunately, because of the differences in life spans between men and women, sexual partners may not be available.

There are some physiological changes in the older woman during and after menopause. These generally include the effects of gradual steroid reduction, such as thinning of the vaginal walls, a reduction of length and diameter of the vagina and major labia, and a decrease in vaginal secretions. As with the male, these normal age-related changes need not affect the pleasure of sexual intercourse, and cultural expectations and psychological reactions play a major role in this regard.

It is important to recognize that the human sexual function is highly idiosyncratic, and the ways in which sexuality is expressed are very diverse (Corby and Solnick, 1980). The task of the social worker is to recognize and support the view that love and intimacy are important throughout life and to seek an acceptable way of discussing this subject, involving highly personal feelings, with his/her clients. Sexual problems in later life include those that may occur at any age, and are an equally important aspect of human relationships. In that sense, they should not be ignored in the counseling relationship. Many clients need to be reassured that their continued sexual interest is "natural"; others may be concerned that a partner is not available; some may be misunderstood by family and friends, and still others may be in

*See A. Whanger, "Summary of Psychoactive Drugs for Geriatric Patients," in A. Whanger and A. C. Myers, eds., *Mental Health Assessment and Therapeutic Intervention with Older Adults* (Rockville, Maryland: Aspen Publications, 1948).

settings, such as nursing homes, where the expression of sexuality is not acceptable. All are entitled to understanding and support of their sexual feelings.

Clients who have had disfiguring surgery, such as mastectomy or colostomy, or have a major illness or have had a heart attack may need considerable reassurance about their sexuality. In addition, they may require realistic medical information and suggestions for how to best continue sexual activity. Such clients can be encouraged to either speak with their physician or give the caseworker permission to consult with him/her.

Any discussion with the client should take into account the fact that human sexuality encompasses more than sexual intercourse. Intimacy may be manifested in many ways, including listening, conversation, holding hands, or giving a hug or a gift. The ability to achieve intimacy, a major developmental task, involves the emotional flexibility to be able to redefine relationships and to invest in new sources of love and friendship. Those elderly persons who have been able to establish consistent relationships and have an intimate friend on whom they can depend for support generally are better adjusted and have higher morale and life satisfaction (Lowenthal and Haven, 1968).

Nervous System. The nervous system consists of the brain, the spinal cord, and the related nerve cells and fibers throughout the body. It keeps us in contact with the world outside our bodies and, along with the endocrine system, provides most of the control functions for the body. It literally receives thousands of bits of information from the different sense organs (see chapter 4), integrates them, and determines the response to be made.

Sleep Disturbance. Wakefulness and sleep, in large part, are controlled by brain activity, although they can, of course, be influenced by environmental factors. Certain sleep changes are common in later life and may be related to changes in biological rhythms. In general, older people sleep less, sleep lighter, and awaken earlier and more easily. They also have a greater tendency to awaken throughout the night. Because many older people retire early when fatigued, they may waken at 3:00 or 4:00 A.M. and then fear they have insomnia when, in fact, they have had an adequate night's sleep (Butler and Lewis, 1982).

Complaints about sleep disturbances should be evaluated from a biopsychosocial perspective. Changes in sleep patterns may be related to illness, chronic pain, anxiety, depression, drug dependence, and the need for more activity during the day. Too many catnaps during the day can result in day–night sleep reversal. A discussion with the client about his/her specific habits can often lead to a differential diagnosis. Consultation with the physician may also prove helpful.

Parkinsonism. Parkinson's disease is a result of a deficiency of dopamine and a loss of brain cells and associated lesions in the brain. It is characterized by rigidity of the body, tremors, and slowness of movement. It may also be accompanied by involuntary movement of the fingers, shaking head, stooped posture, shuffling gait, and depressed "stare."

Major breakthroughs in the drug treatment of Parkinson's have occurred over recent years, which relieve many of the most common symptoms. However, the caseworker should be aware of some possible side effects related to the use of antiparkinsonian drugs, such as L-dopa. While careful monitoring of dosages minimizes the side effects, reactions may include hallucinations, persistent vomiting, hypotension, depression, and confusion (Butler and Lewis, 1982). As these symptoms may mimic other medical and psychiatric difficulties, consultation is advised. It is also important for the caseworker to be sensitive to the physical implications as well as the embarrassment and depression that may accompany the disease.

Alcoholism. Alcohol is a central nervous system depressant which inhibits cortical control and impairs intellectual functions. Alcoholism is a condition resulting from excessive ingestion of or idiosyncratic reaction to alcohol. As the third leading health problem in the United States (after heart disease and cancer), alcoholism can shorten life expectancy, cause heart disease, damage the brain, contribute to falls and accidents, and lead to chronic impotence in men by damaging the central nervous system and upsetting hormonal balance. Chronic alcoholism can also contribute to vitamin and protein deficiencies, liver dysfunction, and general deterioration of the personality (Butler and Lewis, 1982).

While studies show that the overall incidence of alcoholism in older people is lower than among younger people, this damaging disease should be addressed in assessment. Particular groups of older people, such as elderly widowers, are highly prone to alcoholism. Butler and Lewis (1982) suggest that the mental health practitioner look for the following diagnostic clues for the clinical presentation of alcoholism in old age: (1) insomnia, (2) impotence, (3) problem with control of gout, (4) rapid onset of confusional state, (5) uncontrollable hypertension, and (6) unexplained falls (p. 133)

Organic Mental Disorders. Of all the difficulties associated with advancing age, organic mental (see later description and definition) disorders present the greatest challenge for geriatric practitioners in making correct assessments and providing appropriate treatment. Studies indicate that during the decade of the 1970's as many as one half of older patients seen in inpatient and outpatient facilities were diagnosed as having an organic mental disorder (Zarit, 1980). Senile dementia of the Alzheimer type (SDAT) (see later description and definition) strikes more elderly people than any other brain disease, with an estimated 5% of older people suffering from a severe intellectual impairment. This figure may be as high as 15 to 25 to 40% for those who survive into their 80's and 90's (Eisdorfer, 1984; Center for Studies of the Mental Health of the Aging, 1984).

These alarming statistics have resulted in growing public awareness and support, and increased funds for research. At this time, considerable research is underway at governmental agencies and schools of medicine, and there is cautious optimism about recent findings (Crook, 1983, p. 198; Journal of American Medical Association, 1984). While this text presents the most updated information available at the time of publication, it is critical for practitioners to keep informed of the newest developments.

There are major difficulties, however, in keeping abreast of the literature on organic brain disorders. Inasmuch as this is an area of rapidly advancing research, the social worker may find that studies and references are quickly outdated. At the same time, research may be difficult to interpret because findings may be unclear or contradictory. In addition, there seems to be far too little agreement on the use of terms. The difficulty in choice of nomenclature is said to reflect the current lack of consensus among scientists about how various symptoms arise. While some believe that these symptoms reflect a number of "disparate mental and/or physical [underlying] disorders sharing a common neurological pathway," others suggest there is a single disease entity responsible for the degeneration that characterizes SDAT (Journal of American Medical Association, 1984).

The most recent and widely accepted description of organic mental disorders is found in the American Psychiatric Association's Diagnostic and Statistical Manual of Mental Disorders-III (1980), DSM-III. (Practitioners can refer to it for hospital diagnoses, insurance form requirements, and for an in-depth discussion of the six organic brain syndromes.) These diagnostic categories and definitions offer a means of clarifying symptoms and "standardizing" terms, and are used as a reference for this section of the text.

In order to understand the mental disorders of old age, the practitioner must first be aware of the symptomatology associated with brain disorders and understand the distinction between organic brain syndromes (OBS), which are a constellation of psychological or behavioral signs and symptoms without reference to etiology or cause, and organic mental disorders, which are psychological or behavioral abnormalities associated with specific known brain dysfunction (Table 3.1), determined through diagnostic evaluation.

Organic brain syndrome, a general term used to describe abnormal behavior that is thought to be linked to brain dysfunction, may be

TABLE 3.1. Summary Definitions Related to Organic Brain Syndrome

---

Symptoms of organic brain syndrome

    Impairment of memory involving difficulty in registering, retaining, and recalling stimuli.

    Impairment of intellect involving deterioration in the ability to calculate, handle information, and learn.

    Impairment of judgment which refers to an inability to comprehend, weigh options, formulate decisions, and take appropriate actions.

    Impairment of orientation which refers to a diminished capacity to know time, place, and person.

    Lability and shallowness of affect involving excessive emotional reactions (labile) and/or the blunting of response (shallowness). In both cases, the response is inappropriate to the situation.

Symptoms of dementia

    Primary degenerative dementia, also known as senile dementia of the Alzheimer's type (SDAT)—a form of dementia in which there is atrophy of the brain thought to cause intellectual impairment.

    Multiinfarct dementia—damage to the cerebral blood vessels through arteriosclerotic changes causing a series of small strokes which results in impairment of intellectual functioning.

---

recognized by observing or identifying five mental signs. These signs, which may not all be seen at the same time or to the same degree, are extremely important to monitor, as they may be the subtle beginnings of any number of serious conditions (Butler and Lewis, 1982). (See Table 3.1.)

Organic brain syndromes have an extremely varied course and may be (1) acute, with sudden onset, (2) chronic, lasting months or years, (3) reversible, responding to treatment, and (4) irreversible, having a permanent effect. Of the six organic brain syndromes, the most common and, therefore, of primary interest to the geriatric caseworker in assessment, are *delirium* and *dementia*.

Delirium is characterized by a clouding of consciousness, ranging from drowsiness to stupor or coma, and reduced capacity to sustain attention to environmental stimuli. The individual with delirium cannot maintain a coherent stream of thought, is unable to reason, and, therefore, is difficult to engage in conversation. In addition incoherent speech, perceptual disturbances, such as hallucinations and illusions, may be present. The sleep and wakefulness cycle and psychomotor activity are almost invariably disturbed.

Delirium is most often caused by overuse or misuse of drugs, infections, and alcoholism (other causes may include brain lesions, metabolic and nutritional disorders, circulatory and pulmonary diseases, and sensory disturbances). Older persons are especially sensitive to both prescription and nonprescription medications and, consequently, are more likely to react to multiple prescriptions, high dosages and self-medication. Special care needs to be taken with antipsychotic, antihypertensive medications, and insulin (Matteson, 1984). A review of the client's use of medications, with reference to medical and drug directories and appropriate consultation with the physician, is within the realm of good geriatric social work practice.

Delirium has a relatively brief duration; there is a need to identify the cause and treat it quickly. Failure to do so can result in death (40% of the cases) or permanent damage and institutionalization.

Dementia, on the other hand, is characterized by a chronic progressive decline in mental functioning, and is the disorder that most lay persons call "senility." Senility is actually a meaningless term that erroneously implies that all old people become forgetful. Dementia is actually a disease entity and is *not* a normal part of the aging process. It is characterized by a loss of intellectual abilities that interferes with social and occupational functioning. Symptoms include memory loss, impairment of intellectual functioning and abstract thought, impaired judgment and impulse control, confusion, disorientation, and personality changes.

There are two predominate types of dementia: *primary degenerative dementia* with senile onset (also known as senile dementia or senile dementia of the Alzheimer's type, SDAT) and *multiinfarct dementia*. SDAT, which affects 50–70% of all persons with dementia (Matteson, 1984) and therefore is of great clinical and social importance, has pronounced effects on higher cortical brain functioning. Multiinfarct dementia, unlike SDAT, is associated with cerebral arteriosclerosis and a history of multiple small strokes or cerebral accidents. Multiinfarct dementia, which is found more often in men, is generally less common than SDAT and, in addition to cognitive disturbances, has neurological effects including weakness in the limbs, reflex asymmetries, and changes in gait. (See Table 3.1.)

The disease processes associated with dementia can only be diagnosed with certainty via an autopsy, through observation of certain pathological changes in the brain. (These include the degeneration of neurons, and the existence of extensive senile plaques and neurofibrillary tangles.) However, comprehensive medical evaluation is essential to arrive at a diagnosis *by exclusion* of as many symptoms related to other disorders as possible, symptoms that *look like* those of SDAT (which can include, among other things, infections, thyroid problems, nutritional deficiencies, anemias, tumors, multiple sclerosis, head injuries, diabetic acidosis, general surgery, uremia, dehydration, liver failure, and depression). Such an assessment should include a thorough medical workup, neurological and psychological studies, and a home study (Cohen, 1980).

The presence of any of the warning signs of organic brain syndrome calls for immediate attention by the caseworker. Quick and accurate assessment involving differential diagnosis can allow for prompt treatment. As some causes of organic brain syndrome are treatable and the symptoms reversible under proper medical care, the caseworker should not overlook these potentially dangerous symptoms, and should make appropriate medical referrals.

Organic brain syndromes have a very varied course depending upon the underlying difficulty. In the process of assessment, the cause(s) of the organic brain syndrome may be diagnosed. It may then be "reclassified" as a *specific* organic mental disorder and a course of treatment established. For example, the confused and disoriented client whose dizziness, headaches, and sudden confusion are attributed to a series of strokes may be diagnosed as having multiinfarct dementia; while the client suffering from fluctuating levels of awareness and exhibiting a dazed expression may be found to be suffering from delirium caused by dehydration and malnutrition (electrolyte imbalance). Both conditions are amenable to medical care and could also require social services.

Where organic brain syndromes are attributable to specific systemic illnesses—malnutrition, the ingestion of toxic substances, metabolic disturbances—they are more likely to be treatable and reversible. In disorders such as stroke, there may be permanent structural damage to the brain and permanent impairment. However, rehabilitative efforts on the part of physical and occupational therapists, social workers and other professionals are often successful and should not be overlooked.

In short, since organic mental disorders are psychological and behavioral abnormalities associated with transient or permanent dysfunction of the brain where the precipitating factor is *known*, diagnosis should be based upon evidence including a medical history, physical examination, and/or laboratory tests, and *not* from the symptoms alone. (see Table 3.1 for summary.)

One of the most valuable clinical instruments for assessing the cognitive capacity of older persons is the brief mental status type of examination. This instrument is objective, easily administered, and most useful in the differential diagnosis of organic or affective disorders in the elderly (see chapter 4). The Mental Status Questionnaire of Kahn et al. (1960, 1964) presented in Table 3.2 is probably the most widely used and appropriate to include in social work interviews.

Organic mental disorders, then, the most prevalent psychiatric disorders of later life, require prompt and thorough assessment involving a number of professionals, one of whom is the social worker.

TABLE 3.2. Mental Status Questionnaire[a]

---

1. Where are we now?
2. Where is this place (located)?
3. What is today's date—day of month?
4. What month is it?
5. What year is it?
6. How old are you?
7. What is your birthday?
8. What year were you born?
9. Who is President of the United States?
10. Who was President before him?

---

[a]Modified from R. L. Kahn; I. Goldfarb; and M. Pollack, "The Evaluation of Geriatric Patients Following Treatment," in P. H. Hoch and J. Zubin, eds., *Evaluation of Psychiatric Treatment* (New York: Grune & Stratton, Inc., 1964).

Skeletal and Muscular Systems. The skeletal and muscular systems reach maximum size and strength when the individual is in his/her early to mid-20s. With age, as cells are reduced in number and size, bones tend to lose density and become more brittle, joints tend to become less mobile (stiffer), and the cartilage between segments of the spinal column degenerates. These changes, which do not occur at the same rate for everyone, bring about a reduction in height and flexibility, which can contribute to a hunched-over look (Guyton, 1977; Lowy, 1977).

As changes in the skeletal and muscular systems take place, related physical difficulties can occur. Osteoarthritis, bursitis, and a general loss of muscle strength and tone are some common complaints. In addition, lack of protein deposition in the bones can cause osteoporosis with consequent weakness of the bones, particularly in women. The social worker should not attribute these problems simply to "old age," as proper medical care can often alleviate painful symptoms. Expediting an appropriate referral can be an important social work role.

Endocrine System. The endocrine system comprises all internal glandular activity and secretions. The hormones that are secreted play a major regulatory function in metabolism, blood clotting, and body temperature. Malfunctioning of the endocrine system can contribute to high blood pressure, arthritis, arteriosclerosis, and diabetes.

Diabetes, a disease of the endocrine system, is usually hereditary, especially for those who develop it at an early age. Mild diabetes is common in old age, especially for people who are overweight; however, diet can often reduce blood glucose levels and symptoms can be controlled. When improperly treated, diabetes can cause impotence, mental confusion, and/or depression. Testing for this disease is simple and should be part of a general physical examination that all elderly clients should receive regularly.

Genitourinary System. The purpose of the genitourinary system is to bring about the interchange of nutrients and cellular waste between the tissues and circulating blood. Kidney function shows a major decline with age, which can lead to a buildup of waste products in the body. This can have many side effects, including confused mental states and eventual renal failure. The effect of acute or chronic renal failure depends to a great extent on the water and food intake of the person, which means that dietary habits and medication play an important role.

Dialysis of uremic patients with artificial kidneys has been an available treatment for about 30 years. It is now developed to the point that many patients can live normal life spans. However, there are many psychosocial, economic, political, and ethical questions involved that can affect clients and professionals alike.

Older people, particularly women, may have difficulty with bladder control due to poor muscle control. This condition may cause embarrassing "leakage" and sometimes results in social isolation. As the client may not feel free to discuss the subject, the social worker should be alert to this physical condition and the fact that exercise and/or a simple operation may help.

Circulatory System. With age, the circulatory system, which comprises the heart and vascular system, is characterized by a general decline in its capacity to circulate blood. This is due to a buildup of fatty deposits along the walls of the blood vessels that can, when associated with degenerative changes in the arterial walls, obstruct and narrow the passages. This can lead to coronary heart disease and difficulties in other organs of the body, especially the brain, kidneys, liver, and gastrointestinal tract (Guyton, 1977).

Inasmuch as the hardening (arteriosclerosis) and narrowing (atherosclerosis) of the vessel walls interferes with blood flow, strokes can eventually occur. The stroke, which is, in effect, a blocked or ruptured vein in the brain, can lead to temporary or permanent paralysis, confusion, clouding of memory, loss of speech (aphasia), dementia (see discussion of multiinfarct dementia), unconsciousness, and death. Treatment involves a combination of medical care including physical therapy, recreation, and therapeutic and social services; the social worker is an important member of this multidisciplinary team.

Major risk factors in stroke are an elevated or high blood pressure and smoking. About 40% of older white persons and more than 50% of older black persons have high blood pressure. The National Heart/Lung Institute, as a result of a 5-year study of close to 11,000 people, recommends active treatment of even mild hypertension. This may include management of diet (salt and calorie control), exercise, and oral diuretics.

Respiratory System. Changes in the respiratory system with age are closely related to the ability to transfer oxygen to the blood. This capacity declines as the older person has decreased elasticity of bronchial tubes and may breathe faster as a result. These "normal" age-related changes in the respiratory system may be exacerbated by smoking and diseases, such as bronchial pneumonia and tuberculosis (Guyton, 1977; Lowy, 1979).

Digestive System. The primary function of the digestive system is to provide the body with a continual supply of water and nutrients. Obviously, the physical and mental well-being of the older person is closely linked to the digestive function, and disease or changes associated with aging may affect nutrition. Calorie needs decrease as people age because of decreased activity, changes in metabolism, and a decrease in cell mass. However, the nutritional requirements relative to vitamins, minerals, and proteins do not alter. In fact, there is some evidence that as older people experience a decline in digestive secretions and in intestinal absorption, more nutrients may be necessary (Butler and Lewis, 1982), so the need to be careful about proper nutrition is as great or greater in later years.

Obtaining information about nutritional habits and dietary prescriptions is an important part of a multifaceted assessment. Unfortunately, many older people may not be able to shop for and prepare a proper diet. Others may not want to cook for one person or eat alone. Low income, a lack of knowledge of balanced nutrition, and dulled taste and smell may also interfere with proper nutrition. This can have a ripple effect, leading to deterioration in physiological and mental processes. The caseworker can be of assistance to the client and medical team in sorting out these difficulties.

While an assessment of the client's biological age involves an evaluation of physiological processes and is designed to detect medical problems and their psychosocial effects, it cannot stop there. The assessment should also encompass an evaluation of those factors related to an older person's ability to function in the community or a given environment. The following outline is designed to act as a guide to the caseworker in that assessment (see Butler and Lewis, 1982; Gurland et al., 1977–78; Duke University OARS, 1978; Lawton, Moss, Fulcomer, and Kleban, 1982, Tager, 1980 for further discussion):

I.   *Common physical symptoms*
      Pain
      Fatigue

Shortness of breath
Swelling of ankles
Change in skin—pallor
Constipation—diarrhea
Incontinence or bladder problems
Bowel control
Fainting, dizziness
Bleeding
Other (client's self-report)

II. *Physical limitations*
Hearing loss—hearing aid
Vision loss—glasses, cataracts, glaucoma
Dentures
Gait—cane, walker, wheelchair
Prosthetic devices
Posture

III. *Cognitive ability*
Judgment
Communication—use of telephone, knowledge of news events, financial management
Memory
Intellect
Orientation—use of calendar, appointments

IV. *Medical regimes*
General medical history
Chronic illnesses
Acute illnesses
Prescription drugs (see Whanger and Myers, 1984)
Over-the-counter drugs—i.e., laxatives, aspirin (see Whanger and Myers, 1984)
Special diets—low sodium, low sugar, low fat, low cholesterol

V. *Daily living habits*
Alcohol and drug use
Water intake, general nutritional requirements, vitamins, protein
Caffeine use
Smoking
Exercise/activity—regular, exertion level
Eating and self-feeding skills and general appetite
Grooming—shaving, combing hair, teeth, nails, skin care, clothing
Bathing/washing

Sleep patterns—difficulties, naps, average number of hours,
  sleeping pills, day–night reversals, insomnia
Sexual activities—desires, changes, outlets

VI. *Mobility/safety*
General speed of motion
Home environment (manipulation of)
Lighting, stairs, bathtub, location of toilet and bedroom
Architectural barriers (accessing)—ramps, curbs
Ability to handle emergencies—fire, medical

VII. *Home management*
Housecleaning
Kitchen activities—i.e., open cans and meal preparation
Ability to shop for groceries
Safety—lighting, security of carpets

4

Psychological Aspects of Functional Age

Psychology as a science and as a profession examines the behavioral, affective, and intellectual aspects of human experience. Of the many areas of study it encompasses, developmental, personality, and cognitive theories are of particular relevance to geriatric social work practice. This text presents the concepts thought to be most valuable in assessing the older adult's relative psychological adjustment.

Geriatric psychological evaluations include an appraisal of many factors related to personality functioning, including the client's competence to handle his/her own affairs, level of contact with reality, judgment, problem-solving ability, sense of self-esteem, appropriateness of affect, and interpersonal skills. The key to accomplishing such an assessment is to determine how competently the client copes with his/her environment, focusing on those factors that address the client's adaptability. Inasmuch as a major concern of biopsychosocial study is the evaluation of the coping strategies of the elderly client, the primary focus of this chapter is on those mental health issues that are associated with the individual's personal effectiveness in dealing with his/her environment.

INTRODUCTION

Despite the ever-growing body of newly acquired scientific knowledge associated with the psychological, biological, and social processes of growing old, there is still relatively little understanding of the psychological issues of aging. This lack can be traced to the persistence of popular stereotypes about how personality changes as people grow old, and to the many methodological and theoretical problems encountered in the study of personality and aging.

One common notion about age-related personality change (even among professionals) is that as individuals grow older, they become more rigid, irritable, demanding, and set in their ways (Reedy, 1975; Thomae, 1980). While there is no evidence that the normal processes of aging produce substantial changes in personality, many professionals continue to act as if this were the case (Bromley, 1978). Recent studies document the prevalence of such ageist attitudes, and indicate that prejudices and stereotypes applied to older people sheerly on the basis of their age have even become professionalized (Butler and Lewis, 1982; Greene, 1983). Unfortunately, these negative attitudes often go unrecognized and become an insidious part of mental health practice (for further discussion, see chapter 13).

A second problem limiting the understanding of aging and personality is that until recently many psychological studies were based on institutionalized subjects—a small minority of the aging population. Samples of elderly persons living in the community, on the other hand, have often been biased. In many study samples white middle-class subjects are overrepresented, and there is insufficient representation of other classes and racial and/or ethnic groups. In addition, researchers often do not take into account variables such as health status, intelligence, and other important factors that may impact upon personality. As a result, there is little data on the "normal" aging personality.

Another difficulty encountered in the study of personality and aging is the use of research and evaluation instruments of unknown or dubious reliability and/or validity. While there has been some effort to extend psychometric methods into middle and old age, the results are still questionable (Bromley, 1978; Reedy, 1975).

A further difficulty is a lack of agreement on the definition of such basic terms as personality and mental illness. While personality theory is intended to provide an understanding of how normal behavior evolves over time, in reality each theory may begin with a different conception of personality and what constitutes mental illness. This means that both researchers and practitioners are faced with numerous and contradictory conceptual frameworks and perspectives.

Personality, for example, encompasses the omnibus or "ragbag" definitions in which personality is seen as the sum total of just about everything a person is and does, including innate and acquired experiences; integrative definitions that deal with individual differences in patterns of thoughts, motives, feelings, and emotions; and the class of definitions that view personality as the "total response repertoire" (Arndt, 1974; Maddi, 1972; Stagner, 1965).

Definitions of mental illness are just as vague and/or ill-defined. Points of view range from those who argue that there is no such thing as mental illness (Szasz, 1979; Temerlin, 1979) to those who maintain that specific criteria for defining mental illness can be established (Jahoda, 1979).

Despite the fact that our understanding of the psychological issues of aging is at best "diffuse" and "uncoordinated," fraught with stereotypes, and burdened by methodological and theoretical problems, there is still the need to arrive at an appropriate assessment focus. The framework that is selected for this purpose should contribute to as clear an understanding as possible of the biopsychosocial changes of adulthood. It should also shed light on how the aging individual has faced the events and problems of daily living throughout his/her life. The concept of psychological age as it relates to adaptability has been selected as the theoretical foundation for the assessment framework presented in this chapter because it best meets these criteria.

Inasmuch as the assessment of psychological age and adaptability takes into account an individual's lifelong adjustment strategies and how they are affected by recent events, there are several benefits to this approach. The first is that it permits the social worker "to begin where the client is." It also allows the practitioner to have a sense of the elderly person over time, rather than limiting assessment to the here and now. In addition, for the older person sometimes seemingly "unsophisticated" in many aspects of "therapy," it provides an understanding of how central issues were resolved throughout the life cycle. This is an important aspect of assessment because similar conflicts can arise in a modified form in later adulthood. The resolution of the conflicts of the past is a major goal of casework that should not be overlooked as the social worker attempts to alleviate specific concrete problems of the present.

In view of the fact that psychological age is related to the functional capacities of the older adult as he/she attempts to cope with the environment, the psychological age perspective also suggests appropriate intervention strategies that draw upon the client's strengths and resources. This approach has the added benefit of avoiding unnecessary labeling. While there are some settings that may require assessment based on the classification of mental disorders as defined by the American Psychiatric Association in the Diagnostic and Statistical Manual of Mental Disorders, DSM III, APA, 1980 (see later section of the chapter and Whanger and Myers, 1984 for further discussion), most caseworkers need to be able to arrive at a clear picture of the whole person. The practitioner must not be restricted to the use of diagnostic categories. Rather, he/she gathers information related to life history, present difficulties, critical incidents, economic circumstances, living conditions and routine activities of daily living, and psychological and interpersonal attitudes. This information will enable the practitioner to come to conclusions about the client's coping strategies and treatment needs. *This evaluation process provides a picture of how the elderly client is adapting to the life changes, stresses and losses that are often associated with this stage of life.*

PSYCHOLOGICAL AGE AND ADAPTABILITY IN THE OLDER ADULT

Distinguishing what constitutes adaptive behavior or the relative capacity for functioning in a given society is a complex task. There is little agreement among theorists about how to describe this phenomenon. Although there is also some debate about what to consider adaptive, among the behaviors included in this category are those that contribute to effective modes of dealing with reality, lead to a mastery of the environment, resolve conflict, reduce stress, and/or establish personal satisfaction (Bloom, 1984; Maddi, 1972). Here, those points of view which suggest that adaptability is a *lifelong adjustment process through which the individual meets a series of biopsychosocial transitions* are presented.

Birren (1959, 1968) was among the pioneers in addressing the question of adaptability in adulthood in his study of functional age (see chapter 3). As a gerontologist he was interested in how the older person changes over time and in the development of a research strategy for appraising an individual's level of functioning in a given environment relative to others his/her age. His concern with the functional capacities of the older adult led to the delineation of three kinds of aging—biological, social, and psychological (as stated earlier). He defined psychological age as the age-related adaptive capacities of the individual, encompassing the ability to adapt to familiar as well as unfamiliar environments and the capacity to modify the environment. By equating psychological age with adaptability and recognizing that mastery of the environment is a vital personality function, Birren set the stage for our discussion of adaptation in later life.

One of the best-known theories dealing with adaptiveness throughout the life cycle and giving adequate attention to how an individual develops his/her coping strategies in every phase of life is that of Erik Erikson (1950). He proposed eight stages of development from infancy to old age: (1) basic trust versus distrust; (2) autonomy versus shame and doubt; (3) initiative versus guilt; (4) industry versus inferiority; (5) ego identity versus role confusion; (6) intimacy versus ego isolation; (7) generativity versus stagnation; and (8) ego integrity versus despair. Each stage presents a task or psychosocial crisis, and stresses that ego identity *evolves over a lifetime*, with individuals striving to maximize their potential at all life stages. Erikson also proposed that in every society there is a "crucial coordination" between the developing individual and his/her human environment. This optimistic mental health approach emphasizes growth of the "healthy" personality and stresses the role of socioeconomic, ethnic, and institutional factors in meeting human needs.

The theory suggests that the successful mastery of issues at each stage aids in the person's progression to the next. At each stage of development, however, an individual has a new opportunity to deal with the ramifications of earlier developmental issues.

Although Erikson recognized that each of the above-mentioned stages involves an adaptive issue, psychosocial crisis or task (see the next section), he also addressed the more general question of adaptability. He believed that adaptation involves the successful resolution of the various bipolar crises of each of the developmental stages and that what is known as personality is a function of the outcome. In this context, adaptability is seen as directly related to the strength of one's ego and its capacity to unify experience and actions in an acceptable fashion: The ego "guards the coherence and individuality of experience . . . by enabling [the person] to anticipate inner as well as outer dangers; and by integrating endowments and social opportunities" (Erikson, 1950, p. 35).

As noted earlier, Erikson was also interested in the way social organizations support the development of the individual ego. Erikson is sensitive to the fact that if societal institutions become fragmented and unresponsive, they contribute to a disturbance in personal identity. For Erikson, *adaptive psychological development is related to the strength of one's ego as it emerges through the psychosocial stages and the kind of support lent by societal institutions.* The building block nature of Erikson's eight-stage theory, along with these social components, makes it consistent with effective social work practice with the older adult.

Another psychiatrist interested in the circumstances surrounding adaptation in later life is Eric Pfeiffer (1977). In his discussion of psychopathology in advanced years he suggested that adaptation is at the heart of normal intra- and interpersonal functioning. This is reflected in his definition:

> Adaptation in general may be defined as the process of meeting an individual's biological, psychological, and social needs, under recurrently changing circumstances. Failure to adapt, or pathology, may be defined as failure to meet the individual's basic needs, or meeting them only at the expense of pain, suffering and disorder within the individual or within the environment (p. 650).

Pfeiffer maintained that many of the clinical syndromes typically associated with the later years, such as depressive reactions, hypochondriases, and paranoid reactions (see section later in this chapter) ought to be understood as failures in adaptation. He also suggested that adaptation in old age evolves throughout life and results from the successful mastery of age-specific developmental tasks. For

Pfeiffer, *adaptation is associated with adequate intrapersonal and interpersonal functioning; and pathology with failure to adapt to the various crises, problems and losses occurring in the later phase of life.*

While there are differences in emphasis, the definitions of adaptability discussed here clearly point out that the relationship of the individual to his/her environment is at the crux of understanding personality and behavior (Zarit, 1980, p. 66). The recognition that an individual develops relatively predictable and stable patterns of adjustment through his/her long-term relationship with his/her environment is also at the heart of the assessment process. From this perspective, a client's psychological behavior can be understood as a series of personal adjustments that take place over the life span, involving the achievement of phase-specific tasks and leading to an identifiable pattern of adjustment, sometimes called personality. This point of view, which is an outgrowth of stage theory, proposes that adaptation at any given point in the life cycle depends on prior experiences as well as on how the person responds to the demands inherent in a particular stage of life. A summary of adaptability definitions is provided in Table 4.1.

The life-cycle approach to personality development supplies an important focus to social work assessment. Because of its emphasis on

TABLE 4.1. A Summary of Definitions

Author	Adaptability definition
Greene	Adaptability is a lifelong adjustment process through which the individual meets a series of biopsychosocial transitions
Birren	Adaptability is akin to psychological age and manifests itself in the capacity to adjust to and modify the environment
Erikson	Adaptability is directly related to the strength of one's ego and the support of social institutions
Havighurst	Adaptation is related to the lifelong ability to master biopsychosocial developmental tasks successfully
Peck	Adaptation requires "deep" active effort to make life more secure and meaningful through ego differentiation
Pfeiffer	Adaptation is the process of meeting an individual's biological, psychological, and social needs under recurrently changing circumstances

continuity and change, it suggests that caseworkers not limit the assessment to the client's current situation, but consider his/her life-long adaptive strategies. Through the process of inquiring about the client's "typical" patterns of perceiving and responding to new events, the caseworker can achieve a better understanding of the individual's present circumstances. In addition, the practitioner must realize that, while information about past history is important, adaptational styles that come into play at any one time may not work at another. The basic responsibility is to collect sufficient information to account for the client's current behavior and present difficulty.

The aim of developmental theory is to account for both stability and change that is characteristic of human behavior. At one time social scientists did not believe that individuals developed after reaching maturity. Prior to 1940, psychologists and other students of personality generally confined themselves to understanding the early stages of life. Developmental changes were thought to take place until adulthood; the mature individual was expected to decline and deteriorate into old age and death. "True" developmental processes were believed to be limited to ever-increasing changes, reaching their peak in adulthood and stopping there, much as a child reaches his/her full physical growth. As a result, aging became associated with reverse development and decline.

Life-span theorists have rejected this view. They point out that, while there may be growth limits for physical attributes such as height, other qualities such as creativity and abstract reasoning do not fit this model. As life-cycle research provided more knowledge about the process of human change, the thinking about what constituted development was modified. In this new context, development was defined as the process whereby the individual goes from a relatively undifferentiated state or condition and proceeds to a more complex or increasingly differentiated state/condition (Kastenbaum, 1979). Today, change is still seen as directional and largely cumulative, but is understood to involve those modifications that lead to increased complexity and/or greater organization. Behaviors are still said to precede other behaviors in a meaningful, orderly and related way, and these behaviors are usually grouped in stages. However, development is now said to unfold continuously throughout the life span from conception until death, rather than ceasing with the attainment of physical maturity.

Development of all aspects of cognitive and affective behavior is known to take place throughout the life span (Schell and Hall, 1979). Examples of developmental changes in older adults include adaptation to new roles, such as adjustment to retirement or the learning of new skills (e.g., painting). Society has generally acknowledged the accomplishments of famous people, of which Grandma Moses, Pablo Casals, and Albert Einstein are outstanding examples. However, research shows that the majority of "ordinary" individuals continue to make contributions throughout their life (Newman and Newman, 1979).

The life-cycle point of view suggests that personal growth is possible at any age. If growth is possible, so, too, is change. Consequently, the life-span definition of development lends itself to a positive practice approach to social work with the aged and their families. Without this framework, social workers who often must deal with the socially and economically disadvantaged older adult could erroneously assume that aging itself is a social problem. However, with the life-span approach as a point of departure, the aging process can no longer be considered "pathological." Within this framework aging per se is no longer perceived as the cause of all decremental changes. This point of view underscores that, while decrements do occur more frequently in the aged, they can and do occur in younger people as well. It also emphasizes that, while significant functions in older people may show decline, particularly those with a strong biological basis, other functions may show age-related gains. Abstract reasoning ability and creative skills, for example, often tend to increase with advanced years.

Consequently, it is the role of the social worker, in collaboration with other professionals, to evaluate which *specific* age-related or other changes have produced *specific* decrements in client functioning. The practitioner can then assess individual differences with the view that many, if not most, difficulties of the elderly client are treatable. Thorough and holistic assessment is possible only if "problems" are not erroneously attributed to the "inevitable process of aging." Age alone does not cause incompetence or difficulties, or can chronological age *alone* tell us about a specific adult's competence or capacity for change.

The life-cycle approach to development offers more than the suggestion that personality should be studied within the broader context of the life span. It also implies that successful aging need not be measured against a single model of a previous life stage (Pincus, 1967). Rather, personality in the aged should be examined within the same complex of biopsychosocial events used to study behavior at any age. This implies that chronological age in and of itself is not a meaningful measure in assessment; it is not merely the passage of time that is of interest, but the events that have occurred which give meaning to time (Neugarten, 1977). By keeping this in mind, the practitioner is more likely to ask about the way past events impact on present concerns and thereby come to an appreciation of the client's unique adjustment patterns. In sum, assessment from this vantage point encompasses both the individual's life history and present difficulties.

ADAPTIVE TASKS IN LATER LIFE

In the previous section it was pointed out that adaptability is a lifelong process which centers around the ability to master the environment. Developmental stage theory also maintains that at each stage of life the individual encounters a period of heightened vulnerability when adjustment is "threatened." These transition points or crises can be viewed as turning points in the individual's life that are brought about by the normal stresses and strains of the transitional period. While such times are not extraordinary in the sense that they are emergencies, they do require that the individual acquire new skills and competencies which, if achieved, result in increased mastery over the environment.

Adaptive tasks are encountered in the areas of motor, intellectual, social and/or emotional development (Newman and Newman, 1979). The developmental tasks of learning to walk or talk, for example, are related to biological readiness, while tasks such as learning to think in abstractions are related to biological, psychological, and cognitive timing. Other tasks may arise from the demands, constraints and opportunities provided by the social environment and the complex interaction of the biological, psychological and social spheres. However, mastering such tasks is necessary to achieve happiness and success with later tasks; failure leads to unhappiness and difficulty (Havighurst, 1953). In sum, each life phase presents specific adaptations that the individual must face in order to continue functioning in an adequate manner.

Defining the tasks of a particular developmental stage is difficult, and a number have been ascribed to old age. Table 4.1 lists these as delineated by four theorists who have addressed the mature adult. Each offers a somewhat different perspective on the adaptive tasks in later life.

Erikson believed that at each life stage the individual develops a new orientation toward him/herself and toward his/her world. He/she attempts to integrate present and past psychological issues within a social context. Erikson also stated that each psychosocial crisis could have a relatively positive or relatively negative outcome, which, in turn, provides the foundation for further development. For optimum growth to occur, the crisis at each stage needs to be positively resolved.

Erikson termed the polarities of the psychosocial crisis of late adulthood integrity versus despair. He contended that the older person who has achieved a sense of integrity appreciates the continuity of past, present, and future experiences. He/she also comes to have an acceptance of the life cycle, to cooperate with the inevitabilities of life, and to experience a sense of being complete.

On the other hand, the older person who experiences a sense of despair feels that time has been too short and wants a second chance at life. He/she finds little meaning in human existence, having lost faith in him/herself and others. That person has little sense of world order or spiritual wholeness. As a result, he/she is fearful of death. Erikson (1950) concluded

> two end points of the life cycle come together—development of trust in children depends on the integrity of their fathers . . . healthy children will not fear life if their elders have integrity enough not to fear death.

While Erikson believed that the global crisis of ego integrity or despair was sufficient to describe the adaptive issues of the older adult, Peck (1968) thought the tasks of this developmental stage required elaboration. He further defined three major psychological "stages" in old age: transcending the work role, transcending the body, and transcending the ego. Ego differentiation versus work-role preoccupation refers to the ability to secure a sense of self-worth by engaging in activities beyond the "job." Body transcendence versus body preoccupation concerns the capacity to adjust to the decline in physical powers that accompany old age. Ego transcendence versus ego preoccupation relates the ability to face the immediate and certain prospects of death with a "deep, active effort to make life more secure, meaningful, or happy for those who go on after one dies" (Peck, p. 91). Peck concluded that the developmental tasks of old age can vary greatly from one adult to another, and that the timing of life stages cannot necessarily be tied to chronological age.

Havighurst, another scholar dealing with the biopsychosocial crisis of old age, has proposed six developmental tasks for the older adult. These include adjusting to decreasing physical strength and health, adjusting to retirement and reduced income, adjusting to the death of a spouse, adopting and adapting social roles in a flexible way, establishing a satisfactory physical living arrangement, and developing an explicit affiliation with one's age group. Havighurst also pointed out that while most developmental tasks are age-related and must be mastered at special times in life, this is not true of all life tasks. One task, which he suggests is recurrent and must be established anew at each stage of life, is the development of an affiliation with one's own age group. This task begins for most people about the time they start school and is only partly mastered by the age of nine or ten. As the child enters adolescence, the nature of age group affiliation becomes quite different, as it does at subsequent life stages. He concluded that success with a recurring task in the earliest (possible) stages usually argues well for success in later phases. Therefore, the adaptive patterns of aging can be viewed as the consequences of lifelong individual choices and adjustments.

Pfeiffer (1977) has added another dimension to understanding the adaptive tasks of later life. He proposed that while losses can occur at any age, adaptation to loss is one of the principal tasks facing the older adult. Most elderly people face multiple losses, including the loss of a spouse, friend, or colleague, a decline in physical health, bodytone or hair, and loss of status, prestige or income. The task becomes one of "replacing" some of the losses with new relationships; "retraining for lost capacities" and/or "making do with less" (p. 651).

In essence, the manner in which an individual adapts to loss in old age is, in part, an outcome of how he/she has adjusted previously.

> Generally not recognized, however, is the degree to which we are continually subjected to separations and losses which are so subtle or so well disguised that they may never be recognized or acknowledged. To a surprising degree, we are confronted with and tested by loss and separation throughout life. . . . In the change from childhood to adulthood, from helpless dependency to maturity . . . growth is ordinarily conceived of as *becoming*, in the sense of something developing or being added, something more or other than existed previously. Very seldom does one consider that loss, whether of a possession, a function, an ideal, or a relationship, also is a part of development and contributes to it (Carr, 1975, pp. 3–4).

Of the innumerable losses the elderly person must face, one of the greatest is time; in middle age comes the realization that one's time is finite. However, the intellectual realization that one must eventually die is quite different from the task of psychologically accepting the nearness of one's own death. In fact, no other subject may be as full of meaning. In recent years there have been significant inroads in weakening the taboo about the topic of death, resulting in important improvements in the care of the dying. At the same time, there appear to be no specific guidelines for accomplishing this task that fit everyone. Each individual handles it in his/her own unique way if given the opportunity.

Weisman (1972, p. 157) suggests the following questions be addressed in order to come to a better understanding of what the elderly may feel as they confront death:

1. If you faced death in the near future, what would matter most?
2. If you were very old, what would your most crucial problems be? How would you go about solving them?
3. If death were inevitable, what circumstances would make it acceptable?
4. If you were old, how might you live most effectively and with least damage to your ideals and standards?

5. What can anyone do to prepare for his own death, or for that of someone very close?
6. What conditions and events might make you feel that you were better off dead? When would you take steps to die?
7. In old age, everyone must rely upon others. When this point arrives, what kind of people would you like to deal with?

Another important task in later life, suggested by Pfeiffer, is an identity review. It involves self-reflection and reminiscence in the face of approaching death, and is an "evaluative backward glance" at one's life. The task involved is to weigh one's accomplishments and failures and come to a reasonably positive view of life's worth. There has been much clinical interest in this function, which has resulted in a number of treatment modalities to be discussed later in the text.

Another major task of later life proposed by Pfeiffer is the ability to remain active in order "to retain function" (p. 651). He assumed that in order to age successfully the older person must maintain his/her physical and social activity and find suitable intellectual and emotional stimulation. Pfeiffer concluded that where this did not occur a significant decrease in function would take place.

While most people resolve the developmental tasks and psychosocial crises of later life with relative success, others can experience undue stress and difficulty. This can lead to problems that require some form of intervention. It is important to keep in mind that many elderly clients seen at social service agencies may be experiencing difficulty in making the adaptations and/or adjustments required by the tasks of their particular phase of the life cycle (see mental health inventory check list). In large part, the goal of social work intervention is to assist these persons in meeting these crises. For example, while studies of the impact of retirement are contradictory and the general effect is still not clear, many social workers report seeing older persons who are experiencing difficulties with retirement. This is particularly true of persons for whom work has been the primary source of gratification and personal identity. Retirement, therefore, represents a major loss, and in such cases, **new roles** may be difficult to assume. For those who were financially dependent upon their job, reduced income is an additional burden. Understanding these distinctions and helping individuals deal with such transitions within a cultural context is truly a challenge.

RECOGNIZING THE MAJOR FUNCTIONAL PSYCHIATRIC DISORDERS OF LATER LIFE

The mental disorders of old age are generally divided into two kinds: the *organic disorders* that have a known physical cause (see chapter 3) and *functional disorders* for which no physical cause has been found and whose origins appear to be emotional. It should be stated that this division tends to be somewhat artificial, as advances in the neurosciences continue to reveal the biochemical aspects of functional disorders. Organic brain syndromes, which are mental conditions caused by or associated with impairment of brain tissue function, are known to have many psychosocial ramifications (Butler and Lewis, 1982).

Due to the increased risk and greater prevalence of mental disorders in old age, it is important for geriatric social workers to become familiar with the major emotional disturbances widespread in later life. The DSM III, which was revised in 1980, provides a more complete and updated picture of mental disorders in old age than the previous edition, and includes a description of the following major functional disorders: (1) affective, (2) anxiety, (3) somatoform, (4) dissociative (paranoid and schizophrenic disorders), and (5) adjustment.

Affective

Depression, an affective disorder concerning mood, is the most common psychiatric disorder in late life. Affective disorders can be divided into three categories: (1) major disorders, including bipolar disorder (mixed manic or depressed) and major depression (single episode or recurrent); (2) other specific affective disorders including lesser forms of the first; and (3) atypical depressions that cannot be strictly classified.

The term depression is generally used to refer to a wide variety of feelings ranging from a mild indifference to a state of complete demoralization. Depressive illness, according to the Diagnostic and Statistical Manual of Mental Disorders (American Psychiatric Assoc., 1980), is a severe persistent episode of depressed mood in which the person loses interest or pleasure in the usual activities of life. This usually means a long-lasting depression that interferes with everyday activities. While everyone feels "blue" sometimes, feelings of depression that last 6–8 weeks should be considered serious. Of course, any threats of suicide should be taken very seriously and immediate measures taken, including medical/psychiatric and family involvement (Cohen, 1980).

Psychological symptoms of depression include confusion, irritability, feelings of dissatisfaction, emptiness, hopelessness, personal devaluation, and suicidal thoughts. Depression is often accompanied by sleep disturbance, decreased appetite, weight loss, fatigue, and/or agitation (Butler and Lewis, 1982). The exact cause(s) of a particular depression are often difficult or sometimes impossible to identify. Stressful and/or traumatic life events, personal losses, chronic physical

illnesses, continuing financial problems, and biological predisposi-
tions may all play a contributing role. This is why today's treatment
approaches tend to include both psychosocial interventions, drug
treatment, and sometimes shock therapy.

The clinical assessment of depression in the elderly is difficult, as
the symptoms may be mistaken for other problems. Physical problems
can often mimic psychological problems; similarly, psychological
stresses and conflicts may manifest themselves as apparent somatic
difficulties (White House Conference on Aging, 1981, p. 5).

One of the most difficult differential diagnoses to make involves
distinguishing organic mental change from depression. (See chapter 3
for a discussion of the assessment of mental status.) Some older persons
are sometimes considered to be suffering from organic brain disease
when they are actually suffering from severe depression. The older
person who is in a severe depressive state may appear quite confused,
to the extent that he or she may lose bowel or urinary functions. It is
important to note that such difficulties can be treated *if* recognized and
properly diagnosed (Cohen, 1980).

Accurate diagnosis requires an understanding of the client's reaction
to loss, personal and family medical and psychiatric history, recent
traumatic events, history of presenting symptoms, and functional
status (Cohen, 1980; Whanger and Myers, 1984). Special attention
should be paid to other age-related illnesses such as high blood
pressure, since the use of certain medications can cause mood change.

Patterson (1977), in his discussion of grief and depression in older
people, has made some practical suggestions for making a differential
diagnosis between organic brain disease and depression. He emphasizes the need for a complete medical examination, including diagnostic tests, as a precursor to clinical assessment. The following items are
suggested for making further differentiation. (See Table 4.2)

While depression may at first appear difficult to diagnose, it is one
of the more treatable psychiatric disorders, and the elderly often
respond quickly to therapy. The support of family, caring friends, and
neighbors is another important resource. The important thing to
remember is that depression is a treatable disease.

Anxiety

As a symptom, anxiety is a component of almost all psychiatric
disorders. It is typically accompanied by a number of psychophysio-
logical manifestations involving the autonomic nervous system, including palpitations, tachycardia, hyperventilation, respiratory distress, trembling, and dizziness. As a syndrome, or cluster of symptoms,
anxiety has now been classified as a separate class of mental disorders

TABLE 4.2. Signs of Depression and Organic Brain Disease

Signs that may suggest organically caused mental change

  Failing memory
  Disorganized thinking
  Inability to understand instructions
  Unpredictable mood changes
  Inappropriate affect
  Recent fall(s)
  Sudden onset of problems
  History of ministrokes

Signs that may suggest depression

  Sadness
  Changes in sleep patterns
  Changes in activity patterns
  Unfounded physical complaints
  Eating disorders (over/undereating)

(American Psychiatric Assoc., 1980). This diagnosis is made when anxiety is the predominant subjective experience (Herman, 1984). Four subgroups of the disorder are distinguished: (1) phobic disorders (a persistent avoidance behavior due to irrational fear of a specific object, activity or situation); (2) panic disorders (a recurrent attack of intense anxiety with feelings of extreme apprehension); (3) generalized anxiety disorder (a chronic state of generalized anxiety); and (4) obsessive-compulsive disorder (a presence of obsessions or unwelcomed and recurrent ideas and/or compulsions, senseless behaviors outside voluntary control).

Assessment of anxiety reactions, which are more prevalent among the elderly than was originally thought, involves differentiating anxiety disorders from other conditions and determining what factors are contributing to the anxiety. With the elderly, as with any other age group, this requires an examination of current life style and the gathering of a psychosocial history.

Somatoform

This group of disorders has been newly classified in the DSM-III and is identified by the presence of physical symptoms that give the appearance of being caused by an underlying physical disorder. When organic causes are not found and *a psychiatric evaluation* supports it, a diagnosis of somatoform disorder is made. Specific diagnosis is often difficult as symptoms overlap. There are four categories to consider: (1) somatization disorder involving multiple bodily complaints; (2)

hypochondriasis, centering around a preoccupation with the belief that one has serious disease; (3) psychogenic pain disorder, involving pain seemingly attributable to psychological factors; and (4) conversion disorder, relating loss or alteration of physical functioning to psychological conflict (Herman, 1984)

Hypochondriasis, after depressive and paranoid reactions, is probably the most frequent functional psychiatric disorder. It is found more frequently among older women than among older men, and can often interfere with the individual's interpersonal interactions because it may cause annoyance in those who are "not psychologically minded" (Pfeiffer, 1977). The person suffering from hypochondriases may have multiple diagnostic procedures performed and be seen by several primary care physicians.

Dissociative–Paranoid and Schizophrenic Disorders

After depressive illness, paranoid reactions are thought to be the most common psychiatric problem in old age. These feelings may range from slight sensations of mistrust to delusional suspicions, e.g., "my apartment is bugged by the Russians." The major characteristic is the presence of persistent delusions of a persecutory or jealous nature (DSM-III). Paranoid clients attribute to other people motivations that do not, in fact, exist. They are suspicious of others, have unrealistic explanations of events, and are not amenable to the ideas of others (Whanger and Myers, 1984).

Pfeiffer (1977) has suggested that paranoid ideas are more common in persons with various kinds of sensory deficits, particularly decreases in hearing, visual, and intellectual capacities. Paranoid symptoms represent an effort to "fill in the blank spaces in the cognitive map" (p. 656). An example would be the elderly person who misplaces a wallet and accuses those around him/her of stealing it.

Schizophrenic disorders are actually groups of disorders sharing psychotic features (hallucinations and/or delusions), deterioration of the person's level of functioning, thought disorder, duration of at least 6 months, and the absence of organic or affective illness. There is much controversy surrounding this disorder as its etiology is still not certain and there are widely divergent views concerning the impact of aging on the disease. Schizophrenia is rarely first diagnosed in old age, and older lifelong schizophrenics who live in the community are often the most difficult clients to help.

Adjustment Disorders

The essential feature of adjustment disorders is the individual's maladaptive response to an identifiable psychosocial stressor. While the DSM-III no longer classifies adjustment disorders by the person's developmental stage, as was done previously, it is recognized that stressful life events can bring about problems in adjustment. As emphasized earlier in this chapter, the cumulative effects of stressful life events combined with "unmanageable" present difficulties can account for the prevalence of adjustment disorders among the elderly (Whanger and Myers, 1984).

UNDERSTANDING SENSORY AND COGNITIVE PROCESSES IN THE OLDER ADULT

The ability of older persons to acquire new information or concepts, to alter behavior as a result of experience, and to develop new skills are characteristics of interest in assessment that are most related to cognitive and sensory process. While an in-depth discussion is not within the scope of this text, an overview of the major and most pertinent cognitive and sensory functions is presented in this section.

Sensory Processes

It is generally accepted that all five senses tend to decline in old age. However, it is important to remember that the level of functioning of a particular individual depends on his/her state of health and the adaptive strategies he/she has evolved to optimize performance and minimize decrements.

Vision. With age the eye undergoes many structural changes; as a result, visual difficulties tend to increase. In general, starting at the age of 45, the eye gradually becomes less flexible, and in "old age" becomes less able to distinguish levels of brightness, less color sensitive, and more sensitive to glare.

Many older persons adapt to these changes by wearing glasses, using large-print reading materials, and not driving at night. It is important to remember that despite these visual changes 80% of the elderly have fair to adequate visual acuity up to age 90 and even beyond (Butler and Lewis, 1982; Sumner, 1982).

Hearing. With advancing age there are physiological changes in the auditory system, changes usually associated with disturbances in the inner ear and related neural pathways that produce functional changes in hearing. Significant hearing loss occurs in 30% of all older people, more often in men. Sounds in the higher frequency ranges are harder to hear; the intensity level within the range of pitch that older people can hear needs to be greater; and there is more difficulty making fine distinctions in hearing speech (Sumner, 1982).

A hearing impairment is *not* the same, however, as a hearing loss.

For a hearing loss to be considered an impairment, it must actually interfere with the individual's capacity to interact successfully with his/her environment (Lowy, 1979). In such cases, the impairment may be the most problematic of the perceptual impairments, as it can reduce verbal communciation and lead to suspiciousness, reduced reality testing, and even paranoia (Butler and Lewis, 1982). Helping the older person to accept a hearing loss and compensate for it is an important social work function. It may take the form of educating the person to the advantages of wearing a good hearing aid where medically indicated and installing an amplifier on the telephone.

Taste and Smell. The number of taste buds begins to decrease starting in childhood, and sensitivity to taste declines particularly in the 60's. The inability to enjoy the sense of taste is often compounded for those whose health requires them to eliminate salt and other spices, making it even more difficult to enjoy food. The staff of nutrition programs can help older people adjust to this difficulty by offering attractively prepared foods and companionship at mealtime.

The sense of smell also tends to decline with age. Up to 30% of people over 80 have difficulty identifying common substances by smell (Butler and Lewis, 1982). This can result in a lessening of the ability to distinguish unpleasant odors or smoke (Beaver, 1982). The social worker can be most helpful in this instance by evaluating safety aspects of the client's living conditions.

Somesthetic (touch, vibration, temperature, kinesthesis, pain). Studies show a uniform decrease in somesthetic sensitivity with age, including touch, temperature, and pain. Losses in these areas are by no means universal and are often related to specific physical problems or diseases. Therefore, changes should be considered in light of a multifaceted assessment.

Cognitive Processes

Intelligence. Intelligence is a term that is difficult to define and has been used to refer to both the capacity and the ability to perform (and learn) cognitive and behavioral tasks effectively. Intelligence is commonly measured through intelligence tests, and historically those test results have indicated a decline with advancing years. However, the study of intellectual function in old age is both difficult and marked with controversy. This has led to contradictory conclusions: There are those who state that intellectual functions decline with age (Sumner, 1982), and those who believe that the (observed) decline in intellectual functioning is largely a decline in the performance on the standard intelligence tests, which may result from slower performance (Beaver, 1982). The information most pertinent to the caseworker, however, is whether the client's intellectual competence is maintained or has declined as compared with the previous levels of functioning, and how this affects manipulation of the environment (Schaie and Schaie, 1977).

Memory. Memory refers to the ability to retain information about specific events that have occurred at a given time and place. It is a process of storing and retrieving facts or information, involving short- and long-term capacities. Short-term memory refers to recall after a relatively brief delay or time period; long-term to recall of events that occurred in the past and have not been frequently rehearsed or thought of (Craik, 1977). As in the case of intelligence, data on memory changes in old age are complex and difficult to interpret, and contradictory results are reported. The need for further experimental studies is clear, as many questions remain about memory loss in the normal aging individual under nonexperimental conditions (see chapter 3). Of interest to the social worker is how the capacity to recall events affects the client's activities of daily living and/or functional capacities.

Learning. Learning refers to the ability to acquire general knowledge about the world and can occur at all ages. As with the other cognitive functions discussed above, many questions remain about what types of learning disabilities, if any, can be attributed to age, and how to interpret research findings. Differences of opinion exist about whether the ability to learn declines with age and the role of such variables as speed and accuracy, motivation and maturity of judgment. The client's ability to learn new information often comes into play in the casework process. For example, the client may receive a prescription for taking medication, requirements for a particular diet or instructions for self-care. The ability to follow through effectively is a function of the ability to process and learn new information, and the client's ability is "measurable" in observable behaviors.

THE LIFE-CYCLE APPROACH TO CLINICAL ASSESSMENT

This last section addresses the assessment of the older client from a life-cycle perspective as a means of evaluating the client's potential for meeting the tasks of later life. The case of Mary P. and a series of suggested specific assessment questions serve as an example of this approach.

As pointed out in chapter 3, assessment, in its simplest sense, is a method of looking at a problem, arriving at a decision about what is wrong, and deciding what interventions can help alleviate or eliminate it. In order to come to a full understanding of the client's situation, it is necessary for the assessment to be multifaceted and for all aspects of functional capacity to be thoroughly explored. Obtaining a clinical or psychological assessment is only one part of the process.

Schaie and Schaie (1977) suggest that the goals of a clinical assessment are (1) the diagnosis of psychopathology, or the differentiation of psychopathology from "normal" aging; (2) the determination of baseline behaviors (this permits a comparison following intervention); and (3) a review of the present level of adjustment to changed life roles for purposes of counseling or therapy (p. 693).

The following case of Mrs. P. suggests the questions to explore in assessment from this perspective:

> January 1976—Mr. John P. made several calls to various community agencies about his mother, Mary, age 70. She was described as severely depressed and had not left her apartment in 3 months. She complained that her heart and lungs were failing and was afraid she was fading away. No medical problem had been found despite many tests. Mary lives with her husband, Harold, age 73, and two grandchildren, David, 19, and Rebecca, 17.
>
> Mr. and Mrs. Harold P. lived in New York until 3 years ago. At that time, their daughter, Barbara, died of a severe asthma attack. As Barbara's husband, Peter, had deserted the family many years before, the grandchildren came to live with the grandparents. This "new" family unit moved to Washington, D.C. to be near John. (A second daughter, Susan, lives in New York.)
>
> During the caseworker's original home visits, the family indicated that there was little interaction or family plans for cooking or cleaning. David and Rebecca have taken to leading their own lives and ignore their grandmother. David is rarely home and often eats out. Harold is still active in senior citizen groups to which he escapes every day, although he verbalizes great concern for his wife. At the same time, he says Mrs. P. has been depressed before and "it will pass."
>
> John says he has a good relationship with the family. His involvement centers around getting "help" for his mother's depression.

I. The diagnosis of psychopathology
    1. What behaviors, symptoms, lead John to believe his mother is depressed?
    2. What signs of "pathological" behavior does the caseworker observe? (use DSM III)
    3. What does Mary say about "her depression," eating, sleeping habits, weight loss, sad feelings?
    4. What is the duration of the depression?
    5. Have there been other episodes of depression (as suggested by Harold)?
    6. If so, when, under what circumstances, what was the treatment, and the response to it?
    7. Given that no medical reasons have been found for her physical complaints, what are the symbolic meanings?
    8. Does Mary appear to have cognitive losses? (See chapter 3.)

II.   Indications of lifelong adjustment patterns
   1. What type of wife, grandmother, mother, has Mary been over the years? How does her family "remember" her? How does she recall her past life?
   2. Does Mary feel her life has been worthwhile? What does Mary think about having a "new" family to care for?
   3. How do family members describe their relationships? For example, is communication open? Do all members feel they are heard? How do they resolve conflict, deal with crises?
   4. How has Mary faced other major biopsychosocial tasks and life transitions?
   5. How did Mary adapt to previous losses in her life—the death of Barbara, her move to Washington?

III. Present situation and family response
   1. How does Mary spend her day? Specifics.
   2. Does Mary take care of her own needs? For example, does she dress each day, fix her meals?
   3. With whom does Mary interact? How? Specifics.
   4. What has the family response(s) to Mary's behavior been?
   5. What, if anything, have they tried to do so far about her depression? What was the response?
   6. How do other family members feel about her behavior?

CONCLUSIONS

This chapter has emphasized the life-cycle approach to understanding personality development and mental health status in old age. The way in which the individual adapts to life transitions and satisfies his/her basic human needs over the years was seen as a major determinant of how that person eventually adjusts to the conditions of old age. This point of view has important implications for preventive social work practice.

Fulfillment and "good" mental health in later life, as in all stages of the life cycle, require that the person feel useful and in control over his/her life. Social work interventions that are directed toward enhancing the strengths of older people and developing their capacities can contribute to this process. A sense of personal well-being can also be enhanced by programs that encourage interpersonal relationships, reduce unnecessary stress, and strengthen social support systems.

5

Sociocultural Aspects of Functional Age

As issues of content and focus remain critical throughout the assessment process, the question of which factors to include in the biopsychosocial study in order to account for a client's satisfactory performance in the social sphere must first be addressed. Just as with the biological and psychological aspects of aging, there are numerous variables that might prove useful in understanding the client's relative functioning. This text draws upon the concepts of social age and role as the major vehicle for evaluating the social context of how individuals age.

This approach to the study of social interacting not only emphasizes the task-oriented aspects of social functioning, but also includes psychological and biological considerations. It is particularly pertinent to social work practice with the aged client. This section discusses how the concept of *social age as embodied in role performance* is used as an assessment framework for evaluating the older client's situational and environmental circumstances.

There are several benefits to such an evaluation. For example, in gathering data during the assessment or study phase, an analysis of role performance can yield considerable information about the elderly client's social functioning and task performance. Role theory can also be an effective tool in diagnosing and treating families in crisis or conflict. It is particularly useful in making the interactions within the family more explicit and in understanding individual behavior within a family setting. An evaluation of the family role network, as discussed in chapter 8, can provide information about that family's dysfunctional behaviors and suggest interventive strategies.

Another benefit of applying the concept of role to analyze the social context of how individuals age is that it permits the caseworker to focus on different levels of social influence—the person's immediate interpersonal environment (microsystem) and the less immediate social systems of which he/she is a part (macrosystem). The microsystem is generally considered to be made up of family, neighbors, and friends, while the macrosystem is comprised of larger-scale political, economic, religious, and other cultural institutions. Inasmuch as an assessment of the micro and macro levels is important in evaluating the issues relevant to the client's social aging as well as in selecting appropriate interventions, both are addressed in relevant chapters of the text. The concept of role and its emphasis on interaction is particularly applicable to intergenerational family assessment and treatment and serves as a major theoretical underpinning of the functional-age model.

SOCIAL AGE—THE AGING INDIVIDUAL IN A SOCIAL CONTEXT

"Age is an underlying dimension of social organization, for in all societies the relations between individuals and between groups are regulated by age differences" (Neugarten, 1968, p. 3).

"All societies employ age as a social variable by which they prescribe and evaluate what is considered to be appropriate behavior" (Hendricks and Hendricks, 1977, p. 23).

The caseworker who hopes to assess the aging individual within a social context should first understand that social age is a product of our interactions in the society in which we live. Social age refers to the roles and social habits of an individual *in relationship to other members* of his/her social structure; these roles specify the person's rights and responsibilities, what is expected of him/her and what he/she can expect in return from others (Birren and Renner, 1977). This means that *what an individual believes he/she should do and, in some instances, is able to do will be closely linked to what society expects of him/her.*

"I just don't feel old enough to retire, but I guess it's time."
"My family says I'm too old to live in this big house alone; perhaps I should consider moving to an apartment."
"My daughter doesn't think I should get married again (at my age). I guess she's right."

Every society has a system of social expectations regarding age-appropriate behavior (age-grading). These expectations are internalized as the individual grows up and grows old, and he/she generally knows at what age one is expected to work, to marry, to raise children, to retire, and even to "grow old" and to die (Neugarten and Datan, 1973). Age-grading is such a pervasive element of social organization that people are often cognizant of subtle variations in age-appropriate behavior and the timing of major life events. They also, if asked, can give a fairly accurate assessment of their own adherence to the norm (Neugarten et al., 1968).

An evaluation of the sociocultural aspects of aging requires that the social worker be knowledgeable about the changes in social structure that accompany the aging of the individual. From this point of view, aging consists of passages from one socially defined position (status) to another throughout the recognized divisions of life, from infancy to old age, and the obligations, rights and expectations (roles) that accompany these various positions (Bengston and Haber, 1983; Riley et al., 1969).

The process by which a person takes on a succession of roles and changing role constellations, learning the behaviors appropriate to his or her sex, social class, ethnic group and age, is called socialization and occurs at all stages of the life cycle. Socialization is a learning process through which individuals acquire "knowledge, skills, attitudes and values, the needs and motivations, and the cognitive, affective and conative patterns that relate them to their sociocultural setting (Neugarten and Datan, 1973, p. 56).

At each stage of life, as people perform new roles, adjust to changing roles and relinquish old ones, they are, in effect, attempting to master new social situations. Adopting new roles, such as grandparenthood, may often be fulfilling. Giving up well-established and valued roles such as that of a wife or husband can be a painful process, and it is not uncommon for people to experience difficulties in role performance for which they may seek help.

The relative success an individual has moving into a given role or, where necessary, giving up an old one, is at the heart of social functioning. Successful performance at all stages of life is dependent upon adjustive processes that occur *within* the individual and the negotiations that take place *between* the individual and the various social systems to which he/she belongs. In this sense, successful socialization to old age is a complex phenomenon involving the interplay between *psychological adaptations* and *societal expectations*.

New circumstances that may occur in later life and require major role changes include becoming a grandparent, entering retirement, and becoming widowed. How each of these roles is carried out is related to the older person's psychological capacities as well as to the norms and other influences of society. These multiple factors must be taken into account in order for the caseworker to come to a clear picture of the client's social functioning and to arrive at appropriate interventions.

ASSESSING ROLE PERFORMANCE

This section addresses the assessment of the older client from a role perspective as a means of understanding the *social* dimensions of *individual* behavior. The case of Miss V., described later, serves as an example. The concept of role is generally used to indicate the way in which group norms apply to an individual so that each person is able to place him/herself in "the cast of the drama" and have an idea of what he/she should do. For our purposes, role is regarded as "a prescribed pattern of behavior expected of a person in a given situation by virtue of his/her position (designated status) in the transaction" (Shibutani, 1961).

The concept of role can be more clearly understood if one examines the case of a client who becomes seriously ill; he/she must not only learn to deal with physical and psychological changes, but must also learn how to assume the role of patient. As the individual takes on the patient role, many of the behaviors in this well-defined situation will be known to him/her; others will reflect the person's unique interpretation of the role, his/her own culture, and that of the particular group in which the role is enacted. This suggests that although an individual contributes to an ongoing transaction, his/her role must be viewed by the caseworker in reference to or as part of an "organized enterprise related to other roles" (Shibutani, 1961). In other words, the role of a particular patient can only be understood "vis-à-vis the medical establishment" and within his/her cultural context.

Roles should not be seen solely as a set pattern of expected behaviors, but as a pattern of reciprocal claims and obligations. An examination of role behavior includes the person's *conception* of his/her role (how I see myself as patient), others' reactions or *response* to him/her (how we see and treat you as patient), and the *cultural expectations* for that role by the participants (how our group believes patients should act). The relative success with which an individual takes on and plays out his/her various roles from these varying perspectives is a major focus of the biopsychosocial assessment presented below.

> Miss V., a semiretired schoolteacher age 75, was referred to a family service agency by one of her former students, Mrs. P., who explained that her favorite teacher had been in perfect health until she had undergone surgery for a hip replacement; now she was requesting part-time homemaker service and transportation to the doctor for her. It was indicated that Miss V. was a proud, self-reliant woman who would have difficulty asking for help for herself.
>
> When the social worker visited Miss V., who had agreed to be seen at her apartment, she seemed to be a strong, bright, competent, independent person. She explained that she was a retired teacher who chose never to marry, but to "give her whole life to her students." She went on to say that she had taught for over 50 years at a Jewish day school and had seen many of her students grow up and later send their own children to the academy. The worker commented that she must have been much loved, as many of her students continued to be devoted to her and visit her often.
>
> Miss V. lived alone in a neighborhood that was no longer considered safe. Her apartment building had no elevator and no air conditioning. She lived on the third floor, and walking up three flights of stairs had become a problem. She had lived in this apartment for 35 years because it was within walking distance of the school as well as near public transportation.

Furthermore, the rent was very low. Although Miss V. had an adequate income from Social Security, pension, and interest from savings, and could very comfortably afford to move to other housing, she refused, stating that "she wanted to be close to her doctors."

Miss V. gradually recovered from the hip surgery; however, over the next few years, Miss V.'s health deteriorated seriously. She developed heart trouble, became diabetic, lost a lot of weight (20 pounds), developed great difficulty walking, and lost her vision to the point that she could no longer read. During that time, her situation necessitated home health care, with an RN visiting weekly, a health aide providing personal care, and a homemaker doing light housekeeping and shopping twice a week, all of which she grudgingly accepted.

The caseworker became very concerned about Miss V.'s deteriorating health, and shared her concerns with Miss V. She was hoping to get Miss V. "to accept" her situation and consider an alternative, more protective living arrangement. Miss V. would have no part of moving away from the academy and said she did not want to be treated as if she were sick.

Later that same month, on one of her routine visits, the RN found Miss V. dehydrated and confused and hospitalized her. Miss V. remained in the hospital 1 week and was discharged to a nursing home, as she was weak and needed 24-hour care. In the nursing home, her health improved, but she became very depressed. Her main complaint was that she had to wait for the nurses to bring her the medication that she herself knew how to take. "I have been taking this medicine alone for years, and know exactly when and how much to take." Against everyone's advice, she decided to return to her apartment. She insisted that she could manage alone with the help of the health aide once or twice a week and agreed to receive meals-on-wheels until she felt strong enough to prepare her own meals. In her own home, Miss V. continued to be depressed, expressing suicidal thoughts. She indicated that she valued her freedom and independence more than anything else in life. Now she felt she had "lost control and was dependent on others for almost everything." She said she had decided not to marry or have children when she was young because she did not want "to lose her independence." Now she was not sure she had made the right decision. Her former students, demoralized by her poor health and frail appearance, gradually stopped visiting. Miss V. sadly reflected that "she had never felt old before despite her advancing years," and always thought she would be a "white-haired woman walking with a cane, active and with many interests." She had given some thought to traveling to Israel and possibly retiring there. Now this "dream" was no longer possible.

The caseworker, recognizing that Miss V.'s depression might stem from her feelings of helplessness in the patient role, began to put Miss V. to work on her own behalf. This process started with the caseworker asking Miss V. if she could think of the time in her life she would most like to see re-created. Miss V. said that while she knew she was no longer able to teach at the academy, she wished she could once again have students come to her home for tutoring. She felt that now that she "had nothing to offer, they had all deserted her." The caseworker wondered out loud if Mrs. V. still felt she was able to remember her Hebrew. Miss V. adamantly said, "Of course I can." A short time later she mentioned to the caseworker that she was planning to give lessons in conversational Hebrew. She soon discovered that many families remembered her teaching abilities and were glad to refer students to her. As Miss V. began to see herself once more in the teaching role, her depression lifted. She was able to accept the health and other professional services she needed to remain in her apartment. She continued to enjoy teaching a few students each week until she died at age 80.

It has already been stated that role performance involves the person's conception of his/her particular role, the response of others with whom it is enacted, and the cultural context in which it takes place. Therefore, an analysis of role behavior as it relates to the case of Miss V. requires that each of these dimensions be examined.

An evaluation of role performance from the perspective of the person suggests that personality, or the most significant part of it, be viewed as "the sum total of an individual's social roles" (Neugarten and Datan, 1973). However, this is not to say that the concepts of role and personality are synonymous; rather, personality can only be perceived and assessed within a social context, where the individual is him/herself in some role. When personality is defined as a configuration of the individual's performance in a succession of roles, it is much akin to the social self.

> . . . in every age phase, from infancy onward, the continuous exercise of personality functions occurs within the relationship and tasks that are governed by role expectations and their social judgments. These shape and infuse every aspect of the personality. Vital roles are both time-extensive and emotion-intensive. Because they are the social forms in which living is contained and expressed, in which the human quest for steadiness and dependability, for anchorage and linkages with other human beings, occurs, where the sense of self identity and self-connected-with-others is repeatedly experienced, where the powers of mind and muscle and feelings are continuously in play, social roles are the means by which the human personality is expressed and expanded (Perlman, 1968, p. 56).

As Perlman has so clearly stated, the relative nature of role performance is not simply a reflection of social norms and expectations. It also calls into play the person's feelings, emotions, perceptions, and beliefs. A social history related to functional capacity examines the way in which the undertaking and carrying out of critical roles is intimately related to a' person's sense of self and others.

In the case of Miss V., one readily sees that her conception of self throughout her adult life was closely tied to acting out the role of teacher; she seemed to function best when she was called upon to meet this "special claim" that others had on her. Therefore, the loss of such a central role was experienced as damaging to her self-esteem and life satisfaction. When others no longer recognized and counted upon her to teach, she experienced a sense of personal loss, which was reflected in depression.

The nature of the impact of role loss upon the coping resources and the life satisfaction of the elderly has received considerable attention in the literature. In a theoretical model developed by Elwell and Maltbie-Crannell (1981) it is suggested that role loss is not only a producer of stress but is directly related to life satisfaction. As can be seen in Fig. 5.1, income, health, and social participation can act as important mediating factors, helping the individual to cope more successfully with their loss. When the individual has failing health and few social supports, coping resources can be enhanced through medical and social services. These can hopefully lead to an improvement in morale. For that reason, one of the most important therapeutic interventions in the case of Miss V. was to work with her to "repair" social networks and supports, producing a positive result.

In addition to the loss of her work role, as Miss V.'s health failed she had to learn to adjust to the new role of patient. Miss V., who had been accustomed to viewing herself as an independent woman and a contributing member of the community, found this difficult, making her personal adjustment even more tenuous. As the situation became clear to the caseworker, she helped Miss V. take control over as many life decisions as possible so that she could remain somewhat independent. The caseworker also encouraged Miss V. to interpret her own needs to the health professional from whom she received services, only stepping in at Miss V.'s request.

Role performance, however, cannot be understood solely from the perspective of the *person*. Rather, the analysis must examine personality factors in light of an *interpersonal* situation. Ackerman (1957), one of the first psychiatrists to extend the psychodynamic treatment approach to the family sphere, noted that the concept of role "serves as a bridge between the processes of intrapsychic life and those of social participation. . . . Within the frame of this concept, it is possible to express the extensions of psychic processes into social events" (p. 53). Thus, we see that role can act as a tool for making the diagnostic link between intrapsychic and social processes, and enable the caseworker to arrive at a dynamic interactional assessment of the client.

The decision to conduct an interactional assessment is relevant to both the single elderly client and those with family members (see chapter 8). Such assessment permits the caseworker to better understand the relative "health" of the client's social networks and social supports. Examining social networks provides the caseworker with information about the social relationships that surround a person; studying social supports allows for an understanding of the emotional, instrumental, or financial aid that is obtained from the social network. This knowledge is an important part of functional assessments as it is "now apparent that [such] social conditions facilitate functional ability

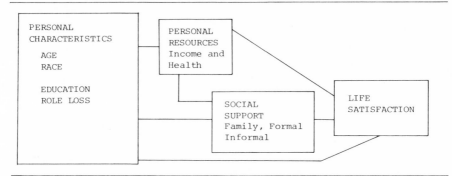

FIGURE 5.1. Impact of role loss. With permission from F. Elwell and A. Maltbie-Crannell, "The Impact of Role Loss Upon Coping Resources and Life Satisfaction of the Elderly," *Journal of Gerontology* 36 (March 1981):223–232.

and independence and, in fact, may make significant contributions to the health and well-being of the elderly" (Berkman, 1983, p. 747).. An assessment of the social networks and supports can be conducted from an individual client perspective or from a community level or public health point of view. These approaches are complementary. An assessment of an individual's social network focuses on the kinds of resources being provided to the individual, his/her unmet needs, and an understanding of what obstacles prevent or inhibit the client from having a stronger support system. An assessment from a community level provides a picture of the social networks of the elderly in a specific target area, usually involving a high-risk population. This information can be used for outreach, case-finding, and for planning new programs and services.

Assessments from an individual perspective look at the structure and the content of a person's social network. Structure includes the number of ties, types of ties (kin, friends, neighbors), and the interconnectedness of ties. Content examines the kinds of assistance the elderly person receives (grocery shopping, house cleaning) and gives (babysitting, volunteer work).

In obtaining information on the content of the client's social network, most social workers are interested in how the older person is able to deal with the activities of daily living (ADL). Clients are generally asked who provides help for them in tasks they cannot do for themselves, and whether they are satisfied with the assistance. Table 5.1 provides questions that can be asked to gather this type of data.

Also relevant to the assessment is the quality of social supports. Though this area of evaluation is seemingly subjective in nature, it is critical to a complete assessment. In the case of Miss V., while there were many professionals involved in her care, she had lost those supports that provide emotional satisfaction. Since a person develops his/her friend-ships and social supports through the various roles performed, role loss can result in a decrease in social participation. After Miss V.'s retirement and the decline of her health, she became more and more socially isolated, which contributed to her sense of alienation and depression. For this reason, the caseworker's interventions were aimed at trying to repair social attachments and community ties.

The last aspect of role performance that needs to be examined is the *structural*. While every society (group) has an age-status system for marking social time and distributing roles, the way in which duties, rights and rewards are allocated is socially defined. In a modern complex society such as the United States, this means that there will be many systems of age status depending upon the particular cultural values and social institutions of the group. Although this issue is only recently receiving sufficient research effort, it is becoming clear that there are diverse patterns of needs and adaptations to aging among the various ethnic groups in American society. Cross-cultural social work practice suggests that knowledge of a client's cultural patterns, ethnic background and traditions constitutes a fundamental part of a thorough evaluation; treatment should also be consistent with those cultural elements valued by the older person (see chapter 12).

As a member of the Jewish community, Miss V. shared in a tradition that stresses learning for learning's sake and views old age as a time when leadership roles should continue. Miss V. undoubtedly experi-enced increasing distress as she was less able "to live up to" these cultural values. At the same time, ethnic communities can often serve as powerful support networks for the elderly (Greene, 1984). In helping Miss V. to reestablish her ties to the Jewish educational community, the caseworker had effectively established a network of professional, social, and emotional support.

Additional structural elements that have been shown to influence the timing of events and patterns of aging are *socioeconomic status*, or work context, and *birth cohort*. Research has shown that an individual's socioeconomic status can influence the age at which major life events occur. In general, the lower the socioeconomic level, the sooner one reaches major life events. This quicker timing of life's course, such as leaving school earlier or being replaced in the work force at a younger age, may lead certain individuals to perceive themselves as "old" at an earlier chronological age (Bengston and Haber, 1983). In the case of Miss V., the client did not view herself as old until she could no longer work at her chosen career. However, fortunately for her, she was a member of a profession in which she could continue to work as long as she was intellectually competent, and she was able to return to part-time activity.

Historical conditions and events have also been shown to influence

TABLE 5.1. Assessment Evaluation[a]

---

1. "Is there any one person you feel close to, whom you trust and confide in, without whom it is hard to imagine life? Is there anyone else you feel very close to?"
2. "Are there other people to whom you feel not quite that close but who are still important to you?"
3. For each individual named in (1) and (2) above, obtain the following:
   a. Name
   b. Gender
   c. Age
   d. Relationship
   e. Geographic proximity
   f. Length of time client knows individual
   g. How do they keep in touch (in person, telephone, letters, combination)
   h. Satisfaction with amount of contact—want more or less? "If not satisfied, what prevents you from keeping in touch more often?"
   i. "What does individual do for you?"
   j. "Are you satisfied with the kind of support you get?"
   k. "Are there other things that you think he or she can do for you?"
   l. "What prevents him or her from doing that for you?"
   m. "Are you also providing support to that individual? If so, what are you giving?"
4. "Now, thinking about your network, all the people that you feel close to, would you want more people in it?"
5. "Are there any members of your network whom you would not want the agency to contact? If so, who? Can you tell us why?"
6. "Are you a member of any groups or organizations? If so, which ones?"
7. "Are you receiving assistance from any agencies? If so, what agency and what service(s)?"

---

[a]Reprinted with permission from D. E. Biegel, B. Shore, and E. Gordon, *Building Support Networks for the Elderly* (Beverly Hills: Sage Publications, 1984).

how roles are socially defined. Sociologists use the terms cohort and generation to deal with concepts of time at this macrosocial level. A cohort refers to those who are born at the same period of calendar time and who enter specific social institutions at the same time intervals (entering school, leaving the work force). A generation is a group of people who are aware of sharing similar sociocultural experiences (sometimes regardless of chronological age boundaries).

Cohort analysis examines how those who were born in each period of time share cultural and historical experiences such as the threat of nuclear war, the "baby boom" or economic depression, and the effects such experiences have on role behavior. The fact that Miss V. was a member of a birth cohort that experienced the Great Depression was important to understanding her attitudes toward her economic situation in old age.

Generational analysis is used to study the contributions of particular age groups to far-reaching social changes in areas such as sexual attitudes, fertility rates and labor force participation. The fact that Miss V. had elected to give up marriage and children for a career had particular significance for a member of her generation. It is also important to note that until there was a breakdown in Miss V.'s social support system she remained happy with this decision. Such information tends to underscore the value of an interactional or systems approach to client assessment, including those individuals without immediate family members.

This chapter has addressed the concept of social age as it is enacted in role performance as a means of understanding the social dimensions of individual behavior. The case of Miss V. was used to illustrate the complex nature of role behavior at the personal, interpersonal and structural levels. The central concept has been viewing the older client in interaction with others, whether they be part of a family system or not. Through the use of the interactional assessment approach, Miss V.'s depression took on new meaning: The sadness and self-reproach associated with it were not seen as symptoms of an "illness"; rather, they were viewed as a signal that the important areas of interaction in Miss V.'s life had broken down. Therefore, the caseworker's efforts were not directed toward "curing" the patient, but toward having some impact on the way the client interacted with others.

The interactional view to assessment is considered throughout the text. In the next three chapters the concepts of social interaction and role will be used to clarify family structure, development and communication patterns. In chapter 8 they will be applied to those aspects of family treatment that deal with difficulties or dysfunctions.

Finally, in chapters 13 and 14, the concept of role will be used to examine issues related to the worker–client casework relationship and supervision.

CHAPTER

6

The Family as a Social System*

General systems theory was first proposed in the 1940's by Bertalanffy, a biologist, in an attempt to provide a comprehensive theoretical model to decribe all living systems. This section describes the general systems model and the rationale for using it to understand and treat the family.

> A model is not a description of the real world. It is only a way of looking at and thinking about selected aspects of reality. It is a map or transparency that can be superimposed on social phenomena to construct a perspective showing the relatedness of those elements that constitute the phenomenon (Anderson and Carter, 1978, p. 10).

In other words, a model is an abstraction or a visual representation of how things work under "ideal" conditions. A model is used as a frame of reference, and it must be complex enough to account for reality. Systems theory has provided such a model; it has been applied to many social phenomena in the behavioral sciences.

A system may be defined as an organization of objects united in some form of regular interaction or interdependence (Bardill and Ryan, 1969). It is a complex of component parts that is best understood by studying the relationships between them. Systems theory suggests that in order to understand a phenomenon one should not view each part in isolation or simply add "views" of each part together, but rather see how the components function together as a whole or as a unit. It also suggests that the unit itself will display properties over and above the simple compilation of the parts. For example, an understanding of each cell's functioning within the brain does not provide a complete picture of the workings of the human mind. In other words, a system "is a complex whole made of component parts in mutual interactive relationship to other parts." To understand the individual part, one must study the transactions among the parts both within the system as well as with other systems (Eyde and Rich, 1983, p. 21).

A social system is a special order of system in that it is composed of persons or groups of persons who interact and influence each other's behavior. In fact, its chief characteristic is the actions and interactions

*Contribution by Jirina Polivka.

of the various people both within and across its environmental borders (Buckley, 1967; Kantor and Lehr, 1975). It is an organization of interacting and interdependent persons. Social systems may include families, organizations, communities, and societies. The social systems model is an approach that can be applied to all forms of human association (Anderson and Carter, 1978).

Many practitioners as well as theorists have adapted general systems theory for use in social work practice because it provides a helpful analytical tool for working with people. It permits practitioners to steer away from simplistic linear approaches (which assume direct cause and effect between relationships) and allows them to integrate many sources of information into a comprehensible whole (Berger and Federico, 1982). Family-centered social workers have looked to systems theory for casework approaches that will provide a better understanding of the family interactional process. The perspective of the family as a system gives them a point of reference for understanding each unique family unit within cultural context.

The family system is one building block of the structure of society and is a basic unit of human organization. The family supplies the milieu in which its members are shaped through an intricate and highly individualized process. It produces new members and readies them to take their places in society. Each family has its own set of rules for shaping its members according to its own customs. This process can be better understood by using systems principles of organization.

> A family is a small social system made up of individuals related to each other by reason of strong reciprocal affections and loyalties, and comprising a permanent household (or cluster of households) that persists over years and decades. Members enter through birth, adoption, or marriage, and leave only by death (Dell and Goolishian, 1979, p. 10).

The caseworker who views the family as a social system recognizes that the family is a very special group possessing unique qualities not shared by any other group. It contains a relatively permanent collection of individuals who have developed their communication patterns over a certain period of time with a particular degree of emotional investment attached to them. It is these organization and communication patterns, as well as the emotional tone of the family, that are the focus of the casework assessment. The term "family" is defined broadly to encompass those persons who constitute traditional or functional family systems. The functional family system is not limited by residence, blood, or marital ties, but is recognized by the long-term nature of the relationships. The use of the functional family concept can assist social workers in recognizing cultural, racial, and/or ethnic factors related to family structure. In short, the term "family" refers here to all persons recognized as operating within the client system.

A family-focused assessment begins with the recognition of the family as a social system. While family systems therapists have differed in their selection of specific properties to use in assessing family functioning, the following basic assumptions provide guidelines for this task:

1. The life of a family group can be studied as a whole system or as a structure of interlocking relationships.
2. A family system is comprised of interrelated members who constitute a unit, or a whole.
3. The life of the group is more than just the sum of its participants' activities.
4. A biopsychosocial change in any one member affects the balance (homeostasis) of the whole family group. Structural changes that occur at family transition points can also disturb its balance.
5. Families under change and/or in crisis seek to reestablish their homeostasis.
6. The family's organizational "limits" are defined by its boundaries or membership.
7. Boundaries give the family its identity and focus as a social system, distinguishing it from other social systems with which it may interact.
8. Transactions (movements) across family boundaries also influence the homeostasis and functional capacity of the group.

As has already been stated, a social system, particularly a family group, is characterized by a relatively high degree of internal organization and interdependence. This means that the individuals are not seen as isolated but as interacting members. It is necessary to understand how members relate to one another in a more or less stable pattern over time in order to assess the family as a group of persons who comprise a causal network. The discussion of the family as a developmental unit and as a center for role allocation provides direction and techniques for achieving this goal.

One major purpose of the family group is to maintain itself over time by meeting the needs of its various members. In order for this to be accomplished, the family group constantly strives for and must achieve balance or homeostasis* both within itself and with other social systems. "Homeostasis refers to the regulatory processes through which the system achieves a state of internal and external balance" (Berger and Federico, 1982, p. 49).

*The terms balance, equilibrium and homeostasis are used interchangeably in this text.

The model used in this text focuses on two major factors that can interrupt or interfere with family homeostasis: (1) biopsychosocial changes in the functioning of an older family member, and/or (2) structural changes that occur at major transition points. The dual-pronged assessment perspective of the functional-age model of intergenerational family therapy addresses these issues, which disrupt the family social system, and seeks to help a family reestablish its functional capacity.

"Systems are always both changing and maintaining themselves at any given time" (Anderson and Carter, 1978, p. 21). Those family systems that are sufficiently organized or functional are able to meet their needs/goals. A disorganized or dysfunctional family is operating in a self-defeating manner. In a functional family, each member has an opportunity to develop separately as a person, to assume a unique identity through the process of individualization. This means that the family allows each member to develop the ability to function on his/her own, even though participation in the physical and emotional life of the family is encouraged. In a dysfunctional family, individualization is obscured.

One of the first tasks of the family caseworker is to delineate the boundaries of the family system. A boundary defines the "edges" of the space or sphere in which the system is located, and describes the extent of the system's organization. Boundaries enable the system to assume its identity and character. For example, a body may be viewed as a system with the skin as its boundary; a tree may be viewed as a system with its bark as a boundary, and so on. The family's organizational limits are also defined by its boundaries.

The family as a social system may be viewed as a group of people who interact with each other as well as with individuals and systems outside the family unit. The caseworker evaluates these patterns of interaction during the assessment process. Interactions within the family system are usually of primary interest to the family caseworker. Each family member will have been socialized to the particular mores and emotional tone operating within that family system. The mores of the family are the cultural expectations, customs, and norms by which the family lives. Emotional tone refers to the shades of intensity assigned to the values. The mores and emotional tone provide the family's organizational fiber. They vary from family to family as well as within each family over time.

The boundary may also be thought of as "separating" the family from other social systems with which it may interact, for example, family, school, church, and agency. In other words, the boundary gives the family its identity and focus as it carries out transactions with other systems. Boundaries vary in density or permeability. Social systems are considered relatively open or closed based upon the extent to which the members interact with individuals in other social systems.

Based upon its interactive modes and patterns, or the density of its boundaries, a family may be assessed as relatively open or closed or somewhere between the two extremes. The density of a boundary influences the ability of the family to alter its functioning and thus be amenable to treatment. A family with a highly dense boundary is likely to exhibit rigid mores and be ruled in a more autocratic manner. It is also less likely to interact with other systems in the environment, restricting the interchange of materials, energy, and information (Berger and Federico, 1982).

If the family is an open system, democratic functioning is more prevalent. There is participatory exchange; each voice in the family is more likely to be heard and respected; decisions are usually made together or on a majority basis. The more open the system, the more potential there is for exchanges with other systems. This allows for a greater use of outside resources and a capacity for action. The case-worker will find that in a closed system with relatively impenetrable boundaries, changes are more difficult to achieve. On the other hand, in an open system that tends to be flexible and amenable to new ideas, change is much more possible to accomplish. In short, the open system is more adaptive and, consequently, is usually more "successful" in therapy.

From a family systems perspective, defining boundaries means that the caseworker ascertains who are considered members of the family group. One of the first tasks of the family-focused caseworker is to determine who the members of the family system are. The importance of belonging is evident when we look at the nature of family member-ship. Family members are a given, and remain a permanent part of the family group. The permanency is felt more through the imprint a member makes on the fabric of the life of the family rather than through his/her physical presence. The family member may have departed from the family in pursuit of his/her independent life or through divorce. Nevertheless, the member remains tied to the original group in some manner, and may participate in family rituals and celebrations or be involved in decision making about the lives of other family members, particularly minor children or dependent elderly. Insofar as an indi-vidual is always part of the group's dynamics, he/she has never truly "left" the family.

The question of who is considered family should be interpreted broadly. The people thought of as family by an older person may change over a lifetime. Families today come in increasingly multiple forms, creating whole new possibilities of kin networks for the older adult. The geriatric caseworker needs to explore all evidence of possible family support for an older person. This is a critical step in the assessment process. The caseworker's approach at this point will strongly influence his/her ability to involve those persons most central in the life of the older person.

While it may seem a simple task, the actors in the client system are not always easy to identify. Most mental health or service agencies receive calls on behalf of an elderly client which suggest that the presenting problem rests *solely* with the older adult. Many families see the older person as "the problem," and are often resistant to discussing other significant persons in the life of the older member. The favorite grandson who is away at school may have the potential for reaching out to the grandfather in a special way. The "adopted niece" who is not viewed as a "true relative" by the family (or by the caseworker) may be a key person in the life of her "aunt." Older couples who are "just living together" but identify themselves as "husband and wife" are an increasing phenomenon, but may not be seen as a treatment unit.

Caseworkers must be culturally aware and sensitive to different life-styles when identifying members of the client system. They must not be bound by traditional nomenclature, and should reach out to those persons who are important in the life of the older family member. A well-established relationship with the older person often allows for direct inquiries of this kind. As the social worker begins to gather a developmental history of the family, the roles of the various members of the client system become clearer.

How changes in the functional ability of any one family member affect the whole system is the focus of the assessment. The organization of the family is a major issue. How is the family arranged or grouped together to form a whole? What respective role(s) does each member play? How does the family work together to achieve its goals? Issues of power, control, authority, and decision making are all of concern. Such "systems thinking" allows the caseworker to evaluate individual behaviors and roles within a family context as well as within the broader environment (Berger and Federico, 1982).

Communication patterns among family members is another major area for evaluation in family-focused casework. Communication, as the next chapters make clear, depends on the interplay of two or more people. A basic rule of communication theory is that communication styles reveal the nature of the relationship between people and the function of the communication for each of them (Parsons, 1964). For example, a statement by an 80-year-old mother such as, "I know you are too busy to see me today," is not merely an "understanding" comment. It expresses something in the way of the relationship, i.e., a self-observation and an expectation of the other family member. The role of the caseworker is to help the family establish and understand the meanings, given and received, in order to improve communication. Since family therapy centers around concepts of interaction, it is essential to observe and understand family communication styles (Satir, 1972). Improved communication between all members of the family and the subsequent improvement in family functioning is the ultimate goal.

Without the benefit of understanding how the whole family functions, the task of comprehensive assessment would be impossible. The role of the social worker is to assess the various life-styles of the individual family members within the system. The caseworker needs to constantly keep in mind that the assessment of any one individual is part of the total assessment of the group that ultimately provides the therapeutic focus.

THE PRESENTING PROBLEM

People seek out mental health and social agencies for a variety of reasons. Clients come for help because they are "in need," "have a problem," are "under stress" or are "in a crisis." While these terms are often used interchangeably, the concept of crisis, which is central to our model, can be more precisely defined: In simplest terms, it is a state of imbalance, or a critical period of disequilibrium (Rapoport, 1963). It is a time of heightened vulnerability and threat. This definition presupposes that individuals and family systems strive to maintain a state of balance through their characteristic adaptive and problem-solving activities. When these adaptive patterns are not adequate, the individual and/or family unit has difficulty functioning.

The social work therapist needs to make an astute assessment of the presenting problem. He/she needs to diagnostically separate a family that is essentially functioning in a balanced manner and finds itself temporarily derailed, needing help to get back on the right track, from a family that has been operating dysfunctionally in its well-accustomed manner for years. He/she needs to be aware of the fact that a functional family can and does draw on its own resources, mobilizing them to right its system. The practitioner also needs to keep in mind that, in a state of crisis, a dysfunctional family may not have many resources from which to draw. In both instances, the therapist should be able to make a judicious use of community resources in conjunction with family counseling.

Because the family system is distinguished by a high level of interdependence, the practitioner can expect that a change in the behavior, status, or role of one member of the family can lead to change(s) throughout the whole group. For this reason, families are particularly vulnerable to disruption during transition points such as birth, marriage, divorce, or death. Families are also in a more precarious situation when faced with a biopsychosocial crisis in an older member, and frequently come into treatment at that time. Successful crisis resolution has been credited with preserving a well-functioning system, and has become the goal of therapeutic intervention with persons and families in a state of temporary stress.

A crisis is a self-limiting period of upset when habitual problem-solving mechanisms fail to meet the needs of an individual and/or family group. This leads to ineffective functioning and disorganization. In essence, a crisis may be defined as an event or circumstance that the family system cannot adequately handle. Factors that may have potential for disrupting family functioning should be identified early in assessment, and a determination made about the presence/absence of a crisis: Was there a stressful precipitating event? Were there rapid cognitive and affective changes in a family member, and have these changes been sustained for an extended period of time? (Bloom, 1963).

Crises often have a somewhat meteoric existence, appearing suddenly. Their resolution is usually equally speedy, even though devastating effects may linger. For example, an aging parent, after being stricken with a stroke and left paralyzed and confused, is confined to a nursing home following the emergency. The daughter continues to feel guilt about sending her mother to an institution, and the mother never really adjusts to her new situation.

Some crises are considered normal because they are a part of family development and, therefore, more predictable: marriage, birth of a first child, children going to school, children leaving the home, retirement from a job, and death of a spouse are such situations. However, even though they are to some extent predictable, they are nonetheless stressful. Because these events are often experienced as "points of no return," the family must reestablish its equilibrium or balance.

Other crises may be neither predictable nor expected. Or, perhaps, the family knows that a problem is on the horizon but elects to put off thinking about it until it is a full-bloomed crisis situation (the ostrich maneuver). For example, the family may have observed changes in the older relative's physical health for some time. He/she may have become increasingly immobile, but left to reside in a large two-story home. No one discusses the matter with the older person. "Suddenly" a serious incapacitating illness strikes. At the time of crisis, the family may seek help. However, far too often the aged person may not participate in the process of decision making that takes place even though he/she may be capable of doing so. In some instances, the older person's home and furnishing are sold and nursing home placement sought before the individual's recovery rate and functional capacity are assessed.

Another hasty decision that may be made is the transfer of the frail aged parent into the home of an adult child. In a variation of this theme, the aged parent may have lived with the family in relative balance for some time, but the onset of illness may place the family in crisis. The unaccustomed responsibility for the extra care for the parent may result in negative feelings on the part of the adult child, including feelings of resentment, martyrdom, and guilt. Crisis prevention and family-centered casework can be instrumental in circumventing and/or ameliorating such situations.

Since the 1960's the stress that accompanies a crisis has been given increased scientific attention, and the identifying elements discussed in the literature. A "stressor" in this context is a situation or circumstance for which the family has had little or no previous experience or preparation. While such events as retirement, cataract surgery, the closing of one's home or a grandson's wedding may first seem to have implications only for the individual, they can produce stress for the entire family.

"Because the family is the bottleneck through which all troubles pass, no other association so reflects the strains and stresses of life" (Hill, 1965, p. 50). A crisis-precipitating event does not have the same impact for every family, nor does every family handle a crisis in the same way. What may be troublesome to some families may be withstood by others without apparent disorganization. The family's capacity to deal with stress is the key to assessing how a crisis will be faced by a particular family. Working to ameliorate the stress associated with events that result in apparent changes in the configuration or pattern of family functioning is at the heart of this text. Such crises threaten the family system, which is dependent on the well-being of each of the individual members and the adequacy with which they perform their roles and tasks.

PRESENTING PROBLEMS AND THE FAMILY SYSTEM

It has already been pointed out that shifts in well-established patterns can occur when an older relative faces a biopsychosocial crisis and/or when the family passes through critical stages of transition. The functional-age intergenerational treatment model suggests that assessment and treatment of these problems should center around a diminution in the functional capacity of the older relative.

A decrease in functional ability can take place in the biological, psychological, or social sphere. Biological decrements may be caused by factors such as the onset of a disease, a stroke, or a hip fracture. Decreases in psychological functioning may be brought about by a change of residence, the onset of organic brain disease, or loss of a loved one. A diminution in social skills may be precipitated by inaccessibility to transportation or fear of incontinence. A realistic understanding of these areas of functioning is necessary in order to assess an elderly person's functional age. One area of dysfunction affects all others and should not be viewed in isolation.

Functional age must then be evaluated in its relationship to the client's functioning *within* the family system. The caseworker's assessment skills should be used to simultaneously evaluate the complex interaction between the changes in the older person's functional abilities and the family's adaptational capacity. When either factor is taxed to the extent that the needs of any individual family member cannot be met, a social service agency may be brought into the picture.

> The older adult who has recently broken a hip may make "excessive" demands on his youngest son. The mildly confused mother may be viewed by her "anxious" daughter as an "appropriate" candidate for nursing home placement. The hospitalized stroke victim may be visited daily for many hours by a "concerned" daughter.

Family problems such as these do not stem solely from either the diminution in the older adult's functional capacity or the family's adaptational ability—a full diagnostic picture requires an understanding of both. Consequently, the caseworker must be prepared to assess these factors simultaneously in order to attain a systems perspective.

Another assumption of the functional-age intergenerational treatment model is that disequilibrium within the family system may be precipitated by an inability to meet the demands of a particular developmental stage. Each stage has certain family tasks associated with it that require the attention of the family group:

> Each stage in the life cycle of the family is characterized by an average expectable family crisis brought about by the convergence of biopsychosocial processes which create phase-specific family tasks to be confronted, undertaken, and completed. These family tasks reflect the assumption that developmental tasks of individual family members have an overriding influence or effect on the nature of family life at a given time and represent family themes that apply to family members as individuals as well as a group (Rhodes, 1980, p. 31).

Throughout the life cycle the family must learn to cope with maturational tasks and demands that require it to adapt and make changes in its internal organization. The intergenerational family, too, must learn to deal with such changes:

> The newly widowed grandmother moves into the oldest son's household "upsetting the routine." The recently retired grandfather becomes a "depressed shut-in," refusing to leave the home. The newly retired grandmother moves to Florida, "abandoning" her daughter and handicapped grandchild.

Presenting problems, whether precipitated by a diminution in an individual's functioning or by a transitional crisis, require assessment skills that address the family as a system. Only then can the social worker select appropriate treatment goals and interventions. Since the goal of family systems therapy is to alter and facilitate interaction among family members, this therapeutic stance should begin early in the assessment period. Thus the family can be helped to reach mutually agreed upon goals, with the caseworker making suggestions about how the presenting problem might be handled.

In order to help a family define the presenting problem, the caseworker needs to encourage each member to disclose his/her views. That which is implicit often can be made explicit by asking, "I wonder if each of you can give me some ideas of why you have come to the agency today." Family members should be encouraged to discuss what each believes to be the nature of the difficulties: What precipitated the problem? What behaviors perpetuate it? What solutions have been tried? What changes in behavior are needed to alter the situation?

Observation skills and reflective listening are critical to assessing the presenting problem. Ongoing/recurrent behaviors usually surface during interviews. Integrating all levels of communication—actual words, tone, posture, and so on—is a major assessment task. The caseworker then conceptualizes the information, paraphrasing it to the family for confirmation.

Reframing the problem in family terms is a most critical step during this casework phase. Helping the family spell out and understand how the older person's problem affects the lives of each family member is the goal. Recognition of the older person's difficulties must be addressed in that a decrement in the functioning of that family member is painful for all concerned. However, the functional capacities of the older adult should be seen in a family context.

> An adult daughter calls for help in dealing with her mother, who is institutionalized. She indicates that the mother puts unbearable pressure on her, in her complaints about the nursing home where she must live until a broken hip mends. The caseworker offers to meet with both women at the nursing home. The caseworker also obtains permission to speak with the head nurse and family doctor about the case. She learns that a physical therapy schedule for the mother has not been made. Consequently, the mother believes "she will never go home." Arrangements are made for a physical therapist to see the patient three times a week.
>
> The worker also finds out that the daughter has a small baby. For the next session, the social worker encourages the daughter to bring the grandchild along. When this three-generational group is brought together, the social worker discovers that the pressure does not come from the aged mother alone. The daughter feels the pressure of being torn between giving her time to her mother and to her child and not having enough time for either. The caseworker knows there may not be many interviews and

moves quickly to help the women understand and resolve their situation through examining the intergenerational pattern of relationships.

In several sessions, the caseworker, through her knowledge of family systems principles, helps both women realize what can be done to alleviate family tensions. The mother is able to lower her demands on her daughter's time now that she is learning to use a walker; the daughter tries not to set her standards too high, i.e., being the perfect mother and perfect daughter. After such a change has been set in motion, mother, daughter, and probably the baby, too, experience less stress. This came about as the mother was able to modify her demands and the daughter to newly define her "filial duties."

Situations like these illustrate how important it is that therapists understand family structure, roles, alliances, and communication styles in order to assess the meaning of an "individual symptom" in family terms. The older relative is not an isolate, but rather a part of a family, and must be evaluated as an interacting member of that social system.

THE GOAL OF THERAPY: RESTORATION OF FAMILY FUNCTIONING ON BEHALF OF THE OLDER MEMBER

There is a diversity of goals among family therapists. Helping the family to establish a new system of relationships, improving communication, enhancing autonomy and individuation, strengthening role performance, and alleviating (individual) symptoms are only a few. The issue of defining therapy goals, at best complicated, is more fully discussed in chapters 9 and 10. However, the functional-age model suggests that a major treatment goal at the time of crisis is to assist the family in reestablishing its equilibrium so that its stress can be lessened and the older member assisted. A family that is experiencing excessive stress, whether induced by a developmental or biopsychosocial crisis, cannot adequately attend to the needs of its members. As a result, the older adult who is experiencing a problem is less likely to receive the support of the family unit. However, once the family has regained its homeostasis, it is better prepared to deal with the tasks that enhance the functioning of all its members.

In order to clarify the nature of the problem, the practitioner needs to establish an atmosphere in which the immediate crisis can be resolved. The caseworker who perceives the family as a social system understands that a traumatic or upsetting event has the potential for bringing about a crisis felt throughout the family system. The empathic caseworker lets the family know that he/she understands the difficulties that are faced. At the same time, he/she gives the members confidence that they have the capacity for change and the potential to regain a reasonable level of functioning.

By employing the family systems principles the caseworker can assess what precipitated the crisis and what can be done to alleviate it. The family-focused therapist realizes that the life of a family group can be studied or assessed as a whole system. The relationships within the family unit form a structure or set of reciprocal roles that he/she can often observe firsthand. As is discussed in chapter 5, the behavior associated with each of these roles in any particular family creates a unique pattern that needs to be assessed by the caseworker. This enables him/her to understand what changes in relationships can lead to better family functioning.

How a family handles a crisis often depends, in part, on how it has met previous challenges. While first responding to the initial request, exploring the family's developmental history can give the caseworker additional insight into the family's past competencies and present potential for dealing with its problems. The worker's knowledge of past adaptive patterns contributes to an understanding of how a particular family may achieve change. However, it should be realized that problems affecting older persons often involve the need for specific services and require fast, practical decisions. In a systems approach to therapy, the caseworker concentrates his/her problem-solving energies and activities on the present, rather than spending them on an exhaustive examination of the past. For this reason, it is a particularly appropriate approach for working with a family experiencing difficulties centered around an older adult.

In clarifying the immediate crisis, the caseworker needs to also consider what influences outside the family boundaries may be affecting the functional capacity of the group. Difficulties with the housing authority, the nursing home staff, or muggers on the streets may result in dramatic changes for a family. Just as events outside the family may engender a crisis, so, too, can outside resources assist in alleviating it. The caseworker who has assessed the family as a system as well as the functional capacity of the older adult is better able to suggest community resources that everyone is able to accept and use appropriately.

To summarize, the therapist who wishes to assist the family to reestablish its equilibrium must be prepared to deal with the major concern(s) that has brought the members to seek help. Most often the family expects a quick solution. Consequently, gathering a family history, understanding family dynamics, and assessing the group's functional capacities must all be done quickly in the interest of clarifying and resolving the crisis at hand.

In discussing the goal of therapy, it should also be pointed out that crisis situations are not the only ones in which family systems therapy may be applied. Its important contribution is increasingly noted in the field of prevention, or when a state of "pre-crisis" exists. Unfortunately, the field of prevention has not been as popular in the Western Hemisphere as it has been elsewhere, particularly in Europe. However, the philosophy is changing, and practitioners are beginning to recognize the value of timely intervention.

It is important to acknowledge that the social work practitioner can help the family effect meaningful changes in its system whether the members find themselves in a state of crisis or whether they are beginning to plan for preventing its occurrence at some future point. Being aware of the usefulness of prevention is particularly important in the field of aging. A wide arena of services is often accessible to enhance the quality of life and the physical rearrangements of an aged individual. The profession of social work is ideally suited to offer the family the right kind of anchor in its search for help. The social worker is well-informed about services and community resources that the client family may need. He/she is educated to make a quick and competent judgment about which resources could be tapped. Finally, he/she is trained to assess and give direction to the family.

Despite the family's need for assistance in selecting appropriate help, they may also resist it. Much of the resistance to change can be attributed to fear of the unknown. A chronic problem has the redeeming value of familiarity. The promise of improvement is suspect due to uncertainty about its outcome, and the family tries to retain familiar behavior patterns even if they are dysfunctional and are the reason the family came for help in the first place. Therefore, family members may sabotage the worker's attempt to promote change. The family may be distressed by the problem that brought them to treatment; while they seemingly wish to rid themselves of the difficulty, they may feel threatened by change. The process is a paradox: overtly the family desires change, covertly they do not.

In assessment, the therapist needs to make a careful inventory of any manifestations of resistance to change. For example, the therapist may notice that the husband persistently changes the subject when the wife begins to complain about his smoking in the living room; or the grandfather has a coughing spell each time the conversation turns to his untidy habits in the house; or the mother shifts in her chair at the mention of the eldest daughter.

Change is often painful, and personal discoveries necessitate much work and effort on the part of family members. For this reason, it may be easier to see the difficulty as resting with one individual—in this instance, the older adult. When working with the intergenerational treatment model, it is necessary to keep in mind that if one member of the family system experiences difficulties, the whole system is thrown out of balance. The goal of therapy is to assist the troubled individual within his/her family group and restore family functioning.

> Family therapy involving everyone from young to old can be a way of helping to understand what is happening to the older person, clarify feelings, review and deal with old conflicts (which may be surprisingly undiluted by the passage of time) and mobilize everyone in the care and concern for older members (Butler and Lewis, 1973, p. 107).

The Family as a Developmental Unit*

This chapter explores family development over the life span. It is concerned with the interrelationship between the changes that are encountered by the aging individual and the role the family plays in negotiating these changes. This chapter looks at the family as a developing social system with its own stages and tasks, and examines what factors lend themselves to continuity and stability within the evolving family group.

The term *development* is difficult to define, particularly as it takes place over the life cycle. Development usually refers to the process whereby an individual goes from a less differentiated to a more differentiated state, from a less complex to a more complex organism or from a lower to a higher stage of ability, skill or trait (Birren and Woodruff, 1973, p. 307). The life-cycle approach is concerned with changes that occur from the time of conception until death. The study of family development explores the "interlocking tasks, problems, and relationships" of the intergenerational family system as it moves through time (Carter and McGoldrick, 1980, p. 11). It is concerned with shifting memberships and the changing status of members of the group in relation to each other.

The fact that aging involves adjusting to ongoing alterations in an individual's biopsychosocial functioning has been addressed in chapter 3. It was pointed out that normal aging is associated with changes in the *individual's* body, self, and roles, and that behavior, at any point in time, is an outcome of a person's history of adaptation within a particular social context (Bengston and Treas, 1980). *Family development*, however, is not merely concerned with the concurrent development of individual family members (or a collection of individual life cycles), but rather with the family as a developmental *unit*. The subject of scrutiny is the family as an adaptive group with phase-specific family tasks of its own (Rhodes, 1980).

> The strengths of this (developmental) framework include the consideration of the internal functioning of the family system(s) without ignoring the external or environmental transactions of the family as a social unit. This

*Contribution by Roberta R. Greene and Jirina Polivka.

framework is particularly helpful in viewing the process of family change. It approaches change as a facet related to the interaction of the individual member within and without the family system, as well as the structural implications of position and role derived both from society and from the internal aspects of family size, age, and sex of its members (Levande, 1976, p. 294).

The family approach to development recognizes that as each family member develops over time, there are alterations in the relationships among the members. The manner in which individual and family development is intertwined has been well described by Kantor and Lehr in 1975. They conceptualized the family as a developmental unit consisting of three interlocking subsystems: (a) the family unit subsystem, (b) the personal subsystem, and (c) the interpersonal subsystem. The family unit subsystem is the total family group or the whole. The personal subsystem refers to the individual members, each having his/her own unique and autonomous development. The interpersonal subsystem deals with the interaction of members in the course of daily living.

The family as a developmental unit can be likened to a house with a grand hallway through which one enters the family system. Each step forward represents a stage of development through which the entire family must pass. There are several staircases in the house leading to the rooms of the individual family members (the personal subsystem). Each member has his/her own set of steps that he/she climbs as he/she moves from one stage of life to the next. All staircases are important to the structure of the house, just as all members are to family development. All members are familiar with the location of the various staircases and know how to get from one part of the house to another (interpersonal subsystem). These subsystems together form an intricate structure of family relationships, constituting a medium for the development of each member as well as for the entire family group.

Each step in the main family staircase is a discrete unit with its own separate identity. The identities represent stages in family development, each requiring specific life tasks called developmental tasks. Each individual needs to master these in order to successfully graduate to the next task. Each step represents a specific and separate developmental task for the family group as well. The family needs to recognize which task lies ahead and how it should be mastered. The family and each person within it must fulfill each task in order to move on to the next one without experiencing future difficulty.

Normally, developmental tasks are specifically prescribed by each family according to its attitudes and approach to life. In that way, the members can know where they stand and how any given situation is expected to be handled. There are certain acceptable "standards" for all of life's tasks: work habits, use of leisure, attitudes toward others, pursuit of hobbies. In families where the developmental tasks lack such identity, orderly progression from one task to another is not easy to accomplish. The staircase structure is blurred and the person climbing it does not know on what step he/she may be or which one he/she has missed.

In a family where the definition of separate developmental tasks is relatively lacking or is imprecise, the individuals respond with inadequate personal growth. In practical terms, it may mean a lack of perception of one's appropriate role in society. The consequence may be a reduction in the individual's level of functioning. In these families, "symptoms" are likely to appear. This is an indication that the family is "stuck" or having difficulty with a developmental issue. Families with such difficulties are often seen in social service agencies. The following case is an example:

> The C. family first came to the attention of a private family service agency in 1975, when the resident manager of the building in which they lived called about their imminent eviction. The resident manager reported that "the mother and son fought every evening and that other residents were complaining."
>
> The household consisted of Mrs. C., who was 76 years old, and her son Ralph, who was 50. Two daughters, ages 52 and 56, lived in the same community but were "not on speaking terms" with either their mother or their brother. Mr. C. had died the previous year, at which time Mrs. C. sold the family home, "wanting to move to a smaller place that would be easier to keep clean."
>
> The developmental history revealed that Ralph was very attached to his father, who had walked him to and from school every day as a child. He "had no other friends." He "was not allowed to go away to college" despite his outstanding academic abilities, and was encouraged to get a job as a clerk nearby upon graduation from high school. Ralph remained at home, and Mr. C. walked with him to and from the bus that he rode to work.
>
> When Mr. C. died, Ralph expected that his mother would now accompany him to the bus; however, her worsening arthritis precluded this. Due to her physical condition, Mrs. C. was able to do less and less around the house, and Ralph "was not about to do woman's work." Arguments and a pattern of family violence escalated when the family agency was finally called.

The problems illustrated in this case reflect the manner in which individual and family development are intimately connected. Ralph, who was not prepared by the family to assume an adult role, was not ready to take filial responsibility for his mother when she became frail in her old age. Five years later, despite the efforts of the social worker to provide home care, the mother was admitted to a nursing home. Ralph visited daily at the dinner hour, insisting that "he wanted to eat dinner with his mother."

SOCIALIZATION

Socialization may be defined as the learning of new behaviors appropriate to a new position (status) or role. In its broadest interpretation, socialization refers to the sum total of an individual's past experiences, which can be expected to influence his/her future social behavior. It includes the knowledge, skills, attitudes, needs, motivations, as well as cognitive, affective, and conative patterns required to adapt and perform in a particular group.

While societies differ in the amount of socialization assigned to the family, it is nonetheless probably the single function universally attached to the family system (Rodgers, 1980). However, other social systems and institutions are also involved in preparing the individual to assume new roles. Socialization is a continuous process of "negotiation between the individual and the social system (including the family) as he or she moves into new positions through time" (Bengston and Treas, 1980, p. 415).

During childhood the process of socialization is more obvious, as children must quickly learn to act in socially acceptable ways. But socialization continues throughout the life cycle whenever new behaviors must be learned. During the middle and later years the individual must continually learn to play new or altered roles and to relinquish old ones (Riley et al., 1969). Supporting the achievement of these negotiations is primarily a function of the family system.

As socialization continues in the later years, the process again involves both the aging person and his or her family. Coping with change has intergenerational ramifications. The family, as an "arena of interacting personalities, and intricately organized positions, norms, and roles," must establish new patterns or reorder relationships in order to meet the needs of its members at each stage of the life cycle (Carter and McGoldrick, 1980; Hill, 1965).

The family remains the major socializing agent for society. While the modern family continues to take many new forms, socialization remains a critical, ongoing family function. The child first must learn the idiosyncratic ways of life of that family into which he/she is born, and interacts primarily within the family group; as he/she matures, more social systems come into play. Through the learning process, the individual gradually incorporates the mores and becomes a full-fledged member of his/her society.

Perlman (1974) calls the process of claiming one's place in society achieving "social security."

> Social security consists not only of a sense of being accepted, recognized, affirmed as an "in," a claimed member of society. By adulthood certainly it depends upon the commitment of one's self to entering and taking on

some place or status in the social system and to carrying its responsibilities (tasks and relationships). . . . He who can be called "adult" is one who has taken on a kind of social contract to occupy a marked out and socially sanctioned niche in society, with its socially designated expectations and its ensuing rewards of social acceptance and affirmation as he meets his "contract" (Perlman, 1974, p. 24).

The need for social affiliation, place, and recognition is very powerful and persists throughout the life cycle. However, there are differences in how socially secure a person may feel at different stages of life. Early childhood is a time when social security is mainly dependent upon caretakers. Many people feel most secure when they reach adulthood, the time of full physical prowess, economic independence, and interaction with one's peers. In the later years of a person's life, there can again appear some lessening in security. Social isolation, crime, economic inequities, and inadequate health care are some of the major concerns of the aging population of our society today.

Socialization is not only a process *within* the individual. It is an outgrowth of interaction *between* the individual and the social systems to which he/she belongs, including the family. "Under ideal conditions, the roles he learns are integral parts of the social structure, embodying widely held values and serving economic, political, and other societal ends" (Riley et al., p. 953). Individuals may experience difficulties changing or learning new roles and/or relinquishing old ones. This is particularly true in a society where ageist or negative attitudes toward old age are more prevalent and socially prescribed patterns for roles are unavailable or inaccessible to a person on the basis of age (Ward, 1979a). Additional stress occurs when accustomed societal roles are lost due to personal, family or societal changes. The ensuing stress can be detrimental to the older person's psychosocial functioning, and may result in the need for mental health and/or social services.

A family can help to alleviate the stress connected with the demands of learning new roles, or resocialization of the older member. The intergenerational family network can serve as a safety net for its older members. It can also serve as a buffer between the older person and his/her society, and offer support to its members, helping to keep them in the mainstream of life: A daughter may take her incapacitated mother shopping; a grandson may accompany his grandfather on a walk; a son may take his father to a ball game. All these transactions between the younger and older family members are part of the ongoing socialization function of the family. They can make it possible for the older person to engage in new activities such as baby-sitting, tutoring, or joining a bridge group.

The older adult must continue to adjust to the new role expectations and societal demands. Families can provide essential support and assistance in making these transitions. Social workers should explore the specifics of how family members work together during critical transition points. In these instances, the worker (and the agency in which service is rendered) should be considered an additional social system involved in the socialization process.

THE FAMILY LIFE CYCLE

As a developmental unit, the family passes through normal, expectable life stages that often test the family's adaptive capacity. At each stage in the life cycle there is a change or modification in the structure and patterning of the family. The structure evolves as the family attempts to achieve mutually satisfying means of meeting the needs of family members. These transition periods have the potential for evoking psychosocial problems in those families that are less able to adjust to new demands (Terkelsen, 1980).

The concept of the family life cycle deals with the family as a basic unit of development. It is a systems concept that refers to stages in the life of the family and to the major transition points that occur as the family group moves from one major event to another. As the family encounters new experiences, the life of the group is modified, each change presenting a new challenge to its members calling for the mobilization of their adjustive capabilities. Each change brings a new set of circumstances to which the system needs to adapt; i.e., its members need to be socialized into a new set of living conditions.

Each event and each task brings a challenge to the *individual's and family's* adaptability. At the same time, each task offers a potential for positive development. Moving successfully from event to event and from task to task contributes to successful lifelong functioning. If all family members function optimally, the life of the family group progresses relatively smoothly. However, life transitions can cause temporary or even permanent dysfunction in a family. The following case of a mother who goes back to work and the grandmother who moves in to assume child-caring functions is such an example:

> The S. family consisted of husband, wife, school-age son, daughter, and grandmother. The wife, who had been a homemaker since the children were born, decided to go back to work as a secretary. The husband invited his mother, who was "tired of keeping up her large home" since the death of her spouse, to come to live with the family "and help out." Two months after moving in, the grandmother, who had sold her home, contacted a social agency, asking for help in securing housing. The grandmother complained that she had "given up her own home only to be made a prisoner in the suburbs." The wife announced that she did not want her

mother-in-law to think she could "take over her children as well as her kitchen."

Two major events that accompany life cycle stages were at issue here, both involving changes in role. The wife was ready to return to work now that her children were "more independent." The grand-mother was hoping to assume a new role as she attempted to deal with the death of her spouse. Both women were grappling with changes in role typical of their respective life stages. When they called the agency for help, they were not aware of how their decisions affected one another or how they had altered the family system. Family members had not discussed their respective roles or established ground rules ahead of time. Helping out had been interpreted differently by all of them. The grandmother hoped "to recapture" what she lost after her own children left the nest and her husband died. It also became clear to the social worker that the family had never come to terms with the death of the grandfather. The extent to which such issues can be brought into the casework process often depends upon the casework-er's skills in pursuing a family focus, at the same time addressing a specific individual's request (in this case, housing).

The changes brought about by transitions in both the grandmother's and mother's roles required that all family members adapt to new circumstances. All family members were involved in the grandmoth-er's need to establish a suitable living arrangement. These shifts also brought to the surface the family's difficulty in accepting the death of one of its members. To the extent that these various issues can be sorted out with the family during assessment, appropriate therapeutic inter-ventions will be effective.

The family development cycle is a key component in viewing the family as a system. "With this orientation, many more families who enter therapy would be seen as average families in transitional situa-tions, suffering the pains of adjusting to new circumstances" (Minuchin, 1974, p. 31).

FAMILY DEVELOPMENTAL TASKS

The developmental task model suggests that different types of issues highlight various periods of the life span. As pointed out earlier in the text, developmental tasks mandate that an individual acquire skills and competencies that permit increased mastery over the environment. As they move through the life cycle, each member of the family encounters his or her own developmental tasks. The successful accomplishment of one person's tasks is, in part, dependent on and contributes to the successful accomplishment by other family members of their appropri-ate tasks (Carter and McGoldrick, 1980, p. 6).

The family system is more than a conduit for age and stage-related developmental tasks. Each stage of the life cycle represents its own *family* developmental requirements or tasks. The developmental task families need to accomplish at each stage of life traditionally have been thought to center around child raising and economic functions. These have included establishing a household, accommodating the birth of a child, and dealing with teenagers, etc. It should be noted that the family, along with its older members, continues to face developmental challenges throughout the life cycle. All such tasks are transition points for the family, a time when stress is at its highest. As a result, difficulties may be encountered in moving through one particular transition phase to the next.

Each family's response to life challenges evolves from earlier family patterns (Walsh, 1980, p. 198). In assessment, the social worker should examine how the family members have coped and the type of system they have created *over the years* in order to appreciate how they adjust to new demands and losses. This will enable the caseworker to better understand the family's present functioning.

S.L. Rhodes (1977) has suggested a multigenerational approach to the life cycle of the family. Her conceptualization of the family as a developmental unit is a synthesis of Erikson's (1950) life cycle of the individual and systems theory. It offers the caseworker a seven-stage framework for understanding the family as "an adaptive unit with the resources for the growth and maturation of its members." As can be seen in Table 7.1, the family is conceived in traditional terms, but the model can be adapted to other family forms.

While the geriatric practitioner may have special interest in later life transitions and tasks, all stages of family development need to be understood. Assessing established family patterns and the changing life cycle needs of members is a critical component of the functional-age model of intergenerational family therapy. Launching the last child from home and establishing a mutual aid system sets the stage for family relationships in the second half of life (Blenkner, 1969; Lowy, 1979; Walsh, 1980). The structural changes of moving from a two-generational household to a single one present developmental tasks for parent and child alike. Both generations must deal with separation; the older generation must refocus on their marriage. While most families successfully adjust to this transition, a failure to do so may interfere with other later life transitions.

Establishing a mutually accommodating parent-child relationship in later life involves the issue of dependency. Interdependence should be viewed as a normal family process and an expected aspect of intergenerational relations. Throughout the life cycle, family members are dependent upon one another for emotional and social support. The resolution of dependency issues in later life, says Walsh (1980, p. 206):

> . . . requires a realistic acceptance of strengths and limitations of the older adult, and the ability to allow oneself to be dependent when appropriate. It also requires the adult child's ability to accept a filial role, taking responsibility for what he or she can appropriately do for aging parents, as well as recognition of what he or she cannot or should not do. This capacity may be constrained by the child's own physical, emotional, and social situation.

Solomon (1973) has examined many of the same family developmental tasks as Rhodes (see Table 7.2). However, Solomon has suggested yet another task for the family of later years—integration of loss. He points out that resolving the losses in economic, social, and physical functioning, which may be experienced by a member of the grandparent generation, is a task for the entire family unit. The process of grieving and investing in future functioning is an intergenerational interaction affecting the whole family group.

In short, the concept of interlocking developmental family tasks is central to intergenerational modes of family therapy. It suggests a framework for the practitioner to use in assessing what is taking place in all generations. As pointed out in the case of the S. family, changes in individual role definition(s) have ramifications for the entire group. In order for families to remain functional and continue to meet the needs of all its members, transgenerational issues must be addressed. The geriatric caseworker cannot focus solely on the family of later years. Events that occurred at any stage of the family life cycle may have precipitated the problem which brings someone to seek help. The relative ages, concurrent stages of family members, and the developmental needs of all must be understood in order for the geriatric social worker to assess the interplay of life cycle issues.

The aware practitioner recognizes that all families can expect time-related changes and as a result can anticipate some degree of stress. The anxiety produced by stress on the family as it moves through the changes and transitions of the life cycle has been viewed as a product of both predictable and unpredictable events (Carter and McGoldrick, 1980). Both types of events bring about a family crisis. In this sense, the term "crisis" is to be understood as an event that causes a disequilibrium in the family system, varies in degree of severity, and occurs as a natural part of the family's development.

Terkelson (1980) classified changes in the family life cycle depending upon their predictability into normative and paranormative events:

1. Normative events occur regularly in the vast majority of family units, arising directly from procreative and child-rearing func-

TABLE 7.1. Rhodes' Developmental Stages of the Family[a]

Stage	Time	Criterion or task	Resolution of task
1. Intimacy vs. idealization or disillusionment	Precedes advent of off-spring	The couple makes an invest-ment in the relationship	A realistic appreciation of one's partner is necessary for intimacy
2. Replenishment vs. turning inward	Childbearing years—from birth of first child to when last child enters school	The development of nurtur-ing patterns among all fam-ily members should take place at this time	The ability to succor de-pends upon the "refueling" of adults
3. Individuation of family members vs. pseudomutual organization	After bearing and rearing of preschool children	Progressive independence and freedom of family members is the concern	Individuation requires an expansion of self and a closeness without fusion
4. Companionship vs. isolation	Families with teenage children	The major crisis for family members rests on the abil-ity to develop companion-ship inside and outside the family	The family negotiates differ-ences through mutual ac-commodation that recog-nizes the child's growing independence

5. Regrouping vs. binding or expulsion	Children are leaving home to establish their own lives apart from the parents	The family needs to cope with advancing independence of offspring and the biopsychosocial pressure for separation	Viability of the marital relationship apart from the parenting function is critical
6. Rediscovery vs. despair	Postparental	Adaptability depends on rediscovery of marriage partner and renegotiation of parent–child interactions	An adult to adult relationship between parent and child requires a rapprochement and reaffiliation as adults
7. Mutual aid vs. uselessness	Postparental and last stage; parent's retirement to death	The development of a mutual aid system through the changing of role pattern is necessary	Successful achievement of a mutual aid system combats generational disconnectedness and supports feelings of usefulness

[a]Summarized by R. Greene.

TABLE 7.2. Stages of the Family[a]

Stage	Task(s)	Goal
I. Marriage	1. Relinquishing primary gratification and/or the fantasy experienced in each marital partner's relationships within the family of origin 2. Investing in marital relationship as the primary need-meeting one	Involving the construction and implementation of the basic male and female roles of the marital partners
II. Birth of the first child	1. Solidifying the relationship of the marital pair 2. Designing and developing the new roles of father and mother to a child	Assuming the parental role without relinquishing the marital one
III. Individualization of the family members (departure of the first child to school through the adolescence of the last child)	1. Modifying roles of all family members	Allowing for independent functioning
IV. Actual departure of the children	1. Relinquishing the primary gratification involved in parenting 2. Assuming the secondary gratification of parents and separated adult-children	1. Stabilizing and reinvesting in the marriage 2. Accepting the child as an "active agent"
V. Integration of loss	1. Resolving the losses in economic, social, and physical functioning experienced by either or both marital partners	Grieving over loss and making an investment in future functioning

[a]Summarized by R. Greene from M. Solomon, "A Developmental Conceptual Premise for Family Therapy," Family Process, 12 (1973), pp. 179–188.

tions. These include: (a) marriage, (b) birth of a child, (c) child entering school, (d) child entering adolescence, (e) child launched into adulthood, (f) birth of grandchild, (g) retirement, (h) senescence, (i) death.

2. Paranormative events are those events that modify the normative momentum of the family unit. Each event occurs frequently but not universally: (a) miscarriage, (b) marital separation and divorce, (c) illness and disability, (d) relocations of household, (e) changes in socioeconomic status, (f) extrinsic catastrophe with massive dislocation of the family unit, and (g) death.*

The concept that life cycle events are either normative or paranormative can be used during the assessment period as the social worker evaluates the nature of the crisis in the family. Is this crisis caused by a normative or a paranormative episode? Is the resilience of the family sufficient to cope? In addressing these questions, social workers must also look at the presenting problem and identify those normative or paranormative events that precipitated or contributed to the crisis. For example, the daughter who calls an agency about "difficulties getting along with mother" may, upon exploration, reveal that her only son has just left for college.

In either a normative or paranormative crisis situation, the therapist needs to evaluate the relative strengths and weaknesses of the family and their coping capabilities. It is useful to explore how the family behaved in previous crises. In this way it is possible to assess how the members are likely to cope in the present. The therapist needs to keep in mind that one of the major purposes of assessment is to understand the developmental history of the family system and its coping capacities.

CULTURE AND VALUES

Culture is produced by persons who live in it, and can be defined as "that complex whole which includes knowledge, beliefs, art, morals, laws, customs and any other capabilities and habits acquired by man as a member of society" (Taylor, 1924); every individual is a product of a particular culture, created by a particular society or group that gives him/her a road map for living; every family is also a product of the general culture, and in addition, every family develops a culture of its own. Culture influences a person's world view, understanding, actions, and feelings. It shapes each person's social recognition, connectedness, and aspiration toward self-realization. Culture binds a particular seg-

*Terkelson classifies death as a paranormative event. The authors suggest death is a normative event.

ment of people who live together and have a common definition of the functions of daily living. The family, as a primary and universal human group, helps to maintain the culture.

Cultures shape the cycle of growth of its members. Within the context of its culture, the family maintains itself throughout its life by adhering to its own particular values, which are a conception, explicit or implicit, distinctive of an individual or characteristic of a group, of that which is desirable (Kluckhohn, 1951). The value system that a family develops influences its life and activity as it moves from one developmental task to the next. For example, in our highly industrialized society there is an emphasis on skills, and functions are highly differentiated and specialized. Members of society as well as families establish norms that constitute success and exert pressure on their members to conform to them. At the time of assessment, the therapist needs to be flexible and understand the family in its relevant cultural constellation. This has particular relevance for minority families, recent immigrants and families that have moved from one part of the country to another.

A historical review of casework with individuals and groups reveals that the worker–client relationship has usually been approached from a white middle-class perspective (Green, 1982). When a client did not come from the same culture or possess values familiar to the social worker, the treatment was in danger of being dissonant and its effectiveness jeopardized. It was as though the client and worker were talking two different languages.

It is paramount for the social work process that the practitioner understand different cultures and respect the client's values. Understanding the client within his/her cultural context requires self-awareness and sensitivity to differences. The social worker needs to accept that beliefs, values, behavioral expectations, communication styles, and language may vary with cultural background. "The greater the cultural distance between help seeker and help provider, the greater the discrepancy in perception, labeling and response to a particular problem" (Green, p. 30).

In our very fluid society changes are continuous and rapid. The professional social worker needs to develop finely tuned observational and listening skills to recognize the cultural nuances of the client family. He/she must develop the ability to step outside his/her own value structure and cultural conditioning and assess the family within its cultural context. The therapist must also remain alert to those cultural features of the client's background that may interfere with treatment. Even highly trained social workers may not be sensitive to the cultural implications and specific variations of a family's problems. For example, placing a parent in a nursing home may have a particular meaning in the traditional extended Chinese family. Where and under what conditions a relative dies can also have particular cultural significance. It is appropriate to ask the client about cultural differences. In fact, the sensitive caseworker knows that the client family is the best source of such information (see chapter 12).

SOCIAL HISTORY

Understanding the existing relationships within the family system requires an evaluation of how that family has developed historically. Family therapy is based on the premise that these relationships provide the optimum arena in which problem-solving can take place. Therefore, their etiological development must be assessed in order to determine how they can be mobilized to benefit family members at any given time (Solomon, 1973, p. 182).

The caseworker needs to address the general questions of where the family is in the sequence of development and how a life cycle event may or may not create disturbance(s) for a particular family. In order to do this, the practitioner needs to be familiar with the process involved in making transitions from one phase of the life cycle to the next. Simon (1980) has suggested that the therapist highlight major life cycle issues related to the presenting problem in order to establish how the family is or is not dealing with them, and to ascertain whether the problems are related to a particular stage or are, in fact, cumulative.

An evaluation of life cycle events demands that the therapist view the family as a system "which spreads laterally in space (extended family) and backward in time (triangles and family themes)" (Simon, 1980, p. 331). An assessment from this point of view asks where the key developmental issue is that may have precipitated or contributed to the presenting problem. The social history is the core tool of this assessment. In one form or another, it has been a part of social work practice since the earliest days of professional social services in America (Shefield, 1924). The particular form of taking social histories varies from agency to agency, from client to client, and social worker to social worker. "The nature of a social case history is determined by the kinds of purpose it is intended to serve" (Shefield, p. 5). Four significant goals are: (1) to provide for more effective assessment of the client system; (2) to provide a record upon which rational interventive, administrative, or legal decisions can be based; (3) to assist the social worker to see systems relationships within and surrounding the client system that might not otherwise be perceived; and (4) to provide research material.

The social history provides information for the clinician to plan and set goals. As work with the family progresses, the clinician may begin to understand clients from a family perspective. As the client system changes, goals may be redefined. The primary purpose of taking a social history is to structure the relevant information about the client system in a way that allows interventions to be selected. The social worker must remember that the social history is not merely for his/her own understanding, but to achieve the professional goal of serving the client family better by perceiving its developmental patterns. The family that has mobilized itself to take action by coming to the social worker is not well served when the energy it has mustered is expended in an exhaustive examination of the past. Extended history taking should never interfere with addressing the identified problem. The social history is not the end product; it develops from the intake process and the worker-client relationship. The social worker must avoid forcing the family life history material into a mold with which he/she is particularly familiar, or which fits his/her own life history.

The practitioner should view the family as a biopsychosocial unit and assume a scientific problem-solving posture in his/her attempt to assist the family in resolving its problem. To this end, the social worker must gather facts with due care not only as to their validity but also as to their subjective meaning for particular family members. The therapist needs to be aware of his/her own conceptual schemes in writing the social history, especially when attempting to assess the patterns of life of families in crisis.

The family as a developmental unit has three interlocking subsystems to be assessed. The following list is offered as a guide in that task:

The Presenting Problem. (a) The problem of the client family should be stated in behavioral terms, that is, in terms that are observable. For example, if the family states that the grandfather has been "depressed" lately, the social worker needs to establish absence of appetite, frequent crying, lack of sleep, loss of energy, and so on, to support this statement. (b) A family-focused statement of the problem should accompany a description of the older person's functional age (as described in the model in chapter 3). (c) The statement of the presenting problem needs to incorporate the interactive patterns among family members.

The Family as a Unit. The focus of a family social history should be the group as a system. One of the first tasks is to define its membership and describe its organization.

Family Life Cycle. Does the family understand the natural events that accompany the family cycle? How do they meet new challenges and demands as well as losses? How does the family meet unpredictable events of the life cycle? What is their coping capacity? How are the events of the later stages of the life cycle addressed?

Developmental Tasks. How are developmental tasks defined in the client family? Are there clear prescriptions (standards, expectations) for the tasks? At what life stage is the family? To what extent does the family's definition of tasks contribute to personal growth? How have previous tasks, transitions (crises) been met? What appears to be the viability of the family group based upon response to crises and coping capacity?

Culture and Values. Has the assessment process defined the problem in culturally relevant terms? Has the problem been described according to the values, attitudes and concerns of the client family?

Socialization. How does the family assume its socializing function? Is it active in helping its members learn new or changed roles and, where appropriate, relinquish old ones? Is the family available in helping to reduce the stress connected with the demands of learning new roles?

8

Assessment: The Family as a Set of Reciprocal Roles*

In chapter 5 the concept of role performance was introduced as a means of understanding the social dimensions of individual behavior. It was suggested that role performance involves the person's conception of his/her particular role, the response of others with whom it is enacted, and the cultural context in which it takes place. It was also proposed that viewing the older client from this perspective, whether he/she is presently part of a family system or not, leads to an interactional dynamic assessment approach.

This chapter discusses the concept of role from a family perspective. It examines the family as a unit that is made up of multiple reciprocal roles and statuses and produces intricate and complex patterns of communication. In this context, the family may be defined as "a unity of interacting persons . . . involving role-definitions" (Burgess, 1948, pp. 28–34).

Families develop some form of interactional system among members to delineate roles for the individuals and to provide social direction for its members vis-à-vis the broader society. Consequently, a family can be viewed as a unit whose members exert mutual influence upon one another. This fluid and dynamic process is carried out through the enactment of social roles both within the family and with other social systems.

In order for the social worker to understand behavior from this perspective, two major principles need to be examined: (1) role and status—a family group is a unit composed of multiple roles and statuses, and (2) communication and interaction—through interaction (mutual influences) the family group produces intricate and complex patterns of communication.

The concepts of role, status, and communication are closely connected and difficult to separate in real-life situations. One may think of them as the building blocks of a bridge. Each block has a different shade of the same color. When assembled, the shades blend. Only upon a closer inspection are the individual shades distinguishable. If the bridge were to be disassembled, the builder would need to know where

*Contribution by Jirina Polivka.

the borders of the individual building blocks were in order to separate them. This is analogous to the task of the therapist in assessment. When the therapist meets the family for the purpose of assessment, he/she needs to be aware that this group is made up of people enacting a complex system of roles and statuses. Many forms of overt and covert communication are operating, all blending together producing an overall effect. The group may appear anxious, phlegmatic, distracted, distraught, and so on. The social worker's knowledge of role theory and interactional processes can assist him/her in formulating a clear definition of the problem by defining which member holds what position in the family and how he/she behaves relative to that position. It also makes it possible for the practitioner to be more sensitive to both the spoken and unspoken patterns of communication between and among members of the group.

ROLE AND STATUS

Role and status are closely connected. The role that a person plays is a result of the status he/she occupies in a given situation. Social role is one of the cornerstones of social work theory and practice, and serves as a conceptual link for understanding an individual's behavior and place in society. Linton described role as the sum total of the cultural patterns associated with a particular status. It includes the attitudes, values, and behavior ascribed by the society to any and all persons occupying that status.

> It is the relation of the individual's perception of his own role to its perception by others that largely determines the nature of his social functioning. Status is a "structural" term indicating the individual's location in a given framework or hierarchy of positions; role is a "functional" concept, indicating how the individual is expected to behave in that status (Linton, 1936, p. 171).

Status is a position in a particular social pattern. It is a collection of rights and duties associated with the various socially recognized positions occupied by an individual (Linton, 1936). The more statuses a person acquires, the more roles he/she is obliged to play. One person may occupy several statuses (positions) concurrently, such as those of a citizen, attorney, husband, father, brother, and so on. The person assumes a set of corresponding roles that he/she then plays out in his/her daily private and business life. As a particular status changes, so does the corresponding role.

Satir (1972) illustrated this point using the analogy of an individual wearing several hats: For example, traditionally a woman first dons her "self hat," the original hat that represents her primary status. This status is an integral part of her person—"she never removes this hat." Depending upon what divergent activities she pursues and statuses she holds, other hats are stacked upon the self hat; a wife hat, a mother hat, a daughter hat, a teacher hat, and so on. She puts on and takes off these various hats associated with her various statuses many times during any single day and appropriately shifts the roles that accompany them.

The concept of the self hat is lodged in Freudian ego theory (Freud, 1953). Freud recognized that particular situations require different roles and create different expectations according to the interactive contexts in which a person finds him/herself. This theoretical conception suggests that each role carries with it different expectations for behavior.

Role expectations are also affected by the particular culture to which an individual belongs. Children quickly begin to assume the various roles modeled around them. They copy the behavior of their parents and siblings and begin to internalize them or accept them for their own. Later, as more people enter their lives, additional role models influence behavior. This process of transmitting behaviors and customs from generation to generation is called socialization, and leads to the development of a group-specific culture.

The process of socialization is not completed by adulthood. Rather, it is a continuous process of development initiated by changes that occur throughout the life cycle. At all stages of life everyone acquires additional statuses that carry with them new role requirements. Each new role is associated with culturally defined values and appropriate behaviors. Social workers need to be aware that interpersonal problems are affected not only by the way an individual interprets his/her role but also by the cultural values of others with whom he/she interacts.

Expectations for role behavior often depend upon whether the accompanying status is ascribed or achieved. An ascribed status is assigned by society. It endows its owner with a stable possession, such as age (year of birth), sex, race, and caste. Society expects individuals to play appropriate roles in the statuses that it ascribes. A mother is expected to care for her baby; an adult is expected to assume responsibility for his/her behavior. Due to its relatively stable nature, ascribed status is difficult to change. Society tends to react punitively and to ostracize the individual that does not fulfill an ascribed status and deviates from the expected norm.

An achieved status is attained by the individual. It is derived from a person's activity and effort, such as acquiring a college education or winning a political office. Society expects certain roles to be attached to achieved statuses, but if these expectations are not met, the individual is shown a degree of tolerance rather than disapproval.

Achieved roles are associated with highly valued social identity. They can be differentiated from ascribed roles by the freedom with which they are chosen and by the high esteem in which people who play them are held. They can also be identified by the extent to which the actors are involved in role enactment. Ascribed roles are associated with behavior which is highly involving and leaves little freedom to enact additional roles. To be cast in the role of a prisoner, or a mental patient in a state hospital, or an unemployed worker means being in the role nearly all the time. At the achieved or choice end of role enactment one may be involved in the role at some times and not at other times (Sarbin, 1968, p. 108).

The social worker making an assessment needs to evaluate the various statuses of the family members in order to make a judgment about the possibility of modifying them through therapy.

ROLE STRAIN

A person whose status is in jeopardy may experience considerable pressure. The literature contains various terms to describe a person who is under stress due to problems around role enactment, such as role pressure, role strain, role confusion, and role conflict.

The family, as the main role-allocating agency for its members, socializes children into their expected roles and continuously guides adult members in their roles. Families "monitor" their members' behavior inside and outside of the family system and hold members accountable to their roles. This means that the family has considerable power to direct and control its members.

The process of role enactment often continues in a relatively smooth, organized fashion in any given family until a crisis brings unexpected pressures on the individual members resulting in role strain. This can be recognized when a person finds him/herself under pressure to change his/her role in some manner. How the individual copes with that kind of pressure depends on his/her personal capacities and the adaptability of that person's system. In chapter 5 the reader saw how a decline in the functional ability of the older adult can lead to difficulties in fulfilling role expectations. For example, the grandmother who has had a stroke may no longer be able to baby-sit or cook holiday dinners; the grandfather who has retired on a small pension may no longer be able to afford financial gifts for extended-family members to the same degree as before.

The family, as "role monitor," is in a strategic position to resolve role strain. The social worker needs to be aware of this potential and to use it in assessment and treatment. If appropriately channeled, the family system can generate the necessary energy to resolve conflicts causing role strain for one of its members.

In situations where roles are not clearly identified and structured, there is too much room for uncertainty and ambiguity. A dilemma of this kind can particularly affect persons in life transition. Someone whose status is changing due to advancing age and a decreasing capacity to live alone may find himself displaced from the familiar. Perhaps the time has come when he/she may have to make crucial changes with critical consequences. Much is unknown and unfamiliar. The reaction can be one of fear or resistance. There may be no clear picture of what lies ahead. The older adults' status becomes more uncertain and less defined. As they give up more and more of their independence, they may feel that they are losing control of their own lives. Common reactions are concern, fear, and even panic. Different individuals and families try to resolve this predicament in different ways. The following is an example of one family's attempt to deal with role strain:

> The household is joined by an elderly aunt. She moves in with the family of her nephew in order to recuperate from a stroke. On the surface, this appears to be straightforward. However, when it comes to the actual events, the seemingly simple plan becomes more complex. The nephew's daughter needs to give up her room to accommodate the aunt. The son resents "the intruder" and the daughter misses her privacy. The nephew's wife finds she needs to pay special attention to menus. As a person fully employed outside her home, she is used to cooking by cutting corners. Now she has to cook "proper" meals and serve them to the aunt in her room. She finds herself shopping for groceries on her lunch break. On several occasions when the nurse's aide did not show up, the niece has had to stay home from work. The nephew has given up his easy chair that was moved to the aunt's room. He is also obliged to spend a good part of his evenings visiting with his aunt, who likes to reminisce. He finds that the nightly visits are encroaching on his favorite evening pastimes of watching TV and working on his stamp collection.
>
> The family contacts a sectarian nursing home on the aunt's behalf. The social worker who makes several home visits learns that the aunt is a single, retired government worker. She has served at the highest echelons and has been accustomed to living on her own at a high standard of living. Until this hospitalization, she had been an active member of the literary guild and local symphony board. While she was paralyzed on her left side, her biggest fear was to be institutionalized with "old people who were out of their minds."

All the members of the family in this case were experiencing difficulties with changes in their respective roles. Their accustomed place(s) in the family and in society were being challenged (my independence, my room, my privacy, my job, my leisure). The social worker's sensitivity in recognizing the losses and demands placed on each family member, whether they appear large or small, is the key to family-focused casework. The aunt who has suffered the greatest loss needs and wants the continued support of her family. Recognition of the stress placed on the family as a caretaking unit is a necessary component of decision-making. Only in this way can adjustments be made in the family system that might accommodate other options for the aunt.

Role Variability

Much has been written about the expectations associated with role and status. Relatively little has been said about the feelings an individual has about the status(es) he/she occupies and role(s) he/she plays. Deasy (1969) amplified the feeling aspects of role and status by stressing the emotional component associated with a particular role.

Some systems theorists are reluctant to deal with emotions/feelings because they are hard to define and difficult to measure. Yet feelings related to particular roles need to be taken into consideration when a social worker makes an assessment of the family. Since each role bestows a particular status in the family group, the members have feelings about their relative positions and what those positions allow them to do.

The meaning or feeling attached to a role is important in a systems approach to assessment and treatment. In systems terms, one may say that the role gets enacted according to what it means to its owner. Stated another way, the behavior of a person in a situation depends on what that situation means or signifies to him/her. It is clear that the attitude toward one's role is a factor in shaping that role. As attitudes differ from one individual to the next, so, too, does the enactment of a particular role. No two individuals perform any given role in exactly the same manner, even roles that seem to be alike. The role is shaped by how its player perceives it and what it means to him/her.

Three degrees of role variability may be distinguished: role as a welcome consequence; role as learned art; and role as life's necessity. Sometimes the acquisition of a new status is welcome and the person experiences pleasure in enacting the accompanying role. With the birth of her grandchild, the new grandmother acquires a new status. This usually is a welcome change in her life. The tasks accompanying the role of grandmotherhood give her great personal satisfaction and are eagerly assumed.

At other times, a new status may not be so welcome, as in retirement. There are, of course, individuals who are delighted with this role since they have waited for this event for years and have plans to last three lifetimes. But then there are retired persons who may be at a loss as to how to enact the new role. Should they switch to another activity that produces income, do volunteer work, pursue hobbies, travel? Whether a person comes to retirement as an enthusiastic, reluctant or unwilling participant, in most cases the status requires some adjusting. Even the enthusiastic retiree may find that life is quite different from the time when he/she was a nine-to-five worker. Socialization into a corresponding and personally satisfying role often becomes a learned art.

At other times, a new status is clearly not welcome or wanted—such as widowhood. Accepting the status and role of a widow(er) is one of the most difficult of tasks. Acquiring the associated role(s) and accepting the loss of a loved one involves the process of grieving. The stages of disbelief, despair, and acceptance must occur before rebuilding can take place. Going through the process of grief is, of course, necessary in order to "normalize" the individual's life. Acceptance of this role becomes a life necessity. Successfully completing the grief work and acceptance of the widow(er) role is necessary before the individual can normalize his/her life.

COMPLEMENTARY FAMILY ROLES

As a person matures he/she must continually learn to play new or altered roles and to relinquish old ones. Normal aging involves many such transitions and the complex process of making them. These changes place many demands upon the individual, and the effectiveness with which they are met is reflected in role performance. An individual is guided in the enactment of a role by his/her own internalized conceptions of what is good and desirable *and* by society's expectations (prescriptions) for what constitutes appropriate conduct. Therefore, successful role performance in adulthood involves arriving at a delicate balance between the individual's internalized values and his/her judgments about what is socially acceptable in each new role situation.

As the major arena where social roles are learned and carried out, the family plays a central part in negotiating the role changes facing its members. Transitions from worker to retiree, from caretaking mother to mother-in-law, from mother to grandmother and from spouse to widow are examples of role changes within the family. Role transitions test the family and its socializing capacities. Throughout the life cycle, family members must be able to negotiate the required changes, shifting and altering their relationships to meet the new needs of all family members. In order for this task to be accomplished, all families establish a "division of labor" and a "code of behavior." The process of defining the rights and duties associated with family membership and deciding what is considered desirable in a particular family results in a network or pattern of *reciprocal claims and obligations*. These role relationships and the accompanying standards for behavior should be examined during assessment.

Understanding mutually dependent and reciprocal roles is the key to understanding family functioning. From this perspective, interpersonal relationships are viewed as the ongoing interplay of the members in their respective family-centered roles. No role exists in isolation, but is patterned with a partner in mind. The claims and obligations involved in role performance should always be examined from this viewpoint.

Because roles are interrelated and by definition reciprocal, claims and obligations must also be examined from an interactional perspective. An obligation is what a person feels bound to do for another by virtue of the role he/she occupies. (As a grandmother, I feel I should baby-sit for my grandchild.) A claim consists of those things that are *expected* by virtue of the relationship. (As your daughter, I expect you to baby-sit for your only grandson.) "What constitutes a claim for one partner is an obligation for the other" (Shibutani, 1961, p. 47).

The interface between role relationships and family adjustment is an important theme in the literature of family analysis. For example, Anderson and Carter (1978) suggest that when role expectations are disrupted or unclear, families become increasingly disorganized; Feldman and Scherz (1967) believe that the disturbed family is experiencing serious difficulty in the management of roles; while Spiegel (1968) proposes that the reciprocal nature of family-centered roles is intimately related to the harmony and stability of the family group. Clearly, the study of how the family functions and maintains itself as a system can be advanced by observation of role interaction. The way in which the family accomplishes needed role changes in response to changed conditions, or fails to accomplish them, is an important factor in assessment. The family's ability to survive such changes is strongly linked to the family's problem-solving capacity and requires flexibility of role definitions and behavior.

The role structure and its effect on the equilibrium of the family can be identified by asking questions such as:

> *What* roles are recognizable in this particular system?
> What is the *content* of the role prescriptions associated with each role?
> What is the *division* of labor?
> To what extent is there *consensus* about roles?
> How does each role contribute to the *maintenance* of the system?
> How does a particular role help to solve problems of *adaptation* and *integration* (Hess and Handel, 1959)?

Among all the issues related to family functioning and role structure, the complementarity of roles is of major importance. The principle of complementarity speaks to the way in which emotional needs are met within the family. It addresses the fit of role relationship(s) and the health, growth, and creative adaptability of the family group (Sherman, 1974). Complementarity exists when "the reciprocal role of a role partner is carried out automatically without difficulty, and in the expected way" (Strean, 1971, p. 320). Discomplementarity reflects an unstable role structure and ambiguous role definitions and expectations.

In order to achieve complementarity of roles, one member of the family acts to provide something that is required by another. As a result, the other person has his/her needs fulfilled. This is an ongoing reciprocal process in which both parties in the interaction expect to have their needs met. When this occurs with sufficient frequency, the relationship may be said to be complementary.

When complementarity fails, mutual needs are not adequately met and the relationship is not fulfilling. Role partners disappoint each other, relationships are experienced as incomplete, and role participants may undergo feelings of anxiety, hostility, and/or tension. Because of their relationship to family equilibrium, sufficient attention must be paid to appraising the positive and negative complementarities among family members.

Spiegel (1968) has suggested five main reasons for failure in role complementarity: (1) cognitive discrepancy, (2) discrepancy of goals, (3) allocative discrepancy, (4) instrumental discrepancy, and (5) discrepancy in cultural value orientations. *Cognitive discrepancy* occurs when one or both parties involved in the relationship are not familiar with the role requirements. Cues are misinterpreted and misunderstandings may result. In this context, difficulties commonly described as the "generation gap" may actually be misunderstandings about the other generation's expectations for a particular role. Misunderstandings between adolescents and their parents can be seen in this light.

Discrepancy of goals refers to situations in which the immediate or ultimate goal of a role is unclear. In such circumstances one of the role partners requires something that the other does not possess. For example, an older woman assumed a demanding role. The original motive was to receive attention/gratification from other family members. However, this motivation was mixed with a defensive need to test whether or not the family is rejecting her. This became a complex family problem when her "true" goal was never acknowledged and hostility resulted. Such behavior eventually led to serious conflict, as family members found they were not able to accommodate each other's needs.

The third cause for failure in role complementarity is *allocative discrepancy*. In any social situation there are questions about how a role is to be allocated or who has the right to a specific role. There are several ways in which roles are taken or given out: Some roles, such as age and sex, are ascribed; other roles, such as occupational roles, have to be achieved; still another way a role is taken on is through adoption.

In this last instance, no one has given permission or approval for the allocation of that role, but the person has adopted it anyway—for example, the role of victim. Or, the older person who adopts the role of patient without it being "allocated to him/her properly" is in danger of that role not being accepted or approved of by others. This may result in his/her being labeled a hypochondriac or malingerer, and treated accordingly.

Roles may also be assumed. In this circumstance the role is not seen as serious and has a playlike quality. The older person who plays the role of martyr may not be seen as truly needy. Assuming a role that is not "real" carries the danger of allocative discrepancy.

A fourth factor that can contribute to a failure in role complementarity is the lack of *instrumental means*. Instrumental discrepancy can occur when the technical equipment, physical facilities or instrumental prerequisites for role performance are not available to the actor. For example, after retirement a grandparent, who had previously been able to be generous to a fault, may find that his reduced income makes this difficult.

The fifth reason for failure in role complementarity is *discrepancy in cultural value orientations*. Roles are always defined with reference to the value orientations of a particular culture or subculture. This may not be as problematic in a relatively fixed or stable society where there are few differences in cultural values. However, in today's America, a society with a diverse cultural base, there may be variations in role expectations. This increases the possibility of confusion about how roles are perceived and carried out. It may also mean that family members experience conflict when important cultural values differ. For example, there are differences in expectations regarding parent caretaking depending upon one's ethnic group and degree of assimilation into the American mainstream. Where family members disagree about these caretaking responsibilities, discrepancy in cultural values may be the cause.

The following case of Mr. and Mrs. B. is illustrative of many of the issues relevant to role complementarity and its impact upon family equilibrium:

> Mrs. B. was referred to the social worker at a nutrition site program for senior adults by a friend who discovered her crying and saying over and over again, "I can't take this anymore." Mrs. B., a youthful, athletic-appearing woman of 65, indicated that she was upset about her husband, who is 75 years old and has Parkinson's disease. The event that precipitated her seeking help was the purchase of a hospital bed for her husband, which was made at the recommendation of his doctor. The bed was delivered that morning and she "suddenly realized that the marital relationship was over and that her husband was seriously ill."

In taking a history, the caseworker soon learned that the marriage had been a stormy one for many years:

> Mrs. B. married when she was nineteen and Mr. B. twenty-nine. They had two children, whom they saw only on holidays. Throughout their marriage, Mr. B. was employed as a tailor and Mrs. B. as a seamstress. Mrs. B. described herself as the major breadwinner who contributed 85% of the household income because "my husband could not always find a job." She appeared very angry and resentful that she had to maintain this role.
>
> Mrs. B. "retired voluntarily" 2 years ago in order to care for her husband. She related bitterly that at work she felt, and was treated like, a real person. By contrast, she said that her husband verbally abused and criticized her constantly. Because Mr. B. was so irritable, friends no longer came to visit. Her social network was now virtually nonexistent. Furthermore, her income had diminished considerably. (The couple lived on Social Security; once again Mrs. B.'s amount was more than her husband's.)
>
> Six months ago, Mrs. B. began sending her husband to a senior day-care program 2 days a week. During that time she would do errands, shop, take long walks, and swim at the Y, and felt that this was her only chance to do something for herself. Mr. B. did not like the program and would make upsetting remarks each morning as he left: "You only want to get rid of me." "Why don't you love me enough to take care of me yourself?" Shortly after she began seeing the caseworker, Mrs. B. received a call from the director of the day-care service, who said the program could no longer meet Mr. B.'s needs. "His rapidly deteriorating physical condition and hostile attitude required too much staff time at the expense of other participants."
>
> Mrs. B. pleaded with the caseworker to make them keep her husband. "Just tell them if they don't, I am going to put him in a nursing home." The caseworker convinced the day-care director to keep Mr. B. for a "trial period" of 3 months. She also talked Mrs. B. into asking her husband to meet with the caseworker and day-care staff in an effort to work things out. Unfortunately, there seemed to be "too many old scores to settle" in the marriage relationship, and Mr. B. entered a nursing home 3 months later.

The restoration of stability or equilibrium in the family system is a complicated process, particularly once complementarity is seriously threatened. In the case of Mr. and Mrs. B., there was a history of low complementarity of roles. Rather than growing and expanding, the relationship became less and less fulfilling and increasingly constricted, until it finally failed.

The meeting of dependency needs was a long-standing marital issue for this couple. Dependency in a family implies someone who is dependent, and someone who is depended upon (complements). Family members may be flexible about how these roles are carried out or they may have more fixed roles. In either situation, each partner must act to reinforce the other's behavior. Mr. and Mrs. B.'s seemingly "lopsided" relationship led to difficulties in communication, and eventually had an overwhelmingly negative effect on the functioning of the family.

COMMUNICATION AND INTERACTION

No discussion of how to conduct a family assessment can be complete without giving serious attention to the topic of communication. It is through the observation of family communications that the caseworker may make a firsthand observation of the family dynamics. In fact, it may be said that a study of a system's communication patterns is a means of examining family role relationships in observable behaviors.

The term communication has been assigned many meanings, and the study of communication systems is often a highly complex mathematical or statistical process. In applying the concept to social work practice, communications can be considered a system of transmitting information between two or more individuals, the cumulative exchanges serving as the basis for evolving relationships between people (Bloom, 1984). From this perspective, communication is viewed as an interchange involving two or more people, each of whom receives, processes, and reviews information (Marcus, 1974).

Communication theory, which can trace its origins to the thirteenth century and its development to a variety of disciplines, can be an important tool in understanding human interaction. Since each family has an identifiable communication system, an analysis of the group's particular communication patterns can be made. These patterns develop through interaction over time and generate shared definitions of norms and roles for its members. This, in turn, influences the nature of relationships and results in the formation of a recognizable family structure which can be analyzed.

It is during diagnostic interviews that the caseworker is able to observe a cross section of the family's various behavior patterns. Through an assessment of communication, including an analysis of why information is transmitted, what meaning it contains, and what inferences are made, many insights into the dynamics of the family system can be gained.

In order to better understand the "laws" and "rules" within the family, it is necessary to clarify when communication is either functional or dysfunctional. Functional communication involves the use of messages that are clear and direct. The individual who is a functional communicator may restate, clarify or modify messages when necessary, is receptive to feedback, checks his/her own perceptions, asks for examples, and acknowledges feelings.

Dysfunctional communication is usually unclear. The dysfunctional communicator leaves out connections, ignores questions, generally responds out of context, and often behaves inappropriately (Satir, 1972).

In a discussion of methodology for studying family interaction, Riskin (1968, p. 257) has suggested that the following aspects of communication be examined:

1. *Clarity*–Is what the speaker says clear to the listener?
2. *Content*–Does the speaker concentrate on the same verbal content as the person to whom he/she is talking?
3. *Agreement*–Does the speaker agree/disagree with the other person's message?
4. *Commitment*–Does the speaker take a stand on the main point or issue when appropriate?
5. *Congruency*–Are the verbal/tonal and nonverbal aspects of the speaker's message consistent?
6. *Intensity*–How forceful or empathetic is the speaker?
7. *Relationship*–What does the message reflect about the relationship? Is the message attacking or accepting of the other person?

When communication occurs between two or more persons, it becomes a shared social experience in which interaction takes place and social communication occurs. "Interaction is a continuous and reciprocal series of contacts between two or more persons who take each other into account" (Gouldner, 1960, p. 161). In that sense, it is a complementary, shared process.

Interpersonal relations involve mutuality. A multigenerational network, for example, contains a multitude of statuses and roles all revolving around reciprocal involvement. The resulting relationships are often difficult to sort out. Tracing the patterns of the mutual exchanges between and among the members can be more easily achieved by following the "two-way traffic" of communication within the client family.

Interaction is realized through communication, which can be verbal or nonverbal. Both are important means of human contact and are valuable in the assessment process. If the therapist is able to understand the nonverbal language of the client, his/her perception of the problem will be facilitated. People use body language to get a point across for which they may lack words, to emphasize what they are saying, or to contradict what they are saying. Thus nonverbal language can be very revealing. For example:

> An older uncle reports to the therapist that his new life is unpleasant since he joined the family of his niece. She thought that he was "getting on in years" and should not live alone. Now he is constantly told to "do this; don't do that; wash up before dinner; hang up your clothes, etc., etc., etc."

This report was given in a calm and measured voice. The therapist noticed that as the uncle talked, he began to tap his fingers on his knees and started jerking his head nervously. Even though the voice of the client seemed unemotional, his body language communicated agitation.

> A family comes into assessment and the therapist invites them to sit down. The family is seated. Suddenly, the mother gets up and moves away from her daughter-in-law and sits close to her son, the young husband. In the ensuing conversation, the mother sweetly praises the daughter-in-law.

This scene may indicate to the therapist that there are contradictions between the mother's words and feelings and behavior. Why did she move away from the young wife whom she says she likes so well? As the situation unfolds, the therapist notices that the mother uses many superlatives when she talks about her daughter-in-law; however, there is invariably a "but" qualifying every one of them. The older woman is actually delivering a series of criticisms of her daughter-in-law, skillfully camouflaged in praise. The therapist is able to pick this up more easily, having been alerted to it through the nonverbal communication that preceded the conversation—the mother repositioning herself away from the daughter-in-law.

Social interaction involves not only those persons who seemingly are in direct participation; it also rests within the total social structure (Cartwright and Zander, 1960; Deasy, 1969, pp. 27–58). In family systems terms, this means that any interaction between or among family members influences the whole group. A family as a system is challenged by a continuous demand for change. As such pressures and demands increase, the family's flexibility is tested. Members of a flexible family interact and communicate with one another positively, sharing happiness and sorrow and solving problems. The communication among them is open and overt, without an abundance of hidden meanings. A family that is less flexible resists change and has a relatively rigid family structure. The family does not face up to its challenges. Communication is dysfunctional, often limited, and may mask the real issues. Double messages are frequently given.

Theoretically, when two persons interact, the direction of their communication should be clear—it is a straight line between two points, from one individual to the other and back. If two persons are joined by a third participant, the messages can go in a number of different directions among the three individuals. This is known as triangulation in communication, and is an important concept in family systems assessment. It has already been pointed out that the family provides a blueprint for the role behavior of its members. In examining the communication patterns between family members, Satir (1972) suggested that roles are positioned and/or enacted in pairs: the role of mother is attached to father; grandchild to grandparent; wife to husband, and so on. Roles in a family fall into three major categories: marital, parental-filial, and sibling. When these major categories of pairs in the nuclear family are joined by others from the extended family, the family interactive patterns, already complicated, become a complex of human relations.

To complicate matters further, the pairs in a family system rarely remain stable. It is by no means unusual that when two members talk, a third person joins in the conversation.

> The benign agreement expressed by the mother with the daughter's comment on the husband's tardiness at mealtime has the potential of a powder keg. No longer is the husband's lack of punctuality an issue between husband and wife. Now the mother gets into the act and the straight line between two points is disturbed. The husband has the option of choosing to ignore the mother and continuing to relate to his wife. Or he may choose to react to the mother's comment and start discussing it with her. He may also tell the mother that it is none of her business. Instead of one possible way of interacting, he now has at least three options. Through the mother's joining the interacting pair, the issue between husband and wife gets diffused and is more difficult to resolve.

When two members engaged in communication are joined by a third, a family triangle is formed and, as we saw in our example, there is, of course, more possibility of interchange(s) among three members than between two. The communication can be redirected and take a turn suited to the needs of a particular member. If the husband does not want to face the issue of his tardiness, he has the option of talking to the mother. Still, the triangular arrangement has the potential for breeding confusion. Family members can send and receive distorted messages and block and garble communication with one another.

In any family comprised of more than husband and wife, the potential for triangulizing is very great and the communication paths quickly multiply. In a family of five, there are 45 possible triangles of communication. How these patterns are enacted depends on what the "third one out" chooses to communicate. In the case of an argument between a pair, the third person has the opportunity to ally him/herself with one or the other member. He/she may try to draw attention to him/herself by verbally joining the conversation or interrupting it nonverbally, by humming or clicking a teaspoon.

> . . . in families we don't live in pairs; we live in triangles . . . triangle is the trap in which most families get caught . . . for a triangle is always a pair plus one. Since only two people can relate at one time, someone in the triangle changes depending on who is the odd man. . . . The odd man in a triangle always has a choice among breaking the relationship between the other two, withdrawing from it, or supporting it by being an interested

observer. His choice is crucial to the functioning of the whole family network (Satir, 1972, pp. 148–149).

An elderly aunt comes to live with the family of her nephew whom she raised. The nuclear family consists of father, mother, and a son. Three different triangles of communication were possible among father, mother, and son: father to mother with the son out; father to son with the mother out; and mother to son with the father out. When the aunt joined the family, the interactive mode increased from three to twelve triangles.

It can be readily seen how an addition of a single person increases the number of interrelationships in the network. Correspondingly, the danger of misdirected communication also increases. The social worker needs to be alert to the fact that the more members in the family, the greater the opportunity for interactional confusion.

THE ROLE OF THE THERAPIST IN ASSESSMENT

Assessment is a crucial part of social work therapy. It sets the stage for all therapeutic processes. At the time of assessment, the therapist and the family members engage in mutual exploration. The newness of the situation is difficult for the client as well as the therapist. Both are embarked on a fact-finding mission. The last three chapters have provided a framework for this task, and the following outline is suggested as a guide in the process:

1. *What is the problem?*
   a. How does the family view the problem?
   b. How differently do individual members view the problem?
   c. How does the therapist's perception of the problem correlate or coincide with that of the family?

2. *Who is the patient?*
   a. Does the family recognize that the whole group is a unit of treatment?
   b. Does the family accept the fact that all its members need help?
   c. Is there an individual member around whom most of the complaints revolve?
   d. How are the family complaint(s) portrayed by its members? Do their descriptions differ?

3. *How and where did the problem originate?*
   a. Has the problem originated in a recent change of roles and statuses within the family?
   b. Can the problem be traced (specifically) to the presence of triangular communication in the family?
   c. Is the problem contained inside the intergenerational network

of the family or does it come in from other systems? Does it reach to systems other than the family?

4. *When did the problem occur?*
   a. Is the problem long-standing?
   b. Is the problem lodged in well-established dysfunctional communication patterns within the family?
   c. Is the problem related to recent developments?
   d. Did the problem arise as a result of a crisis?
   e. Has the problem been brought to therapy at the time of precrisis? (Prevention)

5. *Why is the family seeking help?*
   a. Are there physical obstacles to overcome (such as care of an infirm older member)?
   b. Is the family in economic difficulties?
   c. Are there biological-psychological-social stresses present among the family members?
   d. Is the family on the verge of a breakup?

6. *How is the problem to be worked out?*
   a. Is the family motivated to undertake treatment?
   b. Does the family have potential for successful treatment?
   c. Is the family willing to recognize that all members must change in order to correct the family functioning?
   d. Is the family ready to participate in treatment?

9

The Functional-Age Model and Individual Casework Treatment

The first part of this text dealt with the assessment of the older adult within a family context. Such an assessment requires the ability to consider alternative explanations for behavior, as well as a capacity to examine where in the client system or in the client's life it is appropriate to intervene. From this perspective, assessment is an information-gathering process in which the ordering of data gives direction to the action to be taken by the social worker. In that sense, no clear-cut demarcation of casework phases is possible. However, usually a time does come when the social worker and client recognize that they have reached an agreement about mutually acceptable goals (Northen, 1982). This consensus for working together, sometimes more formally addressed in a contract, provides the mandate for casework treatment.

Social work treatment, which differs according to its specific purpose(s) and the problems, capacities, and life situations of the client(s), has been variously defined. Broadly speaking, treatment, or working on casework tasks, begins with intake and enables clients to improve their social functioning in a way that is consistent with ego capacities in order to better cope with life situations and conditions that present difficulties. Social work treatment encompasses a wide spectrum of activities ranging from interventions aimed at making social institutions more responsive to the needs of people to therapies focused on developing individual insight. Helping people increase their problem-solving and coping capacities, obtaining resources and services, facilitating interaction among individuals and their environment, improving interpersonal relationships, and influencing social institutions and organizations all come under the rubric of social work treatment (Lowy, 1985). In short, what makes social work unique as a helping profession is that interventions may be directed at any number of aspects of a social system or social process with the intention of changing it (Bartlett, 1970). The basic purpose is assisting people to achieve a better match between their needs and situational, environmental conditions.

This eclectic orientation, which involves "the technical flexibility of selecting interventions on the basis of specific client/problem/situation configuration" (Fischer, 1978, p. 237), is most suitable for social work practice with the aged and their families. It allows for the body of biopsychosocial information related to individual functioning to be expanded to include an appreciation of family dynamics and other social systems, which increases the number of intervention possibilities and enriches treatment strategies. Chapter 9 is the first of four that address treatment issues within the framework of the functional-age model of intergenerational therapy. This framework suggests the use of a number of basic social methods of interventions, depending upon the assessment of the functional status of the older adult and the nature of his/her family relationships. Individual, family, group, and community intervention strategies are included.

GENERAL TREATMENT OBJECTIVES

While the functional-age model of intergenerational therapy emphasizes a family-centered approach, it also provides principles and techniques with which to address the realistic need for individual casework services. Older adults who have no family or have outlived them, or reside in a geographic location other than their kin are obvious candidates. In addition, assessment may lead to a decision to modify family therapy techniques, such as supplementing family sessions with separate interviews for either the older adults or their adult children, or counseling older adults without their family members. It should also be noted that more and more adult children are seeking individual therapy for themselves concerning problems related to their older parents.

Because the functional-age model is essentially a psychosocial systems view of treatment (see chapter 1), it suggests a perspective as well as basic therapy techniques that can be applied in varied situations. Six general treatment objectives or elements that are based on the psychosocial method are addressed: (1) engaging the client in treatment; (2) conducting the case study or making an assessment; (3) formulating the diagnosis; (4) formulating the treatment plan; (5) implementing the treatment plan; and (6) terminating treatment.

The first treatment objective or intervention strategy is to bring the client (system) into a problem-solving *relationship* with the social worker. The idea that the client is strengthened and sustained by the worker–client relationship is a treatment principle that is particularly useful in working with elderly clients who have experienced multiple losses and impaired functioning (Beaver and Miller, 1985; Silverstone and Burack-Weiss, 1983). Acceptance, reassurance, encouragement, concern, understanding, and empathy are the qualities that should characterize the relationship (see chapter 2). Such a relationship can not only help engage the client in treatment, but also benefit the client by giving support and minimizing distress.

A second treatment objective is to conduct the *case study* (assessment) in order to formulate a diagnosis and treatment plan. As stated earlier, this does not occur in distinct phases. Rather, treatment goals evolve out of the diagnostic process.

> . . . in casework, the problem-solving means contain the ends; the process and the goal become fused. Within each phase of problem-solving work there is the exercise of the client's adaptation capacities, whether to an idea, a relationship, or a situation, and whether about some small or some large part of the problem (Perlman, 1957, p. 200).

In this way treatment can be said to begin with the request for service and the gathering of information about the problem. As the practitioner works *with* the client to establish a problem definition, she/he may be said to be using a "teaching intervention strategy." By asking questions, making comments, and reframing issues, the social worker not only obtains assessment data, but offers clients a different view of themselves, their situation and events. This new understanding can set in motion the client's "capacities for adaption" (Hartman and Laird, 1983; Perlman, 1957).

The concept of enabling the older client to mobilize his/her own resources and abilities as he/she sees fit is an important treatment principle for geriatric social work practice. By supporting the client's strengths, additional loss of functional capacities may be prevented or minimized. In this way the client can be helped to continue functioning in the least restrictive environment, with respect for his/her autonomy in decision making (see chapter 11). Critical aspects of the case study involve encouraging the client's self-evaluation and helping him/her to reach decisions about treatment.

Formulating a *diagnosis* of the client, the third treatment objective, is also an ongoing process that does not occur at one fixed time during casework. From the very first contact, whether by phone or in person, the social worker begins making tentative evaluative hypotheses. These "hunches" as to the client's difficulties become more refined as the biopsychosocial assessment progresses. Ongoing feedback from the client and information from other professionals invariably bring about changes in the caseworker's initial impressions. Even when the diagnosis has led to the formulation of a treatment plan, modifications in diagnostic statements are likely to occur. This is particularly true when a "trial-run" of the treatment plan leads the social worker to conclude that the plan is not workable.

The term diagnosis should therefore be clarified. While social casework treatment has roots in traditional psychotherapy, caseworkers generally do not use the terms "diagnosis" and "cure" to refer to the therapeutic removal of symptoms that characterize a particular illness. A diagnosis in social work is actually a formalized assessment statement based on the biopsychosocial study. From this point of view it encompasses a wide array of factors from the biological, psychological, and social spheres that may need to be strengthened and/or changed to improve or sustain client functioning.

Establishing the *treatment plan*, which is the fourth element in the casework process, is derived from and focuses on the findings arrived at during the case study. Inasmuch as the functional-age model provides a systematic way of looking at problems and integrating information about the client system, it can serve as a blueprint for formulating the treatment plan. Throughout the study, the social worker is assessing the complex interaction among biological, psychological, and social variables that influence the older adult's level of functioning. The treatment plan is comprised of those interventions related to enhancing adaptational capacities and functional skills that are instrumental in meeting environmental demands.

Functional age is comprised of three basic spheres related to adaptational capacity: biological, psychological, and sociocultural. An assessment of the individual from this perspective allows the caseworker to understand the structure of life and daily living habits of the older adult and to select appropriate intervention strategies.

Biological age refers to physiological age-related changes and the functional capacities of vital organ systems that contribute to life expectancy. As stated earlier in the text, assessment of biological status as it relates to and interacts with personality and social behavior should not be overlooked by the geriatric social worker. Such information as nutritional habits, ease of mobility, availability and use of health care and medication, and understanding of and compliance with medical/health regimes should be obtained. This information is not only related to the client's emotional well-being and use of community resources, but to the client's ability to continue to live as independently as possible.

Treatment interventions in the biological area often include team work and consultation with other professionals. Having a clear understanding of the client's point of view about his/her physical condition and obtaining permission to talk with other professionals is important. Interventions might include inquiries about side effects of medicines, clarification of misunderstandings around medical regime, and counseling for depression and/or anxiety associated with an illness. Referring the client to or obtaining resources is another important intervention. Such services may include locating an inexpensive wheelchair or portable commode, or transportation to chemotherapy or kidney dialysis.

Psychological age refers to the adaptive capacities of the individual and his/her ability to adjust to environmental demands. In this sphere the caseworker is concerned with how the elderly client is adapting to the life changes, stresses, and losses that may be associated with this stage of life. The treatment goal is to draw upon the coping strategies of the client and to select intervention strategies that enhance the client's own internal resources.

In order for this goal to be reached, assessment must provide a picture of the client's lifelong adaptational patterns. Treatment centers around how the individual has lived his/her life, how he/she has changed in the course of time, and his/her view of death. It focuses on the client's subjective experience of the life cycle, including changes in body image and self-concept. Therapeutic activities are concerned, therefore, not only with the immediate psychic, social, and medical situations affecting adaptations in the aged client, but with his/her life history as well. This form of treatment, referred to as life-cycle psychiatry (Butler, 1968, 1969), emphasizes dealing with loss and helping clients face the inevitability of death.

Social age refers to the roles and social habits of an individual with respect to other members of a society. Assessment in this area examines role performance and its effect on the older client's situation and environment. In selecting treatment interventions the focus is on the client's interactions within his/her immediate interpersonal environment and the less immediate social systems of which he/she is a part.

Because of society's system of age-grading (see chapter 5), many older people become socially "disenfranchised." The roles they once played may no longer be available to them, while new roles may seem unattainable. The goal of treatment is to deal with the impact of role loss by seeking alternatives with the client. This is often successful for the more mobile, cognitively alert client who may decide to visit a senior center or to participate in a Retired Senior Volunteer Program (RSVP). But for the more impaired elderly client it may be considerably more difficult to "replace" losses, especially social relationships.

One final and important point needs to be made about individual casework treatment. While the older adult may be seen alone, a family perspective can still be maintained. The older client's family of origin may, on the surface, seem unrelated to current difficulties. However, developmental theory suggests that each stage builds on the previous one, and in that sense past events have an impact on the present. Much therapeutic benefit can be gained as the client recalls such information and puts it into perspective.

The older adult in individual treatment who has (had) a spouse and children can also benefit from a family casework perspective. While they may not be physically present, family may be brought into therapy through a discussion of how the client perceives family patterns and events. The use of life review as a technique can facilitate the therapeutic process. Butler, a major pioneer in the field of geriatric psychiatry, upon reviewing his own clinical practice, was the first to identify the process of life review. In a hallmark article on the subject in 1963, Butler pointed out that the "garrulousness" of the older person is not always an indication of psychological dysfunction, but a naturally occurring phenomenon. He coined the term "life review" to refer to the progressive return to consciousness of past experiences in an attempt to resolve and integrate them. The life review process was seen as having great adaptive value for the client; therefore, it was suggested that the practitioner actively encourage the recall of the past. As seen in the following case, this can help the older person evaluate the meaning of his/her life and provide the opportunity for the ego to reorganize experiences in such a way as to come to terms with past conflicts and relationships.

> Miss R. was in therapy with a family caseworker for several months, having originally been referred by a senior center employee. At that time, she was described as a "small, disfigured woman with a hump, who constantly argued with others at lunch." The other participants complained that she had become more and more belligerent during media discussion groups, insisting that she was "the only one who knew the facts." The caseworker learned that Miss R., age 85, who suffered from severe scoliosis of the spine, was one of four children. According to Miss R.'s description, the first sibling was a brother everyone wanted; the second was a beautiful girl whom everyone admired; she was the third, whom nobody needed, and the fourth was a baby girl whom everyone loved and cuddled. Miss R.'s mother was described as tall and beautiful and her father as strict and reserved. He insisted that she study diligently so that she would be able to go to college and get a good job, implying no one would ever want to marry her. Miss R. said she had shown them all, and had become a librarian at a nationally known library. She was able to spend hours a day reading, becoming an expert on many subjects. She denied that her badly hunched back was ever a concern.
>
> One day, when the caseworker was called to Miss R.'s home because of "an emergency," she found Miss R. rocking and crying before the mirror. She had fallen the day before and severe bruises now appeared on her face. She stood there looking at herself, saying "how ugly, how dumb." When the caseworker first began to talk to her, she said "don't look at me, don't look at me." The caseworker insisted that no matter how ugly Miss R. thought she looked, they were going to have their special talk together anyway. This brought a flood of reminiscences in which Miss R. was able to finally discuss how her disfigurement had affected her life. Painful memories, such as being taunted by children in school and the extravagant wedding of her beautiful sister, all came streaming back. Months of therapy

and the positive regard of the caseworker eventually led to reports from the senior center director that Miss R. was now a more pleasant, contributing member of the group.

Life review is more than simple recalling of the past. As seen in the case of Miss R., it involves a "restructuring" of past events and is conducive to the individual's adaptation to the aging process. Life review can be enhanced through the use of structured interviews, photographs, music, art, poetry, and dance therapy (Greene, 1977; Weisman and Shusterman, 1977). Since it was first advanced, life review therapy has become a well-accepted and widely used clinical technique for working with the aged. Mental health practitioners have found that the technique can be used in a number of different treatment approaches and settings. Not only is it used in casework with individuals and families (Greene, 1977; 1982b), but it has also been employed with groups in nursing homes, senior citizen residences, and community centers (Pratt, 1981; Weisman and Shusterman, 1977). (See chapters on family and group treatment.)

As the above discussion suggests, treatment plans for older adults usually contain both a counseling component and plans for specific health/social services. However, an artificial distinction should not be made between concrete and therapeutic services. The skillful and sensitive practitioner is able to understand the complex interaction between "direct counseling" and "indirect action" (Richmond, 1922), and to help the older adult in ways that are conducive to supporting optimum functioning.

Implementing the *treatment plan* is the next casework objective. Here the caseworker selects strategies that may increase the client's adaptive capacities. Adaptation to loss is one of the principal tasks facing individuals in later life. Loss is often grounded in the biological changes that characterize aging and may be accompanied by deprivation of meaningful social roles and relationships. This can take an emotional and functional toll on many older people and may seriously affect their ability to negotiate their environment (Silverstone and Burack-Weiss, 1983). In short, social workers must recognize that older clients have faced multiple losses: decline of physical health, body tone or hair; loss of status, prestige or income; and death of a spouse, friend or colleague. Psychotherapeutic efforts that work best are directed toward providing an opportunity for older adults to gain a perspective on their lives, and to compensate for and recover from deeply felt losses (Butler and Lewis, 1982).

In order to help the client deal with loss and gain such a perspective, it is important to remember that adaptability is a lifelong adjustment process through which the individual meets a series of biopsychosocial transitions. Therefore, in implementing the treatment plan, the case-worker must not only try to alleviate the current biopsychosocial crisis, but should attempt to draw upon the client's lifelong adaptive patterns (see chapter on life review).

Terminating and *evaluating* are the last objectives of the casework process. They are important and dynamic aspects of treatment, marking the end of the client–worker relationship and the integration of treatment goals. Such endings bring into play both the practitioner's and the client's feelings about loss and separation, and therefore require considerable professional expertise in the resolution of any conflicts. For this reason, it is best if termination can be planned for with the client and be understood as the final step in working together.

Termination can be a difficult time for both the practitioner and the client. Angry reactions or denial that termination is imminent are not uncommon. Dependency needs of the client who must face the reality of separation from an important figure in his/her life constitute a crucial concern (Northen, 1982).

There are some special issues in terminating treatment with elderly clients, many of whom may be chronically ill and/or frail. Such older persons may come to view the practitioner as surrogate family, making it difficult to terminate when casework goals have been achieved. On the other hand, caseworkers may feel they are "abandoning" a lonely, needy person, and thus fail to properly work toward termination. It should be pointed out that there are cases that remain active indefi-nitely, sometimes terminating only at the time of the client's death. But the decision about termination with elderly clients, as with clients of any age, should be made as part of an ongoing review of the client's treatment plans, and should be a professional judgment based upon an evaluation of the case. When difficulties arise, case supervision can be helpful in arriving at a decision (see chapter 14).

An evaluative review of one's own caseload is the professional responsibility of each caseworker, and serves several purposes. First, it assists the practitioner in maintaining professional quality work. Sec-ond, it helps in the identification of cases that may be in need of a supervisory conference or consultation, and finally, it allows the caseworker to "summarize" his/her caseload for agency administration and board members who can use this information in decision making and community planning.

10

The Functional-Age Model of Intergenerational
Treatment: An Introduction to Family Therapy

While the family therapy movement has had a strong impact on social work practice, its influence on geriatric casework has not been as great. Throughout the 1960's and 1970's, in an effort to broaden geriatric services, caseworkers in the field were encouraged to adopt a family-centered approach (Blenkner, 1965; Freed, 1975; Greene, 1977; Spark, 1974). Over the last decades some geriatric social workers have creatively adapted family therapy techniques to fit their practice. However, comprehensive intergenerational family therapy models are just emerging (Eyde and Rich, 1983; Silverstone and Burack-Weiss, 1983). This chapter outlines the history of the family therapy movement and discusses its effect on the conceptualization of the functional-age model. It also suggests how the model can be used in treatment with older adults and their families.

INTRODUCTION

The family therapy movement began in the 1950's. It was, in part, a response to the growing number of family-related problems and to new information available about human behavior. Since its inception, there has been a lack of consensus with respect to its theoretical foundations and treatment techniques. For this reason, it is difficult to provide a concise definition that summarizes both theory and practice. However, the various approaches to family therapy appear to have several elements in common.

Generally speaking, family therapy is indicated when the family's ability to perform its basic functions becomes inadequate. In attempting to alleviate this difficulty, family therapists are concerned with the impact of one family member's behavior on another. They are also concerned with how the family changes, and therapy is designed to modify those elements of the family relationship system that are interfering with the life tasks of the family and its members. Most family therapists also share the view that if an individual changes, the family context in which he/she lives will also change. In that sense, the ultimate goal of family therapy is no different from the goal of all therapies. It is a helping process that is aimed at "improving the lot" (enhance social functioning, restore the equilibrium, strengthen adaptation, etc.) of individual persons (Sherman, 1977, p. 485).

At the same time, family therapy may be seen as a different orientation to working with human problems. It is perhaps a reconceptualization of what therapy is. At the end of World War II, psychiatric treatment was centered around individual psychological functioning; however, family therapists began to realize that it was counterproductive, if not impossible, to work toward individual change without considering the family system. They also recognized that, while it is usually the symptoms or problems of one of its members that brings the family in for treatment, the family group needs to be the unit of attention. By the end of the 1950's, it became clear that family therapy was a different concept of change, not just another method of treatment. The focus of treatment had shifted from changing the individual to altering relationship patterns within the family.

How and in what ways improved family functioning is best achieved is a matter of disagreement among therapists. Today there are many philosophical "schools" of family therapy and a number of practice techniques. Some practitioners emphasize the emotional issues in the family, while others stress behavioral patterns. Some therapists prefer to see the whole family group together on a regular basis, while others may work with only one family member to bring about change in the entire system.

For purposes of discussion, these various methods of family treatment can be viewed as forming a treatment continuum, as depicted in Table 10.1. The two extremes of the continuum, which have been labeled Type A and Type Z, represent two idealized polarities. The concept that the family is comprised of individuals who are emotionally related to one another is central to the Type A form of treatment. In this approach, family therapy is defined as a method for treating individual emotional disorders based upon psychodynamic interventions with the whole family. The therapy is designed for the family unit, which is believed to share a "circular interchange of emotion" (Ackerman, 1972). Insight into problems is gained through interpretations of the psychodynamics of family functioning and of the therapist–client transference. The insight gained and the emotional experience promoted in the family session alleviates distress and promotes health and growth (Ackerman, 1972, 1981). Ackerman (1957), a pioneer in this form of treatment, extended the psychoanalytic treatment approach to include work with families in conflict. He believed that family-centered treatment involved interventions that

TABLE 10.1. Polarities of Family Treatment Forms

Type A[a]	Type Z[a]
Borrows from the psychoanalytic approach and the medical model	Borrows from small-group and systems theory
Emphasizes emotional/affective relationships within the family	Emphasizes structural or behavioral relationships
Suggests that family relationships are influenced by emotional tension/anxiety	Suggests that relationships are influenced by the structural and communication patterns of the family group
Allows for the idea of the therapist–client relationship	Provides for the therapist to remain detached from the family system except for interventive inputs
Adheres to the idea that transference interpretations are therapeutic	Rejects the idea of transference
Encourages the development of insight in family members through interpretation of unconscious processes	Encourages the understanding of behavioral interactive patterns
Attempts to alleviate "interlocking emotional disorders" of the family group	Attempts to alleviate dysfunctional family patterns
Promotes health and growth by contributing to insight and relieving pathogenic conflict and anxiety	Promotes functional behaviors by educating members and altering structural arrangements of the family

[a]Family treatment can be thought of as a continuum, with points along the axis representing the various treatment forms. This Table illustrates the two extremes of the family treatment continuum. The many differing treatment forms actually fall somewhere between the two polarities (A and Z).

focus on individual personalities, an increased understanding of relationships, and a reduction of anxiety and conflict within the family system.

The idea that the family is comprised of individuals who make up an entity, system or group is at the heart of the Type Z philosophy of treatment. Here, family therapy is defined as an interactional process of planned interventions in an area of family dysfunction. The goal is to change family structure by altering behavior. This means that family therapy is seen as a means of changing the family relationship structure by modifying the roles people play. "Symptoms" (of mental illness) exhibited by an individual family member are seen as a response to the pressures of the family system. The practitioners' interventions are designed to help family members understand their interactive style so as to alleviate dysfunctional family patterns that bring about such symptoms. Minuchin (1974) and Bowen (1971), leading proponents of the "systems school," distinguish individual treatment orientations from family therapy by its focus on therapeutic interventions that address the structure of the family group and the functions of individuals within the group.

Needless to say, Type A and Type Z represent somewhat artificial conceptions of family therapy. In reality, family therapy most often is eclectic; various treatment forms actually fall somewhere between the two extremes. Treatment takes many forms, styles, and techniques, and varies with the setting; the specific client group; the therapist's personality, training and theory base; and with prevailing societal and political values. The wide variation in treatment strategies that can be derived from the various schools of family therapy allows the practitioner to establish his/her own focus of treatment. Interventions selected can be based on assessment and treatment goals. In this way, the emphasis may be placed on such seemingly diverse goals as "achieving greater insight" and "altering disturbing behavior patterns."

The history of family casework parallels that of family therapy, which also has no universally accepted methodological approach. Family caseworkers have elected either to adopt one school of therapy as their own or to select particular techniques and interventions as indicated. The *Encyclopedia of Social Work* does offer some guidance in defining this domain of practice in its discussion of family services. Such services are said to encompass a broad spectrum of strategies, methods, and interventions, including:

> Work with individuals, families, small groups or collaterals—work done with or on behalf of clients, young and old, it can include therapy, problem-solving guidance, environmental intervention or advocacy, as well as homemaker services, money relief or other tangible assistance (Sherman, 1977, p. 435).

It is important to note that what distinguishes these modes of service is that the caseworker's *"stated focal concern* is the family and all its members as well as unattached individual persons" (*Ibid.*). This means that the intent of the social worker is to emphasize the client's informal support systems and to actively adapt family therapy techniques to fit his/her practice. In short, family-centered practice is a social work approach to service that views the family as the "unit of attention" (Germain, 1979).

Because family-centered practice involves such a wide range of interventions and treatment possibilities, it is ideally suited for working with older adults and their families. Family counseling, day care, homemaker services, and Meals-on-Wheels—all of which are designed to strengthen and supplement family life—are among the variety of interventions that come under the umbrella of family-centered social work.

The functional-age model of intergenerational treatment is in this eclectic social work tradition (see chapter 1). It takes into consideration both the elderly person's biopsychosocial functioning and the family and other social systems in which it takes place. As a result of that perspective, treatment strategies may range from offering life-review therapy to the older adult to providing three-generational family therapy. Specific interventions may include completing a genogram, transporting an older adult to a nutrition site, obtaining day-care services for an Alzheimer's patient, or working with the staff of a nursing home.

In using the model, the caseworker must be prepared to not only gather and evaluate biopsychosocial data about the older adult, but also assess the family unit. This requires that the caseworker be knowledgeable about the dynamics of aging and the factors associated with biopsychosocial functioning. It also necessitates an understanding of the properties of the family as a system in which development and role allocation take place. *The ability to simultaneously assess the older adult and his/her place in the family unit, and to establish treatment based upon this assessment, is the key to the intergenerational treatment model.*

The dual-pronged assessment and treatment perspective of the functional-age model of intergenerational therapy addresses the factors that disrupt the family social system and seeks to help it reestablish its equilibrium. The basic goal is to restore family functioning by reducing anxiety and stress so that the group can better support and/or care for its (older) member(s).

A family that is experiencing excessive stress, whether induced by a developmental or biopsychosocial crisis, cannot adequately attend to its needs. As a result, the older adult who is experiencing difficulties related to his/her functional capacities and who may have precipitated the family crisis is less likely to receive the support of the family unit. However, once the family has regained its balance, it is better prepared to deal with the tasks that enhance the functioning of all. The next section describes the role of the social worker in this family-focused treatment approach. The major treatment elements include six overlapping phases: (1) connecting with the client system; (2) determining the problem; (3) reframing the problem; (4) setting goals and contracting with the family; (5) mobilizing the family system; and (6) evaluating, providing feedback and terminating.

FAMILY-FOCUSED TREATMENT AND THE FUNCTIONAL-AGE MODEL

Connecting

The first contacts that initiate the therapeutic process are critical in establishing the boundaries of treatment. It is then that the social worker sets the tone of the helping relationship and orients the clients to the process of therapy. During the first interviews, whether by phone or in person, the caseworker's theoretical view of treatment is put into action. At intake, he/she must consider whom he/she will try to involve in treatment, and then attempt to bring those individuals into a working relationship (see chapter 2).

Connecting with significant members of the client system requires that the caseworker be attentive to the information given at intake so that the older (pivotal) client as well as concerned relatives and/or other informal helpers can be included in treatment. This casework focus is based on the knowledge that change in the older person's functioning has an influence on other family members. As noted previously, while events may center around the pivotal client who is in crisis, the entire family group is affected. Therefore, the older person should not be treated without reference to his/her family system. In short, connecting with the client system means that the practitioner must define them as such.

Defining the family as client does not mean that the social worker imposes his/her views; nor does it mean that he/she necessarily sees the family as "inadequate" or "pathological." Rather, the caseworker is aware that the biopsychosocial changes of the older pivotal client may be too overwhelming for the family to cope without support. Questions related to the functional capacity of the family structure can be clarified during the process of determining the problem. However, family members usually need to be sought out early in the casework process.

The practitioner who is able to understand the precipitating problem from a family perspective and identify the persons who comprise the client system at intake is more likely to maintain a family focus in treatment. This has the potential of strengthening the family as an emotional support network and as a caregiving unit.

Connecting with the family system requires specific knowledge and skills on the part of the social worker. An understanding of systems properties is essential (see chapter 6). The clinician must also be able to gain quickly a perspective of the family's view of the problem and the solutions that have been tried or were disallowed. This puts the practitioner in a position to empathize with the difficulties of all family members. For example, the married daughter who calls for Meals-on-Wheels for her frail 89-year-old father and indicates that she is torn between her father, her husband, and her new job is as much the client as her father.

In order to engage the daughter in the helping process, her needs have to be acknowledged. Asking the daughter to participate with her father and the social worker in planning for the future can be a therapeutic intervention. Inasmuch as it is reassuring to the daughter and supportive to the father, it allows the caseworker to connect with the significant "players" in the system. Further information may lead to the involvement of other family members as well.

In summary, connecting with the client system means that the social worker uses the information acquired during intake to identify both the precipitating events and/or presenting problems from a family perspective and the persons that comprise the client system. With this in mind, interventions are made which aim to involve key family members. Involvement can be achieved by asking clients to participate in the way that the practitioner thinks will best benefit the family group, such as family sessions or joint home visits.

Determining the Problem

Families seek help when they have a problem, are under stress, or are in a crisis. In the case of intergenerational families, they often request social work services after a prolonged period of struggling to provide emotional and instrumental support to a functionally impaired older member. Determining the problem, therefore, in simplest terms, is a matter of describing and understanding these family events. This enables the family to learn what family patterns are dysfunctional (not working) and to consider what members can do to change their situation.

During this phase of treatment the family begins to acquire a picture of itself, its goals, and the ways it may change. If treatment is "successful," the family "can learn to become experts in their own family, independently capable of recognizing, commenting on, and thus interrupting dysfunctional patterns" (Hartman and Laird, 1983).

This learning, which is an outgrowth of assessment or problem-determination, is a joint endeavor of family and caseworker. It begins with a clarification of what brought the family into treatment. The more specifically this can be presented the more easily solutions may be sought. Therefore, the caseworker should not be reluctant to ask all family members what they think the problem is: "I wonder if each of you could give me some idea of why you have come today?" Or, "I'm wondering what each of you has to say about the problem?"

Problems in intergenerational therapy are usually first defined as "belonging" to the old family member. Understanding how the presenting problem is viewed enables the caseworker to begin to reframe the definition of the problem from one affecting only the life of the pivotal client to one affecting the lives of each member of the family (Herr and Weakland, 1979). Hearing each family member's point of view can also provide information about what is interfering with the family's problem-solving process. Systems theory (see chapter 6) suggests that when a family becomes dysfunctional it tries to reestablish its equilibrium. Therefore, inquiring about the solutions that have been attempted by the family and older relatives to date is an important aspect of this phase of treatment. It can not only let the caseworker know what resources have been used, but also offer clues about family relationships.

Determining the problem with a family that has come for help "for an older adult" usually must be accomplished in a relatively short time. The family often views their situation as an emergency, and the level of stress may be high. Therefore it is even more critical for caseworkers to keep the functional-age assessment framework in mind. It can serve as a guide for observing family relationships in order to better understand the structure and developmental history of the family system (see chapters 6–8).

Questions related to how family roles are carried out and how these have changed over time are particularly useful in gathering this information. A mother who used to be depended upon to cook a Thanksgiving dinner for her three children and their families and now lets the pots burn on the stove may be seen by the family as "losing her mind" or "incompetent." What turns out to be a slight memory loss may have a ripple effect throughout the family system. By observing the systems properties of the family and coming to understand with them how roles have developed over the years, the caseworker is better prepared to offer interventive strategies.

Reframing

Reframing the problem in family terms is one of the most critical components of family casework. It begins at intake and is a means of helping the family learn how the "older person's problems" affect the lives of each family member. The caseworker can accomplish this by expanding the focus of exploration from the pivotal client to aspects of family organization. Learning how each family member operates in relation to the perceived problem is the goal.

"Reframing the problem may also take place through expanding its meaning, that is, by setting the problematic behavior in the context of the total family or in a historical context" (Hartman and Laird, 1983, p. 308).

The process of reframing the problem becomes clear when examining the situation of families who are caring for an older member with Alzheimer's disease (see chapter 12). Family caregiving to a severely functionally impaired Alzheimer's patient is usually a progressively demanding, all-consuming activity. Because of the stressful nature of caregiving, many family members encounter "problems of their own." Clearly, the client is the family system, and treatment interventions should be aimed at "minimizing the negative effects of the older person's impairment, and increasing the skills and confidence of family members. By providing knowledge about care demands and service needs the caseworker may be able to decrease the anxiety and stress surrounding caretaking (Eyde and Rich, 1983).

Reframing the problem means that the caseworker interprets and organizes the assessment information, arriving at a family-focused biopsychosocial diagnosis. The problem statement contains a definition of the presenting problem from a developmental and family point of view and a description of how the change(s) in the functional capacities of the older adult have altered the balance within the family system. In this way, interventions and services that can help restore individual and family functioning can be introduced.

Setting Goals and Contracting with the Family

When setting goals or formulating a treatment plan with the family, there is a mutual agreement about the direction of therapy. That agreement, called a contract, is sometimes formally established, with goals, content, length, rules, and methods of treatment put in writing. However, in geriatric social work there usually is a less formalized discussion of casework goals, fees, alternative uses of community resources, and general family responsibilities. It is also important for thecaseworkertoclearlyoutlinewhathe/sheandtheagencyhavetoprovide.

The content of the plan and its specific goals are based upon and are an outgrowth of the problem formulation. It is hoped that in this way families can have a more realistic view of what treatment can achieve, as well as an appropriate means of gauging their progress. In short, establishing goals serves to clarify for both the family and the caseworker the reasons for treatment.

In establishing treatment goals, one of the first things that needs to be clarified is the social worker's role. Without a clear understanding, the family may have false expectations about what they can gain from treatment. At the same time, practitioners need to adopt realistic goals for themselves in order to establish professional boundaries, without which well-meaning caseworkers can lose their treatment focus (see chapter 14).

Just as caseworkers must be careful to narrow down a problem, they must also take care to keep their goal(s) realistic. Herr and Weakland (1979) suggest that the practitioner can avoid "overambition" by determining with the family the smallest amount of change that could occur to give them a sense of progress in solving their problem. This may prevent a sense of failure on everyone's part and a recognition that they may not anticipate sweeping changes.

In setting goals, the caseworker also needs to consider how responsive the family is to outside influences. A relatively open family system in which the role expectations are clearer is more likely to accept social work intervention and other community resources. The relatively closed family, where communications are unclear, may be less favorably disposed to treatment interventions (see chapter 6). In the latter case, it is not uncommon to seemingly come to an agreement about treatment goals and later discover that they have not been carried out. For this reason, it is important to arrive at realistic goals that can be modified as treatment progresses.

Mobilizing the Family System

Mobilizing the family system is akin to implementing the treatment goals. Whether the plan is to work with one member or the whole extended family network, the aim is to keep the family in a position where it is best able to meet the needs of its members. It has already been made clear that in order to mobilize family strengths, a careful appraisal of the impaired older person's needs and the family's ability to respond to them is required. This means that the caseworker needs to keep in mind how the family-focused biopsychosocial assessment relates to both the overall therapy process and aims and the specific, concrete treatment tasks.

Understanding the way families have developed and delineated the various tasks relevant to each stage of the life cycle is critical to determining their treatment potential. Ideally, those families that have been able to meet the developmental tasks of earlier years relatively successfully are better able to face later tasks. It is, however, important for caseworkers to consider whether established family patterns that may have been functional for many years have become dysfunctional under stress. It should be noted that the family's ability to cope (namely, to adjust to new demands and losses) depends on the system it has created over the years, as well as the nature of the biopsychosocial crises it is facing. Events such as a stroke or the death of a family member may overload one family system and not another.

Life review with the family as a group is one means of obtaining information about family themes and relationships; at the same time, it offers therapeutic potential. By reconstructing family history, major events, memories, and associations, the caseworker not only clarifies family issues but provides the opportunity for reassessment and reintegration.

While originally designed for practice with younger families, genograms are particularly valuable in gathering information about the client system. A genogram, as seen in Figure 10.1, is an expanded family tree. By using various symbols it allows the caseworker and family to have a visual representation of the family group. If the caseworker is flexible, making modifications as necessary, he/she will find that this tool can simultaneously engage the client(s) and make them collaborators in history-taking and assessment (Gafford and Gates, 1983; Hartman and Laird, 1983). As most older people respond positively to sharing, a genogram also helps make history-taking a pleasant and therapeutic experience, as seen in the following case:

Mr. L., age 89, was brought to a family service agency for counseling by his daughter, Mrs. F. Mrs. F., a woman in her early 60s, explained that her father became depressed following the lingering death of a woman with whom he had a close relationship for 13 years (Sara). Mr. L.'s wife had died under similar circumstances 2 years before he met Sara.

At the first session, Mr. L. expressed a strong reluctance to enter individual therapy. His daughter insisted it would be helpful. The caseworker suggested that both father and daughter attend the counseling sessions together for purposes of gaining a family history.

Mr. L. needed little encouragement to talk about his life growing up in Russia. He spoke of the family's financial difficulties and their struggle to make ends meet. He explained that the family earned a living by having each member sew large aprons, which his mother sold at the market. Mr. L. recalled with sadness his mother's daily trips to the market, especially those in the cold of winter. He remembered waiting alone for her, sometimes late into the evening. Upon her return, he would have some hot

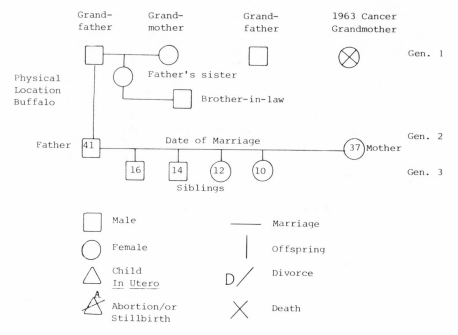

FIGURE 10.1. Genogram.

tea waiting. Mrs. F. said she was not aware of these experiences and appeared touched as he spoke. She said she would imagine that he would have felt scared and lonely waiting for his mother to return.

The exchange of feelings in this first interview established a climate for a family life review, with both father and daughter providing the content of the sessions. Mrs. F. volunteered to bring in a family photo album, which served to facilitate the expression of feelings and exchange of ideas. For example, both Mr. L. and Mrs. F. selected their favorite picture of Mrs. L. They remembered her as a creative and caring person and brought in a book of poems she had written, which was published posthumously. They reexperienced and spoke about their initial grief over her death.

By the sixth session, photographs of Sara elicited feelings of loss from both Mr. L. and Mrs. F. Mr. L. explained how he had nursed Sara through her illness despite great difficulties; Mrs. F. expressed her understanding of her father's loss and concern over his present needs for companionship. Mr. L. was visibly less depressed.

The last sessions of therapy focused on the father and daughter relationship. Mr. L. was able to say that he did not want to join social groups at the community center. He did want his daughter to be available to go out to lunch once a week, as they were doing before attending each therapy session. While she expressed concern over his circumscribed social life, the daughter acknowledged Mr. L.'s right to make his own decisions. They also discussed plans for shopping trips, meal preparation, etc. (Greene, 1982).

It should be emphasized that mobilizing the family as a treatment unit is an ongoing process that occurs simultaneously with other phases of therapy.

An evaluation of the family's capacity to meet the changing needs of its members is made possible by observing them in action. The family's problem-solving style, its capacity to deal with problems and to handle stress become apparent as members enact their respective roles in the "here-and-now." As the caseworker observes these family patterns, he/she then elects when and how to intervene to attempt to modify them. For example:

> The social worker notices that Anna, one daughter in a family of four, is always expected to do her mother's housework and chores. She says she is tired and worn out because of problems with her teenage son. At a family meeting, when everyone says, "Anna will do it," the caseworker decides to ask everyone how Anna came to have that role.

As the family learns about its own behavior patterns, it can decide how to approach things differently. In order to facilitate this process, some family therapists assign tasks to be done at home between sessions. In this case, if all agree that they will share household responsibilities with Anna, a specific week's plan may be drawn up. In this way the "tasks can be used to dramatize family transactions and suggest changes" (Minuchin, 1974, p. 150).

The case of Anna illustrates that as the therapist perceives and analyzes the family system, he/she has the opportunity to assess and modify roles and to interpret the meanings of behavior. As this occurs, the family is helped to see that the current situation can change. This can be a reassuring motivating force, as it helps to restore a family's sense of control over its difficulties.

Another way in which the family therapist works in the here-and-now is to identify roadblocks to effective family communication. As the caseworker "tracks" the meaning, content, and flow of communication, he/she is simultaneously learning about family structure and modifying the communication process (Minuchin, 1974). Communicating more effectively involves family members learning to clarify to whom they are speaking, learning to listen, to repeat what is heard, to request that others respond, and to ask for clarification of messages (Goldstein, 1973).

It has been suggested that the major task in intergenerational therapy is to deal with the issue of dependence/independence. Blenkner (1965) coined the term "filial crisis" to describe the process that takes place in adult children when it becomes evident that their parents are aging and they, as offspring, may at times be called upon to support and care for them.

The successful achievement of this developmental stage involves the renegotiation of the parent–child relationship to one of adult to adult. It does not mean, as some mistakenly believe, that the adult child takes over the parental role. Rather, it requires that the parent wherever possible continue to make his/her own decisions despite frailty or failing health. Caseworkers need to keep in mind that there is no total separation or total independence at any phase of life. Fostering a positive interdependence among family members and helping the adult child to accept what he/she can and should do in the filial role is therefore a major goal of therapy.

Evaluating, Providing Feedback, and Terminating

The last phase of treatment, when mutually agreed upon goals have been achieved and/or service is concluded, is, in many respects, the most difficult. It often marks the end of the casework relationships and a recognition that all that can be done for the present has been done. Sometimes the family may return to the agency when a new crisis flares up. At other times cases seem to remain in service indefinitely, without any clear reason. Such cases should be periodically reviewed in supervision in order to clarify what is still to be accomplished. Cases may remain open because the caseworker has difficulty considering and carrying out termination. On the other hand, the reality of some older clients' difficulties may mean that there is a real need for indefinite service. In either situation, the continuation of treatment should be based upon the assessment of the needs of the client and an evaluation of the progress in meeting casework goals.

Because termination can be so difficult, it is far too often done in a haphazard way rather than as a dynamic and vital part of the social work process. However, "if properly understood and managed, it becomes an important force in integrating changes in feeling, thinking, and doing" (Northen, 1982, p. 270).

For termination to be a meaningful process, it should provide feedback and an evaluation component. Talking with the family about the progress they feel they have made and the services rendered provides feedback for them as well as for the caseworker. A discussion of how community services are being managed is usually needed when a frail and/or impaired elderly individual is involved. The family's ability to continue to manage such resources should candidly be addressed. For some families, there may be a number of family meetings, and the ongoing relationship continues with the older adult. The social worker and the family should be clear about their respective roles, and periodic reevaluations should take place. In summary, the purpose of termination is to help the family clarify the way in which they are going to continue to meet their needs and those of their elderly members.

11

Community Services and Social Work
Group Treatment

Family services encompass a broad spectrum of methods and intervention strategies, including a wide array of community resources. The first part of this chapter examines the long-term care continuum of services and discusses the caseworker's role in their delivery. The second section describes four specific types of group services and outlines their theoretical base and therapeutic value.

THE LONG-TERM CARE CONTINUUM OF SERVICES

Social work has traditionally struck a middle ground between treatment methods that address the clients' psychological development as well as their social and environmental situation. In this way caseworkers have attempted to enhance clients' ego strengths and to mobilize the resources in the environment in an effort to improve the client's functional capacity.

> The essential point seems to be that the function of social casework is not to treat the individual alone nor his environment alone, but the process of adaptation which is a dynamic interaction between the two (Reynolds, 1933, p. 337).

While historically casework treatment has maintained its concern with both the individual and his/her environment, it has not always placed an equal emphasis on both. An intergenerational casework approach, however, requires that the practitioner be a "resource consultant" (Northen, 1982). The majority of elderly clients come to the attention of health or social services agencies when they are in need of some kind of supportive service. The family caseworker must therefore be skilled at assessing clients and helping them to secure necessary resources. This is as important as the counseling component in reducing anxiety and stress and in strengthening and supporting the client system. In addition, "the dichotomization of social work between a psychological and a social orientation and the lack of an integrated conceptual framework can limit the social worker's ability to integrate the family as a psychosocial system" (Hartman and Laird, 1983, p. 21). On the other hand, it is far too often assumed that older people cannot change. Consequently, interventions are usually limited to concrete services and emotional support. It is important to remember that change can occur at any age and that therapy should be an option.

Community resources may be thought of as forming a long-term care service continuum. Long-term care refers to and includes a range of services that address the health, psychosocial, and personal care needs of individuals who are lacking some capacity for self-care. It encompasses resident facilities as well as social service and health programs, and is designed to provide supportive care for an individual over a prolonged period of time at home or in a variety of protective and semiprotective settings.

The focus of a long-term care system is the person (and his/her family) who is frail or has a functional disability and needs assistance with activities of daily living, such as housekeeping, finances, transportation, meal preparation, or the administration of medication. A well-developed long-term care system should provide options to meet the needs for services along a continuum of care. In order to create such a system, sufficient attention must be paid to establishing linkages and filling gaps so that resources include home- and community-based options as well as residential facilities.

The professional staff within the long-term care system assesses the individual, matching the level of impairment with the type of services rendered. This case management process is within the framework of generic social work practice. It is a mechanism for ensuring a comprehensive program for meeting an individual's need for care by coordinating and linking components of a service delivery system (National Association of Social Workers, 1984).

> The concept of continuum of care has emerged in response to the widest need for a model that would integrate different levels of distress and provision of services. . . . Basic to the provision of care along the continuum is a clear statement of need. Old age in itself is not a need. Needs are determined by the complex interaction of biological, psychological, and social variables. . . . The sum total of the biological, psychological, and social person with an individual history defines the need and subsequently the level of care along the continuum (Eyde and Rich, 1983, pp. 34–38).

Long-term care in the past was associated with the institutional care of adults; today, however, the term encompasses a whole range of community services. The continuum of community-based long-term care services as graphically presented in Table 11.1 generally includes the following:

TABLE 11.1. Long-Term Continuum of Care[a]

Access to services	Array of services	Setting
	Least Restrictive	
• Outreach	Monitoring Services	
	Homemaker	— In Home
	Home Health Care	
• Information/	Nutrition Programs	
Referral	Legal/Protective Services	
	Senior Centers	
• Assessment	Community Medical Services	
	Dental Services	— Community
• Case Management	Community Mental Health	
	Adult Day Care	
• Linkages	Respite Care	
	Hospice Care	

• Evaluation/Quality	Retirement Villages
	  • life care
	  • services
	Domiciliary Care
	Foster Home
	Personal Care Home	

Special Housing	Group Home
	Congregate Care
	  • meals
	  • social services
	  • medical services
		— Institutional

FAMILY	• housekeeping	
	Intermediate Care Skilled Nursing Care Mental Hospitals Acute Care Hospitals	
	Most Restrictive	

[a]Adapted from Brody et al., "Planning for the Long-Term Support/ Care System: The Array of Services to be Considered." Region III Center for Health Planning, 7 Benjamin Franklin Parkway, Philadelphia, Pennsylvania, June 1979.

1. Outreach and case findings or screening services—locates the ill but untreated and the still-functioning elderly who may be at risk.
2. Comprehensive assessment services—evaluates the older individual in order to determine the need for service.
3. Primary core; medical, dental and nursing services—provides the core health maintenance in response to acute illness.
4. Home support services—supplies necessary in-home management and personal care of older persons.
5. Home health care services—assists the chronically ill with nursing and related personal health care, including social work services.
6. Day health care or day-care services—provides daytime care to frail or impaired individuals to improve or maintain levels of social, emotional, and health functioning, and to give respite to families.
7. Day hospitals (rehabilitation) services—aims to rehabilitate the older person stricken with physical illness and/or impairments that are amenable to rehabilitation and retraining.
8. Home hospice service—serves the terminally ill with pain management, counseling, and home supports (Iowa Gerontology Model Project, 1982).

The role of the caseworker in coordinating and linking the components of the long-term care service continuum is referred to as case management. It may be thought of as an intensive type of intake service to provide the elderly person with what is appropriate for him/her along the continuum of care. The goal is to coordinate the provision of different services for an individual person who is frail or mentally impaired.

Case managers or caseworkers help their clients by doing a comprehensive needs assessment, drawing up a case plan, facilitating access to services, coordinating the work of a number of professionals, and advocating on behalf of the client. These activities are done in conjunction with the elderly client and his/her family and are intended to improve and/or maintain the older person on an ongoing basis in the least restrictive and safest environment possible.

> Like all aspects of social work practice, case management rests upon a foundation of professional values, knowledge and skills. It is within this dynamic framework that social work case managers establish helping relationships, select problem-solving interventions, and enable client functioning (National Association of Social Workers, 1984, p. 5).

With advanced age comes increased frailty and increased vulnerability to chronic disabling diseases. The delivery of appropriate long-term care services involves an understanding of the specific impairments or conditions that can interfere with autonomous functioning as well as an appreciation of the biopsychosocial aspects of functional disabilities. This knowledge of human behavior allows the social worker to plan and arrange for service(s) most suitable to the client's level of functioning (see chapters 3–5).

Regardless of their age or stage of life, people who find themselves in dependency-producing situations often experience a sense of vulnerability. Chronic health conditions, illness or disease and the attendant need for care may exacerbate these feelings. Social workers need to understand that older adults want to continue to have a sense of control over their own lives, and help clients to better be able to accept help.

In addition to understanding the impact and consequences of functional disabilities, social workers who provide long-term care services need to appreciate the cultural implications of age-specific behaviors (National Association of Social Workers, 1984). As discussed in chapters 5 and 12, in a pluralistic society such as our own, people of diverse cultural backgrounds may perceive and report their experiences differently. These differences can encompass help-seeking behavior(s) as well as methods of problem resolution (Greene, 1982). In order for social workers to become more effective in working with different cultural groups, they must develop cross-cultural communication skills.

The majority of the impaired elderly continue to live outside institutions, receiving primary support and care from family members. It is important, therefore, that social workers be sensitive to the needs of family members. Caregiving systems, whether they be the family, a nursing home, or a day-care center, are a form of social organization that involves the structuring of interpersonal relationships and the division of practical tasks. The social worker who understands that "care is a truly collective action, depending upon direct and indirect contributions from a number of persons including the care for himself" (Daatland, 1983), is better prepared to work with the family and the long-term care system.

Families that assume the caregiving role may experience periods of disequilibrium as they attempt to respond to an illness of one of their members. Many new demands can shift a relatively balanced system of relationships into disequilibrium. The social worker who is alert to these difficulties can play an important role in relieving stress and restoring family functioning.

Other community institutions in which social workers are employed, such as nursing homes, can also be viewed as caregiving systems. Those practitioners who view their role broadly and think of the nursing home staff as a system are better able to act as intermediary among resident, family, and staff in the process of advocating for the older adult (Greene, 1982). In short, social workers in long-term care deal with many types of systems. Among the most commonly encountered are the family, medical, social welfare, community, and political-economic systems. Practitioners need to consider how they can work with these various systems on behalf of the elderly client to provide him/her with the highest quality of care.

SOCIAL WORK GROUP TREATMENT

Social group work places an emphasis on group development so that the group can provide the vehicle by which individuals may improve their interpersonal relationships and/or their environmental or social conditions. The focus is on group process, collective support, and interaction as a means of enabling individual members to grow and develop and/or to achieve a task.

Lang (1981) characterizes the social work group as a unique social form which operates as a mutual aid system that promotes autonomy and benefits individual members through the effective action of the whole group. She also suggests that the social work group is defined by professional and group norms that reinforce acceptance, respect, open communication, tolerance of differences and democratic group functioning (see Table 11.2).

Over the last thirty-five years there has been a growing interest in group services for the elderly. This has produced a number of group approaches, ranging from the recreational and vocational to the physiotherapeutic (Goldfarb, 1971). As a result, group processes in social work with the aged are varied and are offered in many different settings.

While the approaches to working with the elderly in groups are based on a social work philosophy and use social work techniques, each will have its own historical roots and unique methods.

> While there are a variety of group services for the elderly population, there is agreement that some of the same group methods focus on one or more of the following purposes: the enhancement or rehabilitation of the person; improved interpersonal relationships between older people or between and among older people and their families, relatives, friends or peers; problem-solving or achievement of tasks through collective action of elderly people; producing changes in the environment of participants in a group; designing action for changes in institutions or other organizations; creating changes in attitudes, values, social policies, programs and services by and for older people and the population in general (Lowy, 1983, pp. 21–22).

TABLE 11.2. Special Components Contributing to the Formation of the Social Work Group[a]

Component	Specialized requirement related to worker	Specialized requirement related to group
Purpose	Differentiated helping purpose for worker	Differentiated group purpose under the professional auspice
Relationships	Professional norm for acceptance in worker–member relationships	Norm for open relationships system–norm for acceptance, tolerance of difference in member–member relationship
	Professional norm for respect in worker–group relationship	Norm for mutual aid
Structure	Professional norm for activation of group autonomy	Norm for open communication system
	Professional norm for constraining worker power	Norm for open, flexible role system
	Professional norm for activation of democratic group processes	Norm for democratic group functioning
Operation	Professional norm for worker mediation in group interaction	Norm for effective participation
		Norm for participating together
		Norm for development of technical competence of members for agenda-processing
		Norm for productive work
Content	Professional norm for worker mediation in interaction between content, group process, and individual members	Norm for open, flexible program content forms and range

[a]N. Lang, "Some Defining Characteristics of the Social Work Group: Unique Social Form," in S. L. Abels and P. Abels, eds., *Social Work with Groups Proceedings 1979 Symposium* (Louisville, Kentucky: Committee for the Advancement of Social Work with Groups, 1981), pp. 18–50.

Clearly, the use of group methods for work with the aged has many potential benefits. According to Hartford (1980), groups may facilitate continued social growth, provide support through crises, and offer opportunities for rehabilitation, but their general and primary function is to positively affect mental health.

Burnside (1978) suggests that there are some important differences between group work with the elderly and work with other age groups. She proposes that group work with older people is more directive, less confrontive, and more supportive, and that this is a function of the developmental tasks of old age. She goes on to state that group work with older adults should provide the opportunity for teaching and listening to others; dealing with loss, death, and physical disability; and alleviating general anxieties.

While there seems to be widespread agreement about the curative power of groups for older people, there are few systematic well-controlled studies to measure outcome and document their effectiveness. Reviews of group programs for older persons indicate that nearly all examples of group treatment in the literature involve samples of institutionalized persons in nursing homes, old-age homes or state mental hospitals. Therefore, it is not clear whether these group programs treat behavior problems presented by residents before entering the setting, or whether the focus is on the consequences of institutionalization (Zarit, 1980, p. 324).

A second research problem associated with evaluating group programs for the elderly is that while virtually all studies report positive findings, they are usually stated in vague terms and/or reflect measures of dubious validity. Most reports are on case studies, and there are few attempts at establishing comparison groups. Still another problem with present studies is the lack of clarity of goals. Many groups do not have specific, well-delineated treatment programs, making outcome measurement virtually impossible (*Ibid.*). While research on group treatment for the older adult is less than adequate due to difficulties in design, it is nonetheless important to consider group therapy as a form of treatment.

The success of any particular form of group work rests, in large measure, upon the preparation of a practitioner. A well-grounded theoretical framework establishes the rationale and methods for that treatment modality and suggests the role the social worker should play in achieving treatment goals. The following sections present information on the formation of five specific types of groups selected for their suitability for use with older persons and/or their families: (1) reminiscing groups; (2) group psychotherapy; (3) reality orientation groups; and (4) support for caregivers of the elderly.

Reminiscing Groups

Inasmuch as it has been well recognized that reminiscing plays an important role in maintaining psychological health throughout the life cycle, the rationale for establishing reminiscing groups with older adults is apparent. As discussed in chapter 4, it is particularly true that in old age introspection becomes the key to resolving the crisis of integrity versus despair: a process necessary to a positive acceptance of one's life and impending death (Erikson, 1950).

In a hallmark article on life review in 1963, Butler proposed that life review was a "progressive return to consciousness of past experiences in an attempt to resolve them" (Butler, 1963, p. 487) and was a naturally occurring process having adaptive value. Since that time there has been further suggestion that reminiscing can help older persons clarify family roles, cope with stress and grief, experience pleasant images, maintain a sense of adequacy, and give renewed opportunity for ventilation about loss (Greene, 1982; Ingersoll and Goodman, 1980).

Ebersole (1978) maintains that "the major reason to encourage reminiscing among a group of aged people is to produce or enhance a cohort effect" (p. 237). She points out that by sharing reminiscences, individuals can slowly begin to identify their accomplishments, tribulations, and shared viewpoints. They may also have increased opportunities for socialization and multiple interactional possibilities.

Reminiscing groups can be short-term (10 weeks or less) or long-term (more than a year). The group should be kept small (5 or 6, but no more than 10), and each person should be approached individually when given the opportunity to join. The group should meet regularly. Content can be structured at times with visual devices such as "the time line" as seen in Fig. 11.1 (Ingersoll and Goodman, 1980; Jewish Family and Children's Service of Baltimore, 1978). The group process includes beginning, working and termination phases, each of which should be well planned.

The role of the social worker is to encourage reminiscing in a manner that is to the adaptational advantage of the clients (life-review therapy). The accomplishment of this task, which involves the critical social work skills of assessment and diagnosis, can enable group members to work through past conflicts and deal with stress.

Group Psychotherapy

Group psychotherapy refers to all regularly scheduled voluntary meetings of acknowledged clients with an acknowledged trained

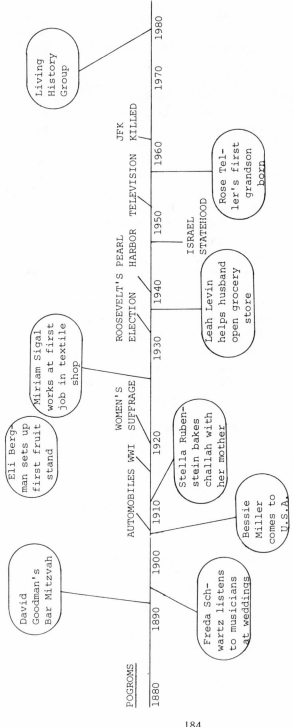

FIGURE 11.1. An example of a timeline (names used are fictitious). From P. J. Guerin and E. G. Pendagast, "Evaluation of Family System and Genogram," in P. J. Guerin, ed., *Family Therapy, Theory and Practice* (New York: Gardner, 1976).

184

leader. The purpose is expressing, eliciting, accepting and working through various aspects of the clients' functioning, and developing healthier and more satisfying modes of behavior. Group therapy, which can be conducted by psychiatrists, nurses, psychologists or social workers, places primary importance on the relationship between the therapist and the patient. The theoretical background of the practitioner, which provides the rationale for treatment, defines the nature of that relationship and the goals of the group.

Among the most widely used approaches are those based upon Freudian psychodynamics and social systems theory. Group leaders with a Freudian orientation help group members to recall and reconstruct events and emotions from their past that may have been hurtful. Efforts focus on assisting the clients to gain insight, which in turn leads to better social relationships (Hartford, 1980). The individual's transference with the therapist (and with other group members) and the interpretations given to it are the keys to treatment.

Group leaders with a systems orientation view "the group as an entity," and focus on its process and structure. Their role is to assist participants in understanding the group culture, norms and values. The educational role of the social worker is central to changing group structure, improving its stability, and increasing its ability to achieve a common goal or task (Anderson and Carter, 1978).

The leader should determine before the group begins what role he/she will play. There is some debate about what it should be. Goldfarb (1971) suggests that while the leader can be passive, functioning as listener and target for the ventilation of clients' feelings; or active, assuming the role of teacher, facilitator, questioner, comforter, and moderator, a powerful leadership position can best tap adaptive capacities (Goldfarb, 1977; Goldfarb and Sheps, 1977).

Group psychotherapy is a difficult technique to employ with a cohort of older people who are not accustomed to expressing personal problems in a group. Therefore, it is not uncommon for group leaders to experience resistance and for members to drop out. Careful preplanning about the purposes, goals, composition, and leadership of the group may help overcome these difficulties.

Reality Orientation Groups

Reality orientation groups are for confused, disoriented elderly persons, and are most often run in nursing homes and other institutions. However, reality orientation programs can be modified to fit a variety of settings, such as day-care and multiservice centers. Reality orientation is concerned with the maintenance and/or relearning of current information, including time, place, names of others, and current events. Verbal repetition, the use of visual aids like weather boards, and stimulation of the senses are the main methods of teaching this information (Wilson and Moffat, 1984).

There are several benefits to working with mentally impaired elderly in a group. According to Wilson and Moffat (1984), many such people believe that they are losing their sanity, and this fear may be somewhat alleviated by their observing others with similar difficulties. By participating in a well-programmed group, participants may hear about the "successes" and "failures" of others and also experience their own accomplishments. This is particularly helpful for people who have become increasingly unable to complete tasks satisfactorily.

The confused elderly person can receive reality orientation in group classroom sessions and/or on a 24-hour basis. Classroom sessions should be planned to include materials that reflect the needs of the group membership: a fundamental group for the most disoriented and withdrawn who require basic information on time, place, and names of participants; a standard group for the moderately disoriented who need discussion and activities to promote interaction; and an advanced group for those with mild disorientation who need more responsibility for determining group activities. Such programming is based upon proper assessment and group assignment.

Twenty-four-hour reality orientation programs, which involve the nursing and dietary staffs, can have dramatic effects when coupled with classroom sessions (Taulbee, 1978). In such an ideal program, the role of the social worker is to engage the entire staff in establishing and carrying out the 24-hour activity. This includes working to improve routines, procedures, and policies, and means the social worker needs to conceive of the nursing home as a system where he/she can help to create an atmosphere that is therapeutic. While nonprofessionals can learn many of the techniques of conducting a reality orientation group, factors that distinguish social work groups include proper assessment of the client, appropriate selection of group members, suitable programming based on cognitive level(s), and timely evaluation of the progress of group members.

Support Groups for Caregivers of the Elderly

It is well-documented that families, not the formal system, provide 80–90 % of medically related and personal care. Research on the effects of such caregiving has dramatically increased. As a result, there is a growing body of literature about the difficulties and strain experienced by the adult children of dependent elderly (Brody, 1985; Robinson, 1983).

> . . . study after study has identified the most pervasive and most severe consequences [of caregiving] as being in the realm of emotional strains. A long litany of mental health symptoms such as depression, anxiety, frustration, helplessness, sleeplessness, lowered morale, and emotional exhaustion are related to restrictions on time and freedom, isolation, conflict from the competing demands of various responsibilities, difficulties in setting priorities, and interference with life style and social and recreational activities (Brody, 1985, p. 22).

Recently, in response to these problems, a growing number of groups has become available to the families of frail and/or impaired elderly (Aronson, Levin, and Lipkowitz, 1984; Cohen, 1983). These groups attempt to provide support, enhance understanding of the older relative's problems and behaviors, suggest plans that can be made for inevitable changes in the older adult, provide insight into the feelings of both the older person and the caregiving relative, and improve coping strategies (Hartford and Parsons, 1982).

Some common themes in groups for caregivers include: (1) relocating a person who becomes too frail or dependent to remain in the original residence; (2) engaging other relatives or secondary caregivers; (3) making decisions and taking responsibility when an older relative cannot do so alone; (4) dealing with feelings of impatience, frustration, entrapment, and guilt; (5) improving communications; (6) reducing conflict; and (7) understanding the biopsychosocial changes of aging (Cohen, 1983; Hartford and Parsons, 1982).

As with the other groups discussed, practitioners should consider in the planning phase the group goals, format, membership, time and size, content and focus, and termination and evaluation procedures. Caregiver groups that often struggle with issues of loss, death and dying, and grief require much knowledge, skill, and emotional investment on the part of the leader. Self-awareness and supervision, both important social work components, are essential (see chapter 14).

CHAPTER

12

Social Work Treatment with Special Populations

Throughout this text, aging has been defined as a complex biopsychosocial process. In the chapters on assessment, the fact that each person ages at a different rate and in different ways was emphasized; in the chapters on treatment the discussions focused on the need for highly individualized plans of intervention. Clearly, the aged are a heterogeneous group. For example, the very old have both a lower average income and a much greater need for health services and living assistance than do somewhat younger age groups. Similarly, many widows living alone and most minority elderly face very different and more difficult situations than do married white elderly couples (Taeuber, 1983).

Geriatric social workers need to be prepared to practice with diverse client populations. This chapter explores some of the issues of serving special client populations. Those that have been selected for discussion include the old-old, the older woman, the minority aged, and the caregivers of persons with Alzheimer's disease or other dementing illness.

THE OLD-OLD

The fact that a steadily increasing percentage of the U.S. population is living past age 65 is well known. [In the past two decades the 65-plus population has grown twice as fast as the rest of the population (American Assoc. of Retired Persons, 1984)]. What is less well known, however, is that the 75-plus group is currently the fastest growing segment of the American population. It is the 85-and-over group that is growing especially rapidly, up 165% from 1960 to 1982 (Taeuber, 1983). By the year 2050, the proportion of those 85 years and older is projected to jump from 1 to 5% of the total population.

Because individuals in the upper age brackets are sometimes frail, they are of particular concern to geriatric social workers. The term frail elderly is generally used to refer to that segment of the community-based older population in need of some sort of attention or care from either formal or informal long-term care systems or both. Frailty is defined as a reduction of physical and emotional capacities and loss of a social support system to the extent that the individual becomes immobilized and/or unable to maintain a household or social contacts without continuing assistance from others (Beaver, 1982; Federal Council on Aging, 1978, p. 2).

The extent to which the old-old may be considered frail is under question. However, it is known that this segment of the population has the greatest need for social services, income maintenance, housing, and health services (American Assoc. of Retired Persons, 1984).

> It is these "old-old"—often mentally or physically impaired, alone, depressed—who pose the major problems for the coming decade. It is they who will strain their families with demands for personal care and financial support. It is they who will need more of such community help as Meals-on-Wheels, homemaker services, and special housing. It is they who will require the extra hospital and nursing home beds that will further burden federal and state budgets (Otten, 1984).

Due to the concern about their impact on the family, the economy, and the health care system, there has been an effort to learn more about the life-style of the "old-old." Gradually a statistical profile encompassing areas such as health, income and living arrangements is emerging.

Today's elderly, even at age 85 or 90, are unquestionably healthier and more active than their predecessors. However, as individuals age they are increasingly likely to suffer from mental and physical health problems and disabilities. Among the disorders that increase with age are senile dementia, diabetes, rheumatoid arthritis, osteoporosis, and cardiovascular and cerebrovascular disease. Moreover, many of these ailments are chronic in nature and require sustained supportive health/social services as well as medical treatment (Brody, 1985).

Among the most incapacitating of chronic illnesses is Alzheimer's disease. As discussed later in the chapter, Alzheimer's is characterized by mental impairment, disorientation, and an increasing inability to function alone. The incidence of Alzheimer's disease, the most prevalent type of dementia, increases with advancing age. The chance of developing a dementing illness roughly doubles every year after age 65. About 1% of the elderly exhibit symptoms at 65 years of age, 2.5% at 70, 5% at 75, 12% at 80, over 20% at 85, and 40–50% in their 90s (Eisdorfer, 1984). Other mental health problems among the old-old include depression and an increased suicide rate—22 per 100,000 for the 75-to-84 age range, and between 14.6 and 16.3 per 100,000 for persons 85 years and over (American Association of Retired Persons, 1984).

While the income level of the over-65 population has improved over the last two decades, in general their economic position is considerably lower than that of younger populations. The average income of the 85-and-over group is at least one third less than that of people between

65 and 70. The old-old may find their pensions exhausted and health bills eating into savings. Among those 85 and older, 21.3% had incomes lower than the poverty level in 1983 (Collins, 1985). Needless to say, lower incomes in the elderly population are associated with factors over which they have little control, such as their gender, race, health, the survival of their spouses, and their own health and ability to continue to work (American Assoc. of Retired Persons, 1984). Such data raise questions about the feasibility of early retirement in view of the fact that individuals are now likely to live longer and will require more income over a longer period of time. The urgency of the situation is brought home by the fact that the proportion of the average man's life spent in retirement increased from 3% in 1900 to 20% in 1980 (Otten, 1984).

The family structure and living arrangements of the old-old are also of interest. Surveys show that although 23.2% of the old-old live in institutions, more than half (54.6%) maintain their own households. Although the percentage of older adults, particularly old women, living with their families does increase with advancing age, a growing number are living alone rather than in family settings. Only 11% of older persons live in intergenerational households.

One of the most striking ways in which increased longevity has altered family structure is the fact that three- and four-generation families are increasingly more common. At present about half of all persons aged 65 and older have great-grandchildren, and 10% of all elderly have a child who is also elderly. This means that family support for the very old may have to come from children who are themselves approaching retirement, or have already retired, and are dealing with their own concerns related to aging. As the following case illustrates, the three- and four-generation family can experience periods of disequilibrium as new demands bring about additional strains on the family system:

> Mr. William Smith, a 98-year-old widower described as fragile, alert, and ambulatory, was referred to the nursing home social worker for counseling. The nursing staff complained that he often refused to get out of bed, would not participate in any group activity, and was nasty about taking his medication. "All he wants to do is stay in bed and listen to the 'good music station'."
>
> The social worker obtained the following case information: Mr. Smith, who was a high school math teacher until he retired at 70, was the oldest living graduate of his university. He and his wife, who was the high school music teacher, were married for 60 years. They lived in a small town in the Midwest until her death, when William moved east to live with his only son, James, and his wife, Edna.
>
> According to William, they all "got along beautifully," for they shared a love of classical music. (Edna was also a music teacher.) Everything turned sour, however, when James, now age 68, retired and Edna, age 62,

wanted "to finally get a chance to travel." They insisted that William was too old to stay alone and "the discussions were unpleasant." A once "perfect" marriage was now characterized as tense, even hostile. About 6 months after James's retirement, Edna suffered a slight stroke.

William told the social worker that it was Edna who had him put in the nursing home "for only a common urinary infection because she wanted to get even with him for preventing her from going on a cruise." William did not believe James when he said he would try to bring him home as soon as Edna was feeling a little better.

Intergenerational problems such as these are increasingly encountered in geriatric social work practice. They require that the practitioner have a full appreciation of the multiple factors that can contribute to problems among the old-old as well as an understanding of their effect on family dynamics. Needless to say, there are elderly over 75 who are not frail, and those under 75 who are. Consequently, a functional assessment of the older adult within his/her family context, as described earlier in the text, is the key to an appropriate plan of intervention.

THE OLDER WOMAN

One of the most dramatic social movements of the last decades has been the women's liberation movement. As a result of its accomplishments, many women have altered the way they see themselves and changed the direction of their lives. Yet for all intents and purposes, these changes have eluded the older woman of the present. She may not only continue to experience sex discrimination, but find that she is a victim of age discrimination as well.

The disparity between the number of older men and women and their respective social and economic conditions becomes more striking with age. By the year 2000, there will be 10 women for every five men over the age of 75. Because of differences in socialization and economic opportunity as well as longevity, many of these women can expect to be widowed, to live alone on relatively low incomes with minimal medical care (Butler and Lewis, 1982).

The probability of older women living longer than men and the differences between the numbers (of older men and women) are significant within every age group. Elderly women now outnumber men three to two. In 1982, there were 80 men aged 65–69 years for every 100 women in this category, and 42 men age 85 and over for every 100 women of this age group (American Assoc. of Retired Persons, 1984). Because the life expectancy of men is less than that of women, the health, social, and economic problems of the elderly, especially those over age 70, are mostly problems of women.

The harsh economic reality of the older woman can be seen by examining income data. The first thing that must be considered is that the general economic circumstances of the elderly are considerably poorer than those of younger populations. In fact, there is a strong pattern of declining income associated with advancing age. This is even more dramatic for older women. Of the elderly poor, 75% are women, with the poverty rate of older women twice that of older men. Income differences between men and women when examined by race are also striking. The median income in 1984 of older black women was $3500; for older white women, $4900; for older black men, $4900, and for older white men, $8600 (Taeuber, 1983). Low economic status was also reflected in the fact that in 1981, 73% of Supplementary Security Income (SSI) recipients were elderly women (Women's Studies Program and Policy Center, 1981).

Living arrangements and marital status differ sharply between elderly men and women. Over 80% of older men live in a family setting, usually with their wives; elderly women are more likely to be widowed, and a substantial proportion live alone. These percentages reflect differences in age-specific death rates and the fact that men tend to marry younger women. In addition, elderly widowed men have remarriage rates that are about seven times higher than those for women (Taeuber, 1983).

The negative stereotyping of the older woman in our society, which is often explicit and socially acceptable, is another reflection of the unfavorable image of older women. They are frequently portrayed in the media as old hags, evil crones, crocks, and old maids. Mother-in-law stories abound.

> Even Grandma becomes a family nuisance as she outlives Grandpa and experiences and expresses the emotional and physical facts of aging. Thus, the message comes across that a woman is valuable for bearing and rearing children and perhaps to nurse her husband in his dotage and often through his terminal illness, but after that it is clearly useless and even burdensome to have her around (Butler and Lewis, 1982, p. 121).

The status of older women is also exemplified in the roles they play (see chapter 5). While each cohort of women may be different, women who are in their 70s and 80s today traditionally have been defined in terms of their roles as wives and mothers. In contrast, men of that cohort have traditionally had the responsibility for the family's economic welfare. This split in responsibilities has brought about differences in life experiences and in sociocultural, psychological, and economic circumstances.

Many women who have spent most of their lives as wives and mothers go through the final stage(s) of the family life cycle as widows.

Of all wives, 85% outlive their husbands. Needless to say, the death of a spouse can be one of life's most stressful events. The circumstances of many of these women can be made even more difficult because they have never worked. Therefore, they live on reduced pensions and may experience difficulty in managing their own financial affairs. Those that have children tend to increase their dependency on them, and some benefit from these emotional ties (Gluck, Dannefer, and Milea, 1980).

There are, however, many older women who have no children. Women now in their 70s and 80s were the cohorts with the lowest fertility rates in history; about a fourth have no surviving children (National Institute on Aging . . . , 1978). Little is known about these childless older women and the nature of their kinship systems. However, what is known suggests that they tend to rely primarily upon a spouse or substitute close relationships with more remote kin. The childless unmarried are also more likely to turn to formal supports in the community.

There is little information available about older people who have never married; therefore, they are often stereotyped as "swingers" or "lonely losers." The data available, however, indicate that single women tend to have higher levels of education, occupational status, and intelligence (Ward, 1979). The few in-depth studies of singles and their life styles suggest that the primary reason for remaining single is a desire to preserve psychological and social autonomy (Adams, 1976). While each case should be assessed on an individual basis, this strong desire for independence may bring about difficulties in later life if the individual becomes frail and/or impaired and is reluctant to accept help, as seen in the following case:

> Ms. S., a tiny single woman 89 years old, came to the attention of a social worker when she fell on the escalator of a subway station. At that time she was taken to a hospital. An observant emergency room clerk noted her disheveled appearance and agitated behavior and notified the social service department. Before she was released that day, Ms. S. was referred to a family service agency. At first, Ms. S. was reluctant to accept the referral. When the social worker called to offer an appointment, Ms. S. sounded weak and confused, and her voice was barely audible. During the social worker's second call Ms. S. stated that she was unable to get out and that there was no food in the house. Ms. S. finally allowed the social worker to visit when she offered to bring her some groceries.
>
> When the worker arrived, she found Ms. S. dressed (in the middle of winter) in a sleeveless summer housecoat with a stained apron on top. Her apartment was cold, dirty, and disorganized, with clothes, shoes, and newspapers in the middle of the floor. The hot water in the kitchen sink was running and was about to overflow. Ms. S. did not seem to notice. The social worker also observed a college degree on the wall and many fine

china cups and plates. When she asked about them, she was able to piece together the following background information:

Ms. S. had moved to the Washington, D.C. area at the age of 21 to become a government worker during World War II. She was viewed as a bright and capable worker, received several promotions, and held responsible positions in her 44-year career. While working, she attended a university at night and earned a degree in business administration. Despite several offers, she had elected not to marry. Ms. S. had had an active social life. She had a circle of friends, mostly single women, with whom she traveled to Europe, Latin America, and the Orient. She was interested in theater, concerts and opera, and wrote poetry. She was a member of the Toastmistress Club and had been president for many years. She did volunteer work at her church and was an active member of the women's auxiliary.

Her income allowed her to do what she pleased. She always dressed in expensive clothes and furnished her apartment in good taste, but ate all her meals out. She also played the stock market and followed it carefully. She often became depressed when the market went down and was in high spirits when the market did well.

Although Ms. S. had an excellent pension and savings, she indicated that she was reluctant to spend her money for services. She wanted to save it "for a rainy day." Ms. S. said that she valued her independence and freedom more than anything in life. She also valued her friends and found comfort in them.

Her best friend is a 91-year-old woman who lives in the same building. She is homebound but very alert, and Ms. S. visits her daily. Ms. S. has no family in the area. Her nephew, who was 59 and lived nearby, died 6 months earlier of cancer. He was very helpful to her and she was very fond of him. Ms. S. cried bitterly when she talked about him. She felt his death was untimely because he was young and that she should have been the one to die because she is old and "miserable."

After several assessment interviews, it became clear that Ms. S.'s problems began when she started having difficulty with her dentures. She made several visits to the dentist, who said she would need a new plate that would cost $2500. Ms. S. who was "shocked" by the cost, never went back. When she realized she could no longer eat "gourmet meals" in her favorite restaurants, she began to subsist on coffee and donuts. Gradually, she became malnourished, depressed, and disoriented. Friends and neighbors, noticing these changes, encouraged her to "take better care of herself." It was not until her accident that she was able to accept help. Based upon this assessment, the goal of treatment was to help Ms. S. cope with her losses and physical changes and to accept minimal services in order to help her to be able to remain independent in her apartment.

FAMILY CAREGIVERS OF OLDER PEOPLE WITH ALZHEIMER'S DISEASE

One of the most documented facts in gerontology is that the family is the primary source of care for the frail and/or impaired elderly. While there are no definitive data on the actual number of people involved in parent care, Brody (1984) suggests that this has become a normative event. For many families the situation may be highly stressful, especially when the older person has a debilitating illness. The following section examines some of the components of this stress, particularly as it relates to family members caring for relatives with Alzheimer's disease.

Family caregiving to a severely, functionally impaired Alzheimer's patient is usually a progressively demanding, all-consuming task. At first, the individual with Alzheimer's disease experiences only minor and almost imperceptible symptoms. Gradually, however, the person becomes more forgetful. She/he may neglect to turn off the stove, misplace things, take longer than usual to complete routine tasks, or repeat already answered questions. Changes in personality, mood, and behavior, including confusion, irritability, restlessness, and agitation are likely to appear. As the disease progresses, memory loss, poor judgment, and an inability to concentrate become more common. Gradually the older person may become unable to write, read, speak, or even eat (Office of the Assistant Secretary . . . , 1985). In such cases, incontinence and excessive burdens on the family can lead to institutionalization (Robinson and Thurner, 1979). In the final stages, muscular twitching and repetitive movements such as lip smacking occur. The patient is finally confined to bed and becomes more prone to infections.

The care of an impaired elderly person encompasses a range of duties. The daily management of problems such as planning a well-balanced diet, seeing that the person does not wander off, getting the person from a bed to a chair, or from a chair to the bathroom, bathing, feeding, or even the handling of incontinence may be involved.

Family caregivers usually have no training in these exacting caregiving skills and often develop strategies by trial and error, at great expense to themselves. Unlike child rearing, in which the level of the child's dependency gradually decreases, the caregiver for a family member with dementia faces continued or increased dependency, with no predictable end of the "36-hour day" (Archbold, 1982; Mace and Rabins, 1981).

Family members who are involved in the patient's care can encounter problems of their own. As it becomes clear that their relative will never get well but will progressively become more dependent, they often experience powerful and, at times, conflicting emotions as they struggle to meet their relative's physical and emotional needs.

> Gone is the patient's ability to work and to love. Only fragments of familiar behavior and personality remain as sorrowful reminders to the family of what has been lost. The healthy spouse and family experience life as an ongoing funeral: the person they once knew is dying, a little at a time. The

family grieves for the loss, yet there are no formalized rituals to help them through this time (Kapust, 1982, p. 79).

Assuming the care of a dementia patient can, in short, result in family members' loss of freedom, privacy, mobility, energy, and time.

Study after study has also identified the many mental health problems that may result from the consequences of the emotional strain of caregiving. These include symptoms such as depression, anxiety, frustration, helplessness, sleeplessness, lowered morale, and emotional exhaustion.

The vast majority of services for demented elderly persons are provided by the spouse, together with adult daughters and daughters-in-law. Many of the daughters are "women in the middle" who find that they are caught between the needs of their parents and the demands of their children and husbands (Brody, 1981). In addition, they may have to adjust their work schedules, with some leaving paid employment to assume parent care (Brody, 1985).

Because of these difficulties, there has been increased concern about the stress related to caregiving. Importantly, the characteristics of the caregiver and those of the elderly family member often influence the quality of relationships and the degree of burden that is felt (Gordon, 1981). The ages, personalities, and health status of the persons involved, as well as the long-term quality of their relationship, are key factors. Severe memory loss or disorientation and urinary incontinence have been identified as especially likely to contribute to a sense of family burden (Robinson, 1983; Zarit, Reever, and Bach-Peterson, 1980).

While still in the developmental stages, several interview schedules have been used to measure caregiver strain [see Tables 12.1 and 12.2 for Robinson's (1983) Caregiver Strain Questionnaire and Zarit, Reever, and Bach-Peterson (1980), The Burden Interview]. These tables address a number of problematic behaviors that may be displayed by the patient, as well as a range of feelings that may be experienced by the caretaker. They also suggest questions for assessment which can be incorporated into the social work interview.

The assessment of the family's ability to cope with the demands of caretaking is critical to proper intervention. Assessment, which should first focus on the extent of emotional stress brought about by the burdens of caregiving, must include all family members (see chapters 6–8). The ongoing care of the Alzheimer's patient, as with all the severely impaired, puts a strain on the family system. This can lead to changes in family homeostasis, stimulate interpersonal conflict and, in severe instances, result in abuse, as seen in the case on p. 200.

TABLE 12.1. The Burden Interview[a]

---

1. I feel resentful of other relatives who could but who do not do things for my spouse.
2. I feel that my spouse makes requests which I perceive to be over and above what she/he needs.
3. Because of my involvement with my spouse, I don't have enough time for myself.
4. I feel stressed between trying to give to my spouse as well as to other family responsibilities, job, etc.
5. I feel embarrassed over my spouse's behavior.
6. I feel guilty about my interactions with my spouse.
7. I feel that I don't do as much for my spouse as I could or should.
8. I feel angry about my interactions with my spouse.
9. I feel that in the past, I haven't done as much for my spouse as I could have or should have.
10. I feel nervous or depressed about my interactions with my spouse.
11. I feel that my spouse currently affects my relationships with other family members and friends in a negative way.
12. I feel resentful about my interactions with my spouse.
13. I am afraid of what the future holds for my spouse.
14. I feel pleased about my interactions with my spouse.
15. It's painful to watch my spouse age.
16. I feel useful in my interactions with my spouse.
17. I feel my spouse is dependent.
18. I feel strained in my interactions with my spouse.
19. I feel that my health has suffered because of my involvement with my spouse.
20. I feel that I am contributing to the well-being of my spouse.
21. I feel that the present situation with my spouse doesn't allow me as much privacy as I'd like.
22. I feel that my social life has suffered because of my involvement with my spouse.
23. I wish that my spouse and I had a better relationship.
24. I feel that my spouse doesn't appreciate what I do for him/her as much as I would like.
25. I feel uncomfortable when I have friends over.
26. I feel that my spouse tries to manipulate me.
27. I feel that my spouse seems to expect me to take care of him/her as if I were the only one she/he could depend on.
28. I feel that I don't have enough money to support my spouse in addition to the rest of our expenses.
29. I feel that I would like to be able to provide more money to support my spouse than I am able to now.

---

[a]Zarit, Reever, and Bach-Peterson, in *The Gerontologist*, 20, 6 (1980), p. 651.

TABLE 12.2. Caregiver Strain Questionnaire[a,b]

I am going to read a list of things other people have found to be difficult in helping out after somebody comes home from the hospital. *Would you tell me whether any of these apply to you?* (GIVE EXAMPLES)

	(Yes = 1)	(No = 0)
Sleep is disturbed (e.g., because ____ is in and out of bed or wanders around at night)	_____	_____
It is inconvenient (e.g., because helping takes so much time or it's a long drive over to help)	_____	_____
It is a physical strain (e.g., because of lifting in and out of a chair, effort or concentration is required)	_____	_____
It is confining (e.g., helping restricts free time or cannot go visiting)	_____	_____
There have been family adjustments (e.g., because helping has disrupted routine; there has been no privacy)	_____	_____
There have been changes in personal plans (e.g., had to turn down a job; could not go on vacation)	_____	_____
There have been other demands on my time (e.g., from other family members)	_____	_____
There have been emotional adjustments (e.g., because of severe arguments)	_____	_____
Some behavior is upsetting (e.g., because of incontinence; ____ has trouble remembering things; or ____ accuses people of taking things)	_____	_____
It is upsetting to find ____ has changed so much from his/her former self (e.g., he/she is a different person than he/she used to be)	_____	_____
There have been work adjustments (e.g., because of having to take time off)	_____	_____
It is a financial strain	_____	_____
Feeling completely overwhelmed (e.g., because of worry about ____; concerns about how you will manage)	_____	_____
Total score (count yes responses)	_____	

---

[a]Scores range from 0 to 13.
[b]B. Robinson, *Journal of Gerontology*, 38, 3 (1983), pp. 344–348.

In the spring of 1980, Mr. B. called a family service agency requesting socialization activities for his wife who was suffering from Alzheimer's disease. Mr. B., a 66-year-old retired man, had Parkinson's disease, and his right arm and leg were impaired. He explained that he was managing "rather well" in spite of his impairments and that he was doing the cleaning, cooking, shopping, etc. Mrs. B., age 72, was unable to help him or to care for herself.

The couple had two children. A married daughter, who lived out of state, called the couple about once a month. A married son, who lived nearby, was interested and concerned. He visited the parents often and took them home for Sunday dinners.

The initial casework goal was to help Mr. B. understand and cope with his wife's mental deterioration. The couple was also referred to a nutrition program and a home health care service in order to provide support to Mr. B., who was carrying the major burden of Mrs. B.'s care.

As Mrs. B.'s mental condition deteriorated, Mr. B., who had formed a positive relationship with the caseworker, was able to express his frustration and anger. He eventually volunteered the information that he had hit his wife when "she refused to take a bath after forgetting to go to the bathroom." He said he was sure this would not happen again. He also said he was embarrassed by his lack of control, but became upset when "she wouldn't listen to him." The caseworker, hoping to reduce the pressure on Mr. B., said that she was sure the tension must be very great and suggested that home health care services be increased to at least twice a week. Mr. B. accepted this suggestion.

Several weeks later, the home health aide reported scratches on Mr. B.'s face and severe bruises on Mrs. B.'s arms. The registered nurse told the caseworker she was considering a referral to protective services. The caseworker invited the family (Mr. and Mrs. B., son and wife) to the office to discuss the problem. The family agreed, at the son's suggestion, to send Mrs. B. to a day-care center twice a week. He also offered to pay for this service. The long-range plan was to place Mrs. B. in a nursing home if and when day-care services were not adequate to meet her needs. The caseworker also used the interview as an opportunity to reinforce the fact that Mr. B. had been a good provider and a caring husband for over 40 years. She suggested that it was undue stress in the care of his wife that led to "this situation." She asked Mr. B. to advise her or his family when he felt under too much pressure so that help could be provided.

Mrs. B. was able to remain at home for almost a year as a result of these services—home health care three times a week and day-care twice a week. Mrs. B. gradually became incontinent, lost bowel control, and was severely disoriented. Mr. B. was able to discuss his feelings about a nursing home placement with the caseworker. He came to the decision that this placement was responsible and meant he still cared about "what was best for his wife."

Following the nursing home placement, the caseworker continued to meet with Mr. B. for about 3 months. During that time, he dealt with his feelings of loss and spoke of his daily visits to the nursing home.

Intervention strategies for caregivers of Alzheimer's patients, as this case so well illustrates, should focus on lessening daily demands and thereby hopefully reducing stress. Assisting the family to obtain affordable respite service, whether in the form of homemaker, day-care, and so on, is therefore a primary goal. Education and support groups can also play a significant role by teaching caregivers specific management skills and techniques as well as providing an opportunity for them to express feelings and to obtain encouragement. Gaining a better understanding of the patient's behavior and suggestions for how to better handle problems can often make a big difference. Finally, as in the case of Mrs. B., where the strains of caregiving became too great, family members may need to be helped to accept nursing home placement.

MINORITY AGED

The literature includes a number of definitions for the minority elderly based on characteristics of race and national origin. The first distinction that should be made is the difference between a minority and an ethnic group. Members of an *ethnic* group think of themselves as being alike, having a sense of shared past and similar origins, and are so regarded by others. This sense of being distinct is most important when members of differing groups are in contact with each other or "cross-ethnic boundaries" (Green, 1982).

An ethnic group is "a dynamic system constantly changing, adjusting, and adapting to the wider environment of which it forms a part" (Holzberg, 1982, p. 254). Many ethnic groups are singled out from others in the society in which they live for differential and unequal treatment. This minority group standing often places members in a relatively less powerful position in society, and they may be denied access to privileges and opportunities available to others.

> By virtue of minority group membership, minority elderly share common characteristics and life experiences with others of their reference group (i.e., history of slavery, experience of segregation, minority status, etc.). However, each individual's experience, response, and coping strategies differ, and may have differed at particular stages of their lives. Thus it is important for students to be aware of the macro influences on aging minorities, reference group responses, and individual responses. These experiences and responses influence problem definitions, behaviors that are considered adaptive, and the configuration of significant others in the client system. The range of definitions of family, and community, may vary from one culture to another, as will values, roles, and relationship patterns (Soniat, 1982, p. 10).

Ethnic group and minority elderly comprise many subgroups with diverse life styles, histories, and cultural strengths and supports. These *cultural patterns affect help-seeking behaviors* and the utilization of social work services. The premise of cross-cultural social work practice is based on the assumption that American society is culturally diverse and efforts must be made to individualize the client. Acquiring accurate knowledge about how the client perceives his/her life situation and problem(s) within his/her individual cultural context is essential. Minority groups should be understood not only in relation to their minority status, but for the richness of their heritage and the benefits they can give to society (Soniat, 1982).

Progress in meeting the social services needs of minority and ethnic clients within a cross-cultural perspective has been slow at best, due to a number of factors. One problem is that until recently most gerontological research has focused on limited samples of white middle-class subjects. As a result, there is insufficient information about the differing cultural patterns and life styles of the minority and ethnic aged, and far too little understanding of how ethnicity and/or minority group status may impact on the aging process.

Discrimination has also been a major difficulty. Minority aged bear a double burden—the devaluation in status associated with old age and the disadvantages imposed by their minority group status. The plight of the minority aged has been characterized by many as one of "double jeopardy" (Dowd and Bengstson, 1978; Jackson, 1971; National Urban League, 1964). Double jeopardy refers to the additive negative effects of being old *and* black (or any other racial/ethnic minority) on frequently cited indicators of quality of life, such as income, health, housing or life satisfaction.

The disadvantaged status of the minority aged is reflected in the data collected in a survey conducted by the American Association of Retired Persons (AARP) in 1984 (Prisuta, 1984). The survey of over 1000 people over 55 years of age focused on quality of life issues and asked respondents to indicate their degree of personal satisfaction with a number of social indicators, such as housing, employment, health and income. It is significant that the minority elderly rated their housing more negatively than other older adults. The biggest differences involved the comfort and location of their homes. Many also felt their homes were less energy efficient, more difficult to maintain, and less accessible to shopping and medical care.

Perceived overall health status was also found to be related to race. More than half (51%) of older minorities reported restricted diets [only one-third (31%) of the general population is so limited]. Minority elderly were also more likely than others to be disabled (11 compared to 4%), and more than half (57%) reported that they had to retire due to poor health.

There were also disparities in income among the elderly. Of the minority elderly, 43% reported an income under $12,000 per year, while that figure was 38% for the general population. Data from other sources are even more alarming. For example, Lowy (1985) reports that four out of five elderly minority women in 1980 had incomes below $2000 per year. Of all elderly female blacks living alone, two thirds were officially classified as poor and 78% were at least near poor.

The AARP survey also revealed that minorities were more likely to note long-run improvements in the quality of their lives than the general population (58 compared to 46%). Minority and female respondents also were more in favor of support from government programs and benefits for the elderly. Of minorities, 91% felt that this was "very important," compared to 77% for older women, 74% for the general older population, and 70% for older men. In summary, minority elderly were generally dissatisfied with their health status, income, housing, and employment opportunities, and ethnicity/race was found to be an important variable in accounting for these differences in standards of living and quality of life.

Another issue of concern in cross-cultural social work is the sensitivity with which services are delivered. "Cross-cultural social work is the utilization of ethnographic information in the planning, delivery, and evaluation of social services for minority and ethnic group clients" (Green, 1982, p. 49). From this point of view, social work with minority and ethnic group clients requires adequate preparation for and alertness to those aspects of the client's cultural background that affect "social service encounters." This is a complex process involving self-awareness and a willingness to carry out one's professional activities in a manner that recognizes the client's cultural integrity.

As a powerful influence on behavior, culture encompasses the values, knowledge, and material technology that people learn to see as appropriate and desirable. Culture establishes the parameters that guide, structure, and often limit thinking and behavior (Berger and Federico, p. 10). Because cultural norms and values are group-specific, the social worker engaged in cross-cultural communication must be cognizant of social boundaries and be prepared to move beyond the limits of his/her own personal experiences. The social worker must make a conscious effort to help the client in a manner that is congruent with the client's cultural values and attitudes (Greene, 1985).

Ethnicity becomes most apparent when individuals meet others who are culturally different from themselves. In fact, it is the interaction across group boundaries that is ethnicity's defining characteristic. Because of the importance of this interaction, "the persons who mediate boundaries are critical social actors in the communication of information and the regulation of resources as they affect those groups" (Greene, 1982a, p. 13). The social worker is, of course, such an actor.

Because cross-cultural social work involves interacting with clients who are ethnically distinct and serving communities that are culturally unfamiliar, the practitioner must be willing to learn how to respond appropriately in such encounters. The acquisition of cross-cultural knowledge is at the heart of ethnically sensitive practice methods.. "A performance-level response of cultural awareness represents a depth of comprehension of others that surpasses the usual injunctions about patience, genuineness, and honesty in client–worker relationships" (Green, 1982, p. 52). Beyond this it necessitates that the social workers know, appreciate, and utilize the culture of another in assisting with the resolution of a human problem. In essence, it means that the practitioner is able to conduct his/her "professional work in a way that is congruent with the behavior and expectations that members of a distinctive culture recognize as appropriate among themselves" (*Ibid.*).

In the following cases two geriatric caseworkers describe their reactions in a cross-cultural social work experience.*

> Mrs. P., a former Ziegfeld Follies showgirl, became a client of ours in 1975, when she was 84. She was a dim reflection of her earlier glory—a withered, wispy-haired old woman, bent over at a 90-degree angle. She needed escort services, which I provided, to get her to the bank and to grocery stores.
>
> When a middle-aged black man was hired as a social work assistant, I decided to transfer the case to him. I was concerned over the possible repercussions—I had heard some negative attitudes expressed by this client in reference to all minority people.
>
> When I approached the subject of the transfer to another worker I said he had more time to give her, and I also pointed out he was a kindly man who was a Negro. I wondered how she felt about this. "Oh no! I'm not going to have some woman calling me up at four in the morning to ask me if her husband was with me!"
>
> This woman, so confident about her sexual attractiveness, became very attached to our worker after an initial period of testing, and was helped by him until she died at 88. (She gave him a picture of herself—a glamorous showgirl.)
>
> Mr. S., a 74-year-old-black male, became known to the agency shortly after being "rescued" from an embarrassing predicament in Landlord-Tenants Court by a Mr. T., a middle-aged white male who operated a local real-estate management company.
>
> These men had become acquainted with each other many years earlier. At the time Mr. S. had been employed at a private country club to which Mr. T. had belonged. They had not been in contact since Mr. S. had retired, until, through an act of Providence, Mr. T. became reacquainted with Mr. S. in Landlord-Tenants Court. Mr. S. had been summoned to the court due to his arrears of rent for a 3-month period.
>
> His deteriorating intellectual capacity precipitated this "crisis," since Mr. S.'s short-term memory evidenced signs of increasing deficit. Due to Mr. T.'s existing working relationship with the court in his business capacity, he intervened successfully on Mr. S.'s behalf by assuring court officials that he would assume personal responsibility for payment of the

*Special thanks to the social work staff of Family and Child Services of Washington, D.C.

rent in arrears in order to prevent eviction action. Mr. S. understandably felt indebted to Mr. T. for his efforts. The sense of gratitude was intensified by his feelings regarding the "protectorate" position that Mr. T. had assumed in relationship to him. The fact that Mr. T. was a member of a racial group with greater power and status endeared him to Mr. S., who was born in an era when the state of race relations generated a tremendous degree of distrust and fear intermingled with a curious mixture of respect and admiration.

Sometime later, Mr. T. initiated a referral to the agency once it became clear to him that Mr. S. needed protective casework services. Subsequently, when Mr. S. was initially introduced to the assigned social worker, his resistance and defenses were high since he perceived that Mr. T.'s status and position could not be matched by the credentials of an agency representative who was unknown to him. The same racial group identity, the gender, and the younger age of the assigned social worker served to heighten Mr. S.'s defenses. Predictably, a period of client nonacceptance followed that required a combination of social worker determination, nonjudgmental acceptance, and continuity of effort to combat the high level of resistance. Later, a strong therapeutic alliance developed between the client and social worker, which facilitated working through feelings about the dynamics regarding the racial group identity and the gender differences.

13

Barriers to Service Delivery

Career opportunities for geriatric social workers are on the increase. By the end of this century, it is estimated that 700,000 jobs will have become available for social workers in the field of aging. Yet, despite the growing opportunity and interest in the field, serious barriers to service delivery remain. This chapter discusses some of these major obstacles, including ageism; negative attitudes, stereotypes, and myths; countertransference and death anxiety. It examines both the attitudes of therapists in direct practice with the elderly and their families as well as social values as they are reflected in public policy.

AGEISM

The impact of ageism on the client–worker relationship can not be understood without first realizing its historical and societal import. Throughout history, in every society, certain qualities have been selected to distinguish the elderly from younger members of the community. For example, respect for the aged has always been considered a virtue in China. For centuries, the Chinese aged have represented knowledge and life experience, and have been given authority and status. The ancient Jewish nation also respected their elderly, incorporating obedience and respect for the aged in the Ten Commandments and passing down in the Judaic-Christian tradition the value of children honoring their fathers and mothers.

In ancient Greece old men tutored the young, and laws gave all the power to the old. However, in private life the authority of the old was much diminished, and they were shown little respect. The Egyptians cherished the hope that they might defeat physical decline and the inevitability of death. They recognized, as did the Babylonians, that the passage of time brings about eventual decline and decay. As a result, these societies developed rites of regeneration. This dream of rejuvenation has persisted throughout history and is said to have brought Ponce de Leon to the New World in 1512 in search of the Fountain of Youth.

Reviews of contemporary American literature indicate that negative attitudes toward the aged are widespread (McTavish, 1971; Butler, 1975, Butler and Lewis, 1982). In our youth-oriented society, the image of an old person as weak, infirm, feeble, helpless, and nonproductive is common. In fact, this view is so pervasive that the term "ageism" was coined to describe the prejudices and stereotypes that are applied to older people solely on the basis of their age (Butler, 1969).

Ageism is a form of blatant prejudice and discrimination against the elderly. It is:

> . . . a process of systematic stereotyping of and discrimination against people because they are old, just as racism and sexism accomplish this with skin color and gender . . . ageism allows the younger generations to see older people as different from themselves. Thus, they subtly cease to identify with their elders as human beings (Butler, 1975, p. 12).

This prejudice toward old people, which is found to some degree in all of us, is a way of pigeonholing people and not seeing them as individuals. Ageism is similar to other forms of prejudice, such as sexism and racism, in that it pervades social institutions as well as individual belief systems. This means that discrimination in areas such as employment can be widespread. In his Pulitzer Prize-winning book Butler (1975 pp. 2–3) poignantly captured the plight of many older citizens:

> For many elderly Americans, old age is a tragedy, a period of quiet despair, deprivation, desolation and mutual rage . . . old age is frequently a tragedy even when the early years have been fulfilling and people have everything going for them. Herein lies what I consider to be the genuine tragedy of old age in America—we have shaped a society which is extremely harsh to live in when one is old. The tragedy of old age is not the fact that each of us must grow old and die but that the process of doing so has been made unnecessarily and, at times, excruciatingly painful, humiliating, debilitating and isolating through insensitivity, ignorance and poverty. The potentials for satisfactions, and even triumphs, in late life are real and vastly underexplored. For the most part, the elderly struggle to exist in an inhospitable world.

The fact that ageism exists in the mental health field and has even become professionalized has been well documented in numerous studies showing the reluctance of allied health professionals to enter the field of aging. This lack of interest in providing mental health and social services to the aged has been of concern for several decades. A 1966 study of doctoral students in clinical psychology revealed a decided preference among the respondents to work with young adults (Wilensky and Barmack, 1966). Two thirds of those students not only held negative attitudes toward work with the aged, but also viewed clients with physical defects and organic pathology with disdain. Such findings have been disclosed in other studies in which older people tend to be perceived as ill, disagreeable, inactive, economically burdensome, dependent, dull, socially undesirable, and dissatisfied.

In a 1967 study of hospital staff including physicians, dentists, physical therapists, nurses, and social workers it was found that old age was viewed as a time of irreversible degenerative change. These professionals often saw the aged as rigid, dependent, and lonely rather than adaptive or having problem-solving ability. As a result, the services offered were seen as custodial or palliative (Coe, 1967).

Throughout the 1960's, articles were written urging social workers to enter the field of aging. They attempted to counteract negative societal attitudes by appealing to the social consciousness of the caseworker (Posner, 1961; Soyer, 1960; Wasser, 1964). Social workers were reminded of their professional Code of Ethics, which underscores the right to service for all in need. At that time the resistance of the majority of trained professionals to work with older persons was said to have contributed to both the segregation of geriatric services and the unsatisfactory treatment of the older client (Wasser, 1964).

In the 1970's, as the field of geriatrics became recognized and better funded, more professionals entered this area of practice. Journal articles began to define social work techniques suitable for working with the elderly. Some journals emphasized the special and unique aspects of working with the aged (Bloom, 1971; Schmidt, 1975), while others stressed the similarities of working with the aged and other populations (Pincus, 1967). At the same time, there was a burgeoning of continuing education programs in gerontology. The goal was to develop an increased level of awareness regarding the needs and strengths of the aged and their capacity for change.

Despite these efforts to eliminate the stereotypes about the aged and the aging process, many misconceptions and barriers to service have remained. Reports from the 1981 White House Conference on Aging confirmed that, despite their growing number and increased risk of mental disorder and social dysfunction, the elderly continue to be underserved by mental health workers. Studies indicate that while some professionals no longer subscribe to the more blatant stereotypes about aging, subtle prejudices still exist. An attitude survey conducted at a mental health clinic in New York City examined the treatment views of psychologists, psychiatrists, social workers, and students. Attitudes toward the aged held by these therapists were found to be generally positive. However, other more subtle evidence of negative stereotyping of older clients was revealed. Most of these mental health workers agreed with the questionnaire statement, "Old people usually don't talk much." The researcher went on to say:

"Here we see what may be a new, insidious stereotype insulating the "reluctant therapist." After all, if the elderly do not talk much, how could we—who are engaged in essentially verbal therapy—possibly help them. They do not talk much so they do not require interaction with us. It is not that we, as therapists, avoid the elderly because we do not like them or because they have low status, or because they are a poor investment of our time (having fewer years left to live than younger patients)—oh, no! "Old people don't talk much"; "the old people do not need us, do not want our services, cannot benefit from our skills" (Garfinkel, 1975, p. 137).

Garfinkel concluded that the choice of treatment approaches, and the expectations and outcome of therapy were undoubtedly affected by these beliefs.

Because of her concern about such prejudice in the social work profession, Roberta Greene (1983) designed a study to explore what differences might exist in attitudes toward the aged and death in two groups of caseworkers—one group with a geriatric caseload, the other with a nongeriatric caseload. This study also found no difference between the two groups in subscribing to everyday stereotypes of aging: Both groups of caseworkers held positive attitudes toward the aged. However, it was found that there were striking and significant differences between the two groups in their preferences for working with particular population groups. Geriatric caseworkers preferred to work with the frail elderly and cancer patients, while the nongeriatric caseworkers generally expressed a negative preference for these same clients, as shown in Table 13.1. Those practicing in the field of aging revealed a significantly greater level of death anxiety as indicated by measures of fear of the dying of others. Results also pointed to a relationship between death anxiety and the number of years of social work practice with the aged.

Greene concluded that while caseworkers may elect to practice in the field of aging, they may nonetheless bring with them stereotypes, misconceptions, and/or fears of aging and death. She further concluded that it is important for educators and supervisors to provide an opportunity for social workers to explore their personal attitudes and concerns about working with the aging and learn to use these to the best advantage.

ATTITUDES, STEREOTYPES, AND MYTHS

It has already been said that the attitudes, stereotypes, and myths held by social workers can have a major impact on the casework process. An *attitude* may be defined as an enduring organization of motivational, emotional, perceptual, and cognitive processes with respect to some aspects of the individual's world (Bennett and Eckman,

TABLE 13.1. Preference Ranking of Six Client Populations by the Two Groups
of Social Workers

Rank	Geriatric case workers	Generic social workers
Most 1	Frail elderly	Young married couples
2	Middle-aged widows	Middle-aged widows
3	Cancer patients	Disturbed children
4	Young married couples	Frail elderly
5	Disturbed children	Adolescent offenders
Least 6	Adolescent offenders	Cancer patient

1973). Attitudes reflect a readiness or predisposing tendency to respond to an object or stimuli in a particular way. This suggests that how
a person *perceives* another can influence how he/she behaves toward
that person.

Stereotypes are sets of beliefs that claim to describe typical categories of people. Those holding stereotypes act as if their beliefs are true
(Seltzer and Atchley, 1971). Traditionally, stereotypes of "old" are
factually incorrect, rigid, and illogical; stereotypes can be either negative or positive. As with attitudes, stereotypes can predispose the
professional to act in either a positive or negative way toward a
particular client group.

For example, the professional may have a stereotypic positive view
of his/her elderly clients and tend to see them only as nice, wise, or
loveable; on the other hand, the practitioner may have a stereotypic
negative view and tend to see most of his/her elderly clients as senile,
isolated, infirm, or helpless. Such views are learned and originate early
in the socialization processes. They often continue if limited relationships with older people fail to provide an accurate frame of reference
for understanding the client as an individual. Without further, more
insightful socialization experiences, such as supervised geriatric field
work and ongoing supervisory conferences, these attitudes and stereotypes may be brought into the professional social work relationships.
Although there appears to be considerable unanimity about the prevalence of negative attitudes toward older people, it should be pointed
out that positive attitudes about the aged are also evident. Researchers
such as Tibbetts have suggested that, from a historical perspective,
stereotypes of middle and old age are on the decline; Seltzer and
Atchley have proposed that gerontologists may be oversensitive to
stereotypes of old age, anticipating them where they may not, in fact,
exist. Nonetheless, the tendency to categorize all older people into one

homogeneous, undifferentiated group should be addressed in social work practice. Although social workers have taken on many of the myths of society, research indicates that these stereotypic views are challenged as practitioners gain experience in working with the aged. The Palmore "Facts on Aging: A Short Quiz" (1977) and N. Kogan's Old People Scale (1961) are presented in appendixes A and B for those who would like to examine their own attitudes toward the aged and the aging process.

Myths are reflections of how a society views human nature and relationships. Of particular interest for discussion here are the myths and stereotypes that can interfere with the successful application of the functional-age intergenerational treatment model. In order to apply the model appropriately, the practitioner must avoid the tendency to accept unsubstantiated ideas about the aged. To this end, the following facts and fallacies were selected from the literature:

Myth: Being "old" is merely a matter of chronological age.
Fact: Aging refers to the processes of change in individuals that occur after maturity. Not all aspects of the human organism show the same age-related changes as the person advances in chronological age. Therefore, it is well to distinguish three aspects of aging: biological age, referring to organic changes and life expectancy; psychological age, referring to adaptive capacities; and sociocultural age, referring to social roles and expectations of the group. These are interrelated and together comprise an individual's functional age (Birren and Sloane, 1980, p. 4).

Myth: Older people talk about the good old days because they are garrulous or "senile."
Fact: The introspective qualities of older people are a result of a naturally occurring return to past experiences, reassessing them in an attempt to resolve and integrate them. This provides the opportunity for the ego to reorganize these events and come to terms with past conflicts and relationships. The process of reminiscing can occur at any age, particularly at times of transition. However, this takes place more frequently in some elderly who are not as actively involved in the present and may not be able to draw upon interesting current experiences. The tendency to reminisce also increases as the older person begins to deal with his/her own mortality. This process can be tapped as a therapeutic tool in life review (Butler, 1963).

Myth: Older people do not develop or grow.
Fact: Life span theorists reject the view that growth ends with adulthood. They point out that, while there may be growth limits for attributes such as height, other qualities such as creativity and abstract reasoning do not fit this model. In this context, growth refers to differentiation, increased complexity, and greater organization, and can occur at every age (Schell and Hall, 1979).

Myth: Older people cannot learn new roles, skills or competencies.
Fact: Unfortunately, mature individuals are usually thought of as having reached a stage when no further socialization takes place. However, research on aging and the life cycle indicates that, as people mature,

they must "continually learn to play new or altered roles and to relinquish old ones" (Riley, Foner, Hess and Toby, 1969). It is now understood that at every stage of life the individual must master certain developmental tasks requiring new skills and competencies.

Myth: Older people are not suitable candidates for insight therapy.

Fact: Because of their introspective qualities, capacity for growth, and lifelong coping styles, many elderly clients have great adaptational skills to draw upon in a crisis. Butler (1968) suggests that "the possibility for intrapsychic change may be greater in old age than at any period in life" (p. 237).

Myth: Older people are alienated from their families.

Fact: The family continues to be the primary source of social support in old age. While most Americans do not live in three- or four-generation households, the family continues to be the primary caregiver for the frail and impaired elderly. Research affirms that there is frequent contact between the elderly and their families, particularly at times of illness. "Exchange of services and regular visits are common among old people and their children whether or not they live under a single roof" (Shanas, 1979).

Myth: Older people are cared for by their families but do not give anything in return.

Fact: Survey data suggest there is a high degree of interdependence between generations in today's families. There is generally ongoing contact between adult children and their parents in the form of shared social activities and the *mutual* exchange of material and emotional support (Bengston and Treas, 1980).

Myth: When older people experience a biopsychosocial crisis, they are *best* helped without the involvement of the family.

Fact: A family system is composed of interrelated members who constitute a group. A change in the life of one of the members brings about change throughout the system. Therefore, a biopsychosocial crisis in one of the members can be expected to result in change affecting everyone in the family system. An awareness of this phenomenon can enhance casework services to the aged and their families.

COUNTERTRANSFERENCE

Freud (1966) was first to give insight and prominence to the psychotherapeutic interpersonal experience between patient and therapist. Freud called attention to the patient's irrational feelings for the therapist (transference), and also suggested that the therapist's inappropriate responses (countertransference) need to come under study. He believed that the curative nature of the therapy itself stemmed from the analysis of this emotional exchange between patient and practitioner. The Freudian view that all of our relationships, including the one between patient and practitioner, are patterned by our relationships with significant people, has been a dominant theme in the psychiatric and social work literature and often is used to examine the counseling relationship.

At the same time, Freud's less than positive attitude toward the older patient is reflected in his statement that " . . . near or above *the fifties the elasticity of the mental processes, on which treatment depends, is as a rule lacking.*" Freud's legacy of skepticism as to the value of psychotherapy for the aged has long influenced the delivery of psychiatric services to this population group. Far too often, therapy with the aged is viewed "as only supportive," "a second-rate procedure," having "no systematic theory" or "not worth a long-term investment" (Butler and Lewis, 1982; Cohen, 1977; Mutschler, 1971).

The literature has little to offer on the specific nature of countertransference mechanisms in psychotherapeutic work with the aged; consequently, one must apply what has been said about other client groups. Countertransference in traditional terms is defined as the therapist's distorted reaction(s) to the patient. This reaction is based on the past relationships of the therapist rather than on the real attributes of the client, and may include anxiety, anger, even defensiveness and oversolicitousness, and can be noted when the practitioner finds him/herself perceiving and reacting to clients in inappropriate ways. Countertransference behaviors reflect disturbances or distortions in perception and in the communication process (Langs, 1974). These disturbances are considered to be related to conflicts within the therapist and, once examined, can be clues to understanding the dynamics of the client–worker relationship.

The concept of countertransference has been expanded over the years to include an examination of more aspects of the interactional processes of therapy. According to Parsons (1951), the therapeutic encounter may be viewed as a social system of complementary roles to which each person brings a set of attitudes, beliefs and expectations regarding how he/she and the other person should behave. From this perspective, countertransference behaviors are seen as reflecting disruptions in the system's communication process. The expansion of the concept of countertransference to include additional interactional processes means that the caseworker can achieve a better understanding of his/her relationship with a particular client and eliminate counterproductive responses that are based on distortions in the communication process.

The use of the interactional approach to analyze communication in therapy allows for a broader perspective and for the concept of countertransference to be applied more freely. The concern goes beyond the practitioner's so-called personality conflicts with the client. The interactional approach recognizes the potential for certain groups of clients to evoke countertherapeutic responses. This means that certain client groups, such as the mentally retarded, handicapped or aged, may be more likely to elicit problematic responses from a particular social worker. In interactional terms, countertransference is also viewed as a disruption in the communication process of therapy. It comes about when there is a divergence in role expectation or role enactment between therapist and client.

As early as 1957, Perlman recognized that the management of irrational elements in the relationship is one of the most difficult aspects of the casework process. She suggested that the social worker would be less than human if he/she did not respond naturally to "emotion-exciting" situations. However, subjective involvement with the client may reflect a countertransference problem that needs to be handled with professional skill.

The practitioner needs to become aware of his/her special vulnerabilities and what he/she brings to the therapeutic encounter (Schwartz, 1978). This self-awareness is at the core of the casework process. When countertransference feelings are displaced onto the client, the caseworker is no longer able to effectively hold the position of listener, observer, and therapist. The sense of professional objectivity is diminished, as is the ability to perceive and to clarify the client's needs and feelings (Perlman, 1957, p. 81). Practitioners need to accept responsibility for what they contribute to the client–worker interaction, and be able to determine when such contributions are constructive and when they are not. Because of its importance to effective casework intervention, this will be addressed further in the following chapter on supervision.

DEATH ANXIETY

Despite the fact that death has been a prominent theme in philosophy, literature, and religious thought throughout the ages, there has been a systematic examination of the relevance of death anxiety as a psychological variable only in the last decade.

Themes of aging and death are closely related. Ambivalence toward aging and death can be traced back to some of the earliest myths and legends, which reflect the concepts of both life prolongation and acceptance of finitude. For centuries, the death theme has been played out in sacred and secular spheres. The Gilgamesh Epic, known to the Sumerians as early as 3000 B.C., expressed both the intense desire to triumph over death and the doubt that magic, cunning, virtue, and strength could achieve this objective. The faithful of Old Testament times knew a God of life. They believed that the way in which a person meets death is the product of the way in which he/she has lived life. Renewal or rebirth has also been a salient theme, as seen in the *Egyptian Book of the Dead*, the *New Testament*, and Ponce de Leon's search for the Fountain of Youth (Kastenbaum and Costa, 1977).

The classical psychoanalysts were among the first to discuss the meaning of death as a psychological concept. Freud (1925) maintained that " . . . no one believes in his own death . . . in the unconscious everyone is convinced of his own immortality" (p. 310). Jung (1964) argued that death contributes meaning to life and that the collective unconscious seeks to prepare us for it. He perceived death as the central problem of the latter half of life, as is sex in the first half.

In the mid-1950's a scientific interest in the subject of death began to emerge. By 1977, bibliographic resources at the Center for Death Education and Research contained 3000 entries on the topic. Among the current literature are studies attempting to relate basic demographic variables such as age, sex, educational background, and so on to death anxiety or fear of death (Dickstein and Blatt, 1966; Donaldson, 1972; Feifel and Branscomb, 1973; Lester, 1970).

While not all theorists might view death anxiety strictly as a countertransference phenomenon, it has long been recognized that negative attitudes about death can play a role in the health profession-al's attitudes toward his/her clients (Berezin, 1977; Soyer, 1960). In fact, the reluctance of professionals to interact with the dying person has been widely documented (Feifel and Branscomb, 1973; Kübler-Ross, 1971; Nelson and Nelson, 1975; Wolff, 1966). Working with the aged often brings the practitioner face-to-face with the decline and end of individual life; one of the key issues for social workers and other professionals in the field of aging is that the practitioner must con-stantly face the reality of his/her own mortality. It has been suggested that prejudice toward the elderly is, in part, an attempt by younger generations to shield themselves from the anxieties of their own aging and death (Butler and Lewis, 1982).

Death anxiety can be related to the process of dying itself or can be focused on one's own death, the death of another and/or the effects of death. Death anxiety has been defined in a number of different ways. Hoelter (1979) has suggested the following operational definition: death anxiety is "an emotional reaction involving subjective feelings of unpleasantness and concern based on contemplation or anticipation of any of the several facets related to death" (p. 996).

The terms most frequently used to characterize orientations toward death are ambivalence, fear, denial, concern, and anxiety. Many theorists have asserted that the most pervasive attitude toward death is one of concern. However, empirical studies have demonstrated that there is actually a wide variety of attitudes toward death, which can range from extreme fear to a complete acceptance and a welcoming of one's own death without fear or anxiety.

Recent research has suggested that death anxiety is not a unidimen-sional concept, but that concern about death is multidimensional.

There is evidence that geriatric caseworkers as well as other professionals engaged in work with dying persons experience higher levels of death anxiety (Greene, 1983; Livingston and Zimet, 1965; Weinstein, 1978). This is not surprising, as there continue to be almost daily humanistic and ethical questions for practitioners about how clients may experience death with dignity. The following case illustrates some of these dilemmas:

> Mrs. T., a social worker at a nursing home for many years, received a request to help plan for "a living will" with an alert resident and her husband (Mr. and Mrs. Q.). Mrs. T. felt she would have no difficulty with this request because her many years of experience had allowed her to develop a "comfortable philosophy about death with dignity." She reported to her supervisory consultation group that she "did not believe in heroic measures such as forced feeding."
>
> As the details of the case emerged, it was learned that Mrs. Q. had had a tracheotomy, a gastroscopy, and was constantly on oxygen. There was also a history of mental illness. The resident required a round-the-clock companion for the last 2 ½ years. In discussions with the husband, the caseworker found that "his questions could only be answered medically." Mrs. Q., who could speak using a "special buzzing electrical device," had not been brought into the discussion. The husband felt that his wife's life should not be prolonged through hospitalization, but was not sure he was "making the right decision." Mr. Q. sought out the social worker several times to ask questions about "the arrangements." "Will my wife be in pain?" "Will I have to give permission at the time of the medical emergency?" He was referred back to the physician for "correct information."
>
> Mrs. T. had serious questions about her role as a social worker. Should she "impose her views about keeping people alive under such untenable situations?" The group supported her by suggesting that the social work role lay in helping the husband deal with the emotional component of this seemingly medical matter. (Questions were also raised about Mrs. Q.'s participation in the decision.) The group concluded that intellectually Mr. Q. appeared to have realized that he did not want his wife rushed to the hospital if her present "supports" were not sufficient to sustain her. However, emotionally he was not prepared to face that eventuality. Once the caseworker could sort out her own anxieties (about imposing her views), she would be better prepared to help Mr. Q. examine his feelings. The caseworker indicated that the discussion had served as a catalyst in this regard and that she would seek further supervision if needed.

It is obvious that the ongoing care of frail, ailing or dying clients and their eventual death can affect the caseworker's attitudes and perhaps even his/her ability to perform on the job. Whether the care of such clients leads to dissatisfaction with practice in the field, burnout or ineffectiveness, only further research will determine. The importance of exploring the therapist's personal feelings toward death through clinical supervision and staff consultation is crucial. There is sufficient evidence to support the view that unresolved and/or ambiguous attitudes can lead to countertherapeutic difficulties for the worker. The practitioner must recognize this and not allow a false sense of inadequacy to stand in the way of raising the issue in supervisory or group consultation. This issue is discussed further in the next chapter on supervision.

CHAPTER

14

Supervision

The preceding chapter discussed some of the major barriers to establishing a satisfactory client–social worker relationship. Countertransference, death anxiety, stereotypes, and myths were defined as some of the major obstacles that could disrupt the therapeutic alliance, and thereby interfere with effective casework. This chapter describes ways in which supervision can help the practitioner better understand why he/she is having difficulty with a particular client (family) and what can be done to promote a more professional therapeutic response. Of particular interest are those factors that may be unique or more pertinent to geriatric social work practice.

AN OVERVIEW OF SUPERVISION

Supervision as it is practiced today had its origins in the Charity Organization Society movement in the nineteenth century. During that time there was a concern that limited funds go to the neediest families. Financial aid was given only after a lengthy investigation, with the initial psychosocial study conducted by a paid employee of the Society. In addition to receiving financial assistance, families were also visited by volunteers who offered personal support and "moral counseling." These "friendly visitors" discussed their cases with paid personnel who, in turn, discussed their disposition with district committees. As the first supervisory structure, this system provided a basis for decision-making, gave continuity to the work of staff and volunteers, offered an administrative point of contact, and served as a channel of communication (Kadushin, 1976).

The supervisory conference has since become an integral social work function. Most caseworkers first become familiar with supervision as students in field practicum. The purpose of supervision during that period is to review the students' work in order to teach practice skills and techniques. However, supervision generally continues in some form throughout the caseworker's professional career and serves a number of different purposes. Supervision has been viewed as both an administrative activity and an educational process in which the supervisor helps the supervisee to accomplish his/her job better within an agency framework. It has also been viewed as an institutionalized built-in mechanism through which the attitudes and performances of the social worker are examined. In brief, supervision may be thought of as a means of getting the work done and maintaining organizational control and accountability (Hollis, 1977; Torren, 1972; Towle, 1945).. Kadushin (1976) best summarizes the major characteristics of social work supervision:

> . . . a social work supervisor is an agency administrative staff member to whom authority is delegated to direct, coordinate, enhance, and evaluate the on-the-job performance of the supervisees for whose work he is held accountable. In implementing this responsibility the supervisor performs administrative, educational, and supportive functions in interaction with the supervisee in the context of a positive relationship. The supervisor's ultimate objective is to deliver to agency clients the best possible service, both quantitative and qualitative, in accordance with agency policies and procedures (Kadushin, 1976, p.21).

In other words, supervision in social work serves three major purposes. These include overseeing the activities of staff to assure that the mandate of the organization is properly carried out; evaluating the work of supervisees to guarantee the best quality service for agency clients; and supporting the efforts of practitioners to reduce stress and maximize job satisfaction/performance.

The tasks related to administrative supervision include planning and assigning work; organizing, coordinating, and facilitating the use of personnel and agency resources; reviewing work performance; placing the worker, acting as a channel of communication and as an administrative buffer; helping formulate agency policy and facilitating intra-agency coordination (Kadushin, 1976). Supervisors in the administrative role derive their authority to execute these tasks from their strategic positions in the agency structure. In this way power is delegated, decisions are enforced, the activities of a number of people are coordinated, and common agency objectives and goals are achieved.

Educational supervision, which is the second responsibility of the supervisor, has been described as "post-facto teaching," or a retrospective scrutiny of client–worker interactions and their reciprocal effects (Fleming and Benedek, 1966, p. 238). The process involves a "systematic, explicit analysis" of the practitioner's work so as to provide a "structured learning situation which facilitates maximum growth and frees potentialities" (Eckstein and Wallerstein, 1972; Kadushin, 1976). While this activity is aimed at instructing the social worker in what he/she needs to know in order to do his/her job, the goal of educational supervision, as with administrative supervision, is to further the objectives of the agency in meeting client needs.

There are several distinct orientations toward educational supervision. Among the supervisory models that might be considered are the existential and the didactic. The focus of the existential (supervisee-centered) model is the development of the supervisee's self-understanding, self-awareness, and emotional growth. It is akin to the ability to recognize and manage countertransference issues (see chapter 13). In this instance the supervisor is interested in the practitioner's response to working with a particular client and its effect on service delivery. The didactic (task-centered) approach is primarily concerned with the development of the supervisee's professional expertise. Here the supervisor focuses his/her attention on imparting a particular skill to the supervisee. This might include techniques for interviewing the hearing or cognitively impaired client. It should be pointed out, however, that the distinction is somewhat artificial, as most supervision encompasses both the existential and didactic perspectives.

The third major component of supervision, which is support, is associated with techniques to help supervisees cope with job-related stress. Inasmuch as excessive stress can adversely affect the practitioner's ability to provide services, the supervisor's goal is to prevent, reduce, and/or alleviate the stress of a supervisee. This process includes procedures such as "reassurance, encouragement, and recognition of achievement, realistically based expressions of confidence, approval and commendation, catharsis—ventilation, desensitization and universalization, and attentive listening which communicates interest and concern" (Kadushin, 1976, p. 202). The next sections discuss supervision in social work with the aged from the educational and supportive points of view.

EDUCATIONAL SUPERVISION: THE DEVELOPMENT OF SELF-AWARENESS

Developing a higher level of worker self-awareness is the major goal of educational supervision. Self-awareness or self-management involves the conscious assessment and control of those feelings that have no helping value in the client–social worker relationship. Perlman (1957) suggests that while management of the rational and irrational elements in the relationship sounds so reasonable and simple, it actually is one of the most difficult, discipline-demanding parts of any therapeutic process. The caseworker must be able to observe and feel with the client and simultaneously be responsible for his/her own feelings and the business at hand.

The caseworker must also try to identify when countertransference or inappropriate feelings toward the client are interfering in the relationship. In order to develop a therapeutic relationship with the client the therapist must honestly face his/her feelings, recognizing that each client has a particular meaning for him/her. The conscious recognition of these attitudes allows for the assessment of how they affect the relationship and treatment process. Unless the worker can come to recognize these countertransference reactions, it is unlikely that he/she can be effective as a therapist. The practitioner may be able to recognize and resolve some countertransferences for him/herself. However, as seen in the following case, the supervisory conference is often a necessary aid to preserving quality services either by a private practitioner or in a clinic or social agency.

> Mrs. L. was a middle-aged social worker assigned to the fifth floor of the nursing home. Many of the residents on the floor were described as "not mentally alert"—suffering from various stages of organic brain disease. The case Mrs. L. presented in supervision involved a resident "who looked just like her mother both in physical appearance and in her mannerisms." Mrs. L. described her relationship with her mother as "distant." She asked if such feelings would really get in the way of helping the resident as "there was no need for casework in this situation anyway."
>   Further examination of the facts revealed that Mrs. L. found at least one fourth of her confused patients able to engage in an in-depth casework relationship despite some cognitive limitations. The supervisor inquired about any significant recent events in the life of the resident. It was learned that the resident's roommate had died several weeks earlier. Worker and supervisor concluded that countertransference ('she looks just like my mother') might be standing in the way of reaching out to this resident whom the practitioner perceived as "not needing casework."

The need for trying to achieve this type of sensitivity is readily apparent. If the social worker remains involved in his/her own feelings, he/she is not in a position to perceive the client with any clarity or judgment. Awareness of one's own values is particularly important because they influence choices and actions, including goals, percep- tions of capacities and problems, and the interventions to be used in the helping process (Northen, 1982). The practitioner needs "to realize that he sees others through the screen of his own personality and his own life experiences" (Konopka, 1963, p. 94). As seen in the following case, without self-management a practitioner can unwittingly impose his/her own values or views on a client:

> Ms. P., a young inexperienced social worker, was assigned to work with an elderly couple (Mr. and Mrs. Y.) in marriage counseling. Mrs. Y. was a "temporary" resident of a nursing home, following a referral from a local psychiatric hospital where she had been treated for agitated depression with suicidal overtones following a stroke. The social worker stated that the husband was not willing to participate in counseling from the

beginning and their 40-year-old daughter was fed up, wanting no more involvement.

During supervision, the social worker acknowledged that "I wanted to be all (things) to Mrs. Y." Ms. P. described the Y.s' 40-year marriage as "never being good." Mr. Y. was described as "thriving on Mrs. Y.'s mental illness for years." While the caseworker's goal was to help the family decide where and how best to care for Mrs. Y., she really felt that "he (Mr. Y.) could not take care of her." The social worker was convinced that the daughter was "no longer interested" in the mother's problems. When the whole family decided to move to Florida to retire, the caseworker called to tell Mrs. Y., "You can always come back." The last communication with Mrs. Y. revealed that "she was doing great" with live-in help and physical therapy. Mrs. Y. also reported that she and her husband were once again sharing a bedroom.

Because personal values can at times make it difficult for the practitioner to implement professional values, an awareness of one's own values is essential to the casework process. The process of self-management, or perceiving ourselves with a reasonable degree of accuracy, may not always be as effective as it might be. On those occasions the supervisory conference can help the practitioner more realistically understand how others view him/her.

In order for the process of educational supervision to be effective, both the supervisor and the supervisee must respect the limits and restrictions of their mutual roles. The supervisor's responsibility is to help the supervisee become a better prepared employee, not to intrude into the personal life of the supervisee. The responsibility of the supervisee, on the other hand, is to attempt to analyze client-worker interactions and to bring to supervision those cases that present unrealistic or conflict-ridden communications. Where the supervisor believes there are difficulties, he/she should ask about a case. It is important to recognize that a seemingly nonadaptive or inappropriate client response is not always a reflection of the client's problem.

SUPPORTIVE SUPERVISION: THE DEVELOPMENT OF STRESS MANAGEMENT

The major goal in supportive supervision is to help social workers deal with job-related stress, thereby enabling them to offer the client the most effective and efficient service. The provision of emotional support as part of supervision is an acknowledgment of the fact that in order to do an effective job the practitioner must have the opportunity to allay anxiety and restore his/her own emotional equilibrium (Kadushin, 1976). Supportive supervision can therefore be defined as those interventions on the part of the supervisor that reinforce ego strengths and enhance the capacity of the ego to deal with job stresses and tensions.

Supportive supervision is concerned with social workers who, hour after hour, day after day, are involved with troubled human beings. Ideally, these practitioners are able to remain objective without losing their concern for their clients. However, there are occasions when feelings of frustration, inadequacy and disillusionment can occur. At times practitioners need reassurance that such reactions may be a normal part of the job and that their response is not a sign of inadequacy. Otherwise they may compound the difficulty by feeling guilty and failing to bring their concerns to the attention of the supervisor or discussing their concern with peers. Needless to say, it is more difficult to do an effective job when undergoing such stress, and eventually the practitioner can experience job dissatisfaction and burnout.

Burnout, the term used when the helping professional gradually loses concern for the people with whom he/she is working, is a syndrome of emotional exhaustion resulting from excessive demands on energy, strength, or resources. Over time, the practitioner may increasingly think of his/her clients in derogatory terms, and lose enthusiasm, creativity, and commitment. Eventually there is a psychological detachment, as a result of which the quality of the service that the client receives deteriorates. Minimal attention and effort is given to each case, and a callous, even dehumanizing processing of clients may take place (Freudenberger, 1974; Maslach, 1976).

Geriatric social workers may find that the burden of their caseload is not the only source of job-related tensions. Practitioners can experience the stress related to the conflict between what Kadushin (1976) calls a bureaucratic and a service orientation. In this instance the social worker is caught between the regulations and/or red tape of the agency and a desire to serve the client. This can, over time, contribute to a breakdown in the relationship between the individual social worker and the organization. However, a willingness to deal with these administrative issues in supervision has the potential of alleviating job-related stress and obtaining the appropriate service for the client. Where this does not occur, there is the danger of burnout. Burnout rates are lower for those who express, analyze, and share their personal feelings with their professional colleagues (Maslach, 1976). There is also evidence that incorporating special training to assist professionals in recognizing and understanding their work-related problems can reduce stress. Formal or informal programs in which professionals can get together to discuss problems and get advice and support also are effective in coping with job-related stress.

It is the responsibility of both the supervisor and the practitioner to try to prevent burnout. The social worker who begins to feel unable to effectively do the job, to cope with the full range of client demands, who is tired all the time and/or feels that his/her life is out of control, is experiencing common feelings of burnout. Supervisors may notice excessive absences, excessive use of drugs and/or alcohol and/or a general deterioration of work and social performance. Both supervisor and supervisee should bring these early warning signals to the supervisory conference.

Supervisors and supervisees should examine what they can do to actively counter high stress situations that often lead to burnout. The supervisor can be helpful by trying to provide a clear definition of the scope of work of the agency—what can and cannot be done with existing resources. Examining the administrative system and questioning situational factors, such as excessively high social worker-to-client ratios and excessive continuous direct contact with clients, can be useful. Providing time to share personal feelings with colleagues and adequate ongoing training for continued professional development are positive steps that should be taken.

Practitioners, on the other hand, cannot take a passive role. It is the caseworker's responsibility to advise supervisors about the work environment and the resources direct service workers need to do the job. In this way they can realize that they may make positive contributions to the group processes that shape the organizational/administrative structure. Practitioners also have the responsibility of analyzing their caseloads to identify and bring to supervision problematic and/or difficult practice issues.

In its most positive sense supportive supervision aims to maximize the practitioners' potential:

> In this sense the supervisor, in implementing the responsibilities of supportive supervision, not only relieves, restores, comforts, and replenishes, but more positively, inspires, animates, and exhilarates. The supervisor "motivates towards excellence," helping the worker develop those feelings and attitudes which are conducive to their best efforts, rather than "merely protecting against incompetence." Such supervision makes the difference between joyless submission and eager participation, between playing notes and making music (Kadushin, 1976, pp. 203–204).

SUPERVISION IN SOCIAL WORK WITH THE AGED AND THEIR FAMILIES*

It has been suggested that geriatric social work practice may present special supervisory issues. In general, geriatrics has been viewed as "less prestigious," "less rewarding," and "more demanding." Obser-

*This section is based on a workshop given by R. Greene, E. Fleshner, G. Kraft, and M. Rafner at the 37th Annual Scientific Meeting of the Gerontological Society of America, November 1984.

vations are often made about the "slow rate of change of the elderly client," "the overwhelming nature of this population group" and the "high stress level" of practitioners in this field (Greene, 1984, 1985; Lerea and Li Mauro, 1982).

There is, in fact, little information to date about geriatric social work career patterns or the characteristics of those who work with the elderly. In addition, there has been little progress in identifying those persons best suited to work with the aged, or in understanding what can be done to ensure that those who work in this area are effective and satisfied to remain in the field. While research may eventually clarify some of these issues, clinical experience suggests the importance of exploring these concerns in supervisory conferences.

One of the first practice issues which needs to be considered is the fact that, in most instances, the social worker is considerably younger than the client. These generational differences may mean that practitioner and client have divergent historical views and/or cultural values. Age differences can also present problems of role reversal, with the younger worker being pressed inappropriately into the parent role. At the same time, elderly patients may arouse the therapist's conflicts about his/her relationships with parental figures. In addition, clients and practitioners who are in different phases of the life cycle are facing different life tasks that can affect their time perspective and view of treatment. Elderly clients who are in the final stages of life are dealing with the task of integrity versus despair. They are undergoing a life review in which they are trying to reaffirm their past, come to terms with life, and face death with dignity. The younger worker, who may be dealing with issues of intimacy or generativity, may be busy planning for future careers and/or families. Therefore, it is important to consider how this may affect the therapy.

Another practice issue to examine in supervision in social work with the aged and their families is the fact that the request for help is not always initiated by the older person. Family members and other professionals are often the ones who ask for a particular service for the older adult. Unfortunately, the older person's thoughts and feelings may not always be considered. As a result, he/she may appear to be a "resistant" client. Most importantly, the actual request may not reflect the real need. Therefore, care must be taken not to "take over" and move ahead without consideration for the family system and without involving the older adult. Being alert to these difficulties and bringing problem cases to the attention of one's supervisor can help prevent inappropriate services and infantilization of the client.

Another therapeutic issue with older clients is the fact that they are often seen in nontraditional settings such as their own homes, at a hospital bedside, in senior centers or in institutions. This may make it difficult for the practitioner to establish "professional boundaries." She/he may be asked to buy a loaf of bread, be offered a cup of tea or a piece of cake. It is often difficult in these circumstances to speak privately with the client. There are times when shopping for the client or assisting in a more personal way is appropriate. However, there is also the possibility that the social worker is not acting professionally. Resolving these concerns in supervision may involve an examination of the case dynamics as well as the setting in which casework takes place.

While most older people are able to continue to live independently throughout their lives, many of those who are seen by geriatric social workers are frail and to some degree dependent. Caseworkers can sometimes feel overwhelmed by the multiple physical, emotional, and social problems and the intensity of the dependency needs that an older individual can experience. While social workers may feel a sense of urgency that something be done, they must also keep in mind how much clients are able and willing to do for themselves. Then too, it is sometimes essential in life-threatening situations to be "forceful" with a dependent client. This calls for the practitioner to acknowledge the realities of the client's life and to set reasonable, limited goals. Supervisors can play an important role in helping supervisees to accept that they must find a balance between acting as if there is nothing they can do and feeling they must do everything.

Because older clients often sustain multiple losses, they may present a threat to the younger worker. The severely handicapped or the terminally ill client can present particular issues or problems for practitioners. As physical decline, sensory loss, changes in body image, and social adjustment are seen as an inevitable part of life, it is not unlikely that the practitioner may ask, "Will I be in that situation?" This is an important issue to address in supervision. Supervisors can be helpful by letting practitioners know that it is not unusual to identify with clients in this way. By resolving such problems in the supervisory conference the practitioner is more likely to be helpful to the client.

Geriatric social workers often practice in settings in which ethical issues are likely to occur. The older client who doesn't want his/her life prolonged by heroic measures or the family who places the severely deteriorated Alzheimer's patient in a nursing home are bound to raise quality of life issues for the practitioner. Therefore, it is important for caseworkers to acknowledge any value conflicts. It is in these situations that supervisors can be most supportive to their staff and help them deal with the question: "Would I want to live like that?"

Some general questions that may elicit discussion during supervisory conferences include:

1. What would it be like for you to be in that client's situation?
2. What do you see as the potential for change in working with this client?
3. What future do you think this client will have?
4. Does the client remind you of someone?
5. What feelings does the client evoke for you?
6. What do you think is the client's perception of you?

While geriatric social work practice can be demanding because it forces practitioners to look at issues of dependency, mortality, and the quality of life, it can also be rewarding. Younger social workers can learn much from elderly clients who continue to struggle to be independent despite great difficulties. Practitioners can also gain much from clients who are adjusting to multiple losses, have come to terms with their lives, and are preparing to face death. It is the supervisory conference, sometimes supplemented by peer review and psychiatric consultation, that allows the caseworker to put these benefits into perspective.

A supervisory conference ideally takes place regularly, at a fixed time, and within the context of a positive supervisor-caseworker relationship in which there is mutual respect and a judicious use of authority on the part of the supervisor. Confidentiality as well as the other ethical standards of the social work profession are maintained. Both participants are prepared to use the time effectively, whether the task be administrative, educational, or supportive in nature, and both social worker and supervisor take responsibility for the content of the agenda. Wherever possible, it is best to have defined educational goals based upon an open, clearly stated evaluation of the practitioner's performance.

When the social worker is new to the agency, supervision may center around socialization to the agency and community and the development of service skills. As the practitioner becomes better acquainted with procedures and acquires additional skills, supervision may revolve around issues of professional judgment. From this perspective, supervision may be seen as consultation between colleagues.

Supervisory consultation centers around the "teaching of a case," and the supervisor is looked to for expertise in diagnosis and treatment. The supervisor should also know the worker and sense what kind of help he/she may need to enable him/her to assist the client. Supervision proceeds in a way that extends the practitioner's knowledge and deepens his/her perceptions, feelings, and self-understanding (Austin, 1979).

In order for these ideals to be met, both supervisor and supervisee must be prepared when they go into conference. Social workers should review their caseload and select case situations with which they think they need help; supervisors may want to raise questions about practice issues specifically related to that practitioner's casework "style." The checklists in Appendix C and D are designed to served as guides in that regard. Some question the need for supervision in the case of social workers who have practiced for many years. However, it is such accountability that not only guarantees the best quality services, but also contributes to personal growth and the expansion of our professional knowledge base.

Bibliography

Ackerman, N. "An orientation to psychiatric research on the family." *Marriage and Family Living*, 19 (1957), pp. 68–74.

Ackerman, N. "Family psychotherapy—Theory and practice." In G. D. Erikson and T. P. Hogan, eds., *Family Therapy: An Introduction to Theory and Technique*. Monterey, California: Brooks/Cole Publishing Company, 1972, 1981.

Adams, M. *Single Blessedness: Observations on the Single Status in Married Society*. New York: Basic Books, 1976.

American Association of Retired Persons. *Aging America. Trends and Projections*. Washington, D.C.: AARP, 1984.

American Psychiatric Association. *Diagnostic and Statistical Manual of Mental Disorders*. Washington, D.C.: APA Press, 1980.

Anderson, R.E., and I. Carter. *Human Behavior in the Social Environment*. Chicago, Ilinois: Aldine Publishing, 1978.

Ansello, E. "Children, the media, and images of the elderly." Testimony Before the U.S. House of Representatives Select Committee on Aging, Washington, D.C., 1977.

Archbold, P.G. "All-consuming activity: the family as caregiver." *Generations* (Winter 1982), pp. 12–14.

Arndt, W.B. *Theories of Personality*. New York: Macmillan, 1974.

Aronson, M.; G. Levin; and R. Lipkowitz. "A community-based family/patient group program for Alzheimer's disease." *The Gerontologist*, 24, No. 4 (1984), pp. 339–342.

Austin, L. "Basic principles of supervision." In C. E. Munson, ed., *Social Work Supervision*. New York: The Free Press, 1979.

Baltes, P.B., and L.R. Gaulet. "Status and issues of a life-span developmental psychology." L. R. Gaulet and P. B. Baltes, eds., *Life-Span Developmental Psychology: Research and Theory*. New York: Academic Press, 1970.

Baltes, P., and K. Schaie. "On life-span developmental research paradigms: Retrospects and prospects." In P. Baltes and K. Schaie, eds., *Life-Span Developmental Psychology: Personality and Socialization*. New York: Academic Press, 1973.

Bardill, D.R. and F.J. Ryan. *Family Group Casework*. Washington D.C., National Association of Social Workers, 1973.

Bart, P. "The loneliness of the long-distance mother." In J. Freedman, ed., *Explorations in Psychiatric Sociology*. Philadelphia, Pennsylvania: F. A. Davis Co., 1974, pp. 139–157.

Bartlett, H.M. *The Common Base of Social Work Practice*. New York: National Association of Social Workers, 1970.

Beauvoir, Simone De. *Coming of Age*. New York: Putnam's Sons, 1972.

Beaver, M.L. *Human Service Practice with the Elderly*. New York: Prentice Hall, 1982.

Beaver, M.L., and D. Miller. *Clinical Social Work Practice with the Elderly*. Homewood, Illinois: The Dorsey Press, 1985.

Bengston, V., and D. Haber. "Sociological perspectives on aging." In D.

Woodruff and J. E. Birren, eds., *Aging: Scientific Perspectives and Social Issues.* Monterey, California: Brooks/Cole Publishing Co., 1983.

Bengston, V., and J. Treas. "The changing family context of mental health and aging." In J. E. Birren and R. B. Sloane, eds., *Handbook of Mental Health and Aging.* Englewood Cliffs, New Jersey: Prentice Hall, 1980, pp. 400–428.

Bennett, R., and J. Eckman. "Attitudes toward aging: a critical examination of recent literature and implications for future research." In C. Eisdorfer and M. P. Lawton, eds., *The Psychology of Adult Development and Aging.* Washington, D.C.: American Psychological Association, 1973, pp. 575–597.

Berezin, M.A. "Psychodynamic considerations of aging and the aged: An overview." In S. Steury and M. L. Blank, eds., *Readings in Therapy with Older People.* Rockville, Maryland: National Institute of Mental Health, U.S. Department of HEW, No. (ADM 77-409), 1977.

Berger, R. and Federico, R. *Human Behavior. A Social Work Perspective.* New York: Longman, Inc., 1982.

Berkman, L. "Assessment of social networks and social support in the elderly." *Journal of the American Geriatric Society,* 31 (December 1983), pp. 743–749.

Berrien, F. *General and Social Systems.* New Brunswick, New Jersey: Rutgers University Press, 1968.

Biegel, D.; B. Shore; and E. Gordon. *Building Support Networks for the Elderly.* Beverly Hills, California: Sage Publications, 1984.

Biestek, Felix B. *The Casework Relationship.* Chicago, Illinois: Loyola University, 1957.

Binstock, R. "Aging and the future of American politics." *Annals of the American Academy of Political and Social Science,* Vol. 415.

Birren, J. E. "Principles of research on aging." In J. E. Birren, ed., *The Handbook of Aging and the Individual.* Chicago, Illinois: University of Chicago Press, 1959. (*Abridged in Middle Age and Aging.* B. Neugarten, ed. Chicago, Illinois: The University of Chicago Press, 1968.)

Birren, J. E. "The concept of functional age, theoretical background." *Human Development,* 12 (1969), pp. 214–215.

Birren, J. E., and V. J. Renner. "Research on the psychology of aging: principles and experimentation." In J. E. Birren and K. W. Schaie, eds., *Handbook of the Psychology of Aging.* New York: Van Nostrand Reinhold Company, 1977.

Birren, J.E., and V. J. Renner. "Concepts and issues of mental health and aging." In J. E. Birren and R. B. Sloane, eds., *Handbook of Mental Health and Aging.* Englewood Cliffs, New Jersey: Prentice-Hall, 1980.

Birren, J.E., and R.B. Sloane (eds.) *Handbook of Mental Health and Aging.* Englewood Cliffs, New Jersey: Prentice-Hall, Inc., 1980.

Birren, J.E., and D. Woodruff. "Human Development Over the Life-Span Through Education." In P. Baltes and K. Schaie, eds., *Life-Span Developmental Psychology: Personality and Socialization.* New York: Academic Press, 1973.

Blenkner, M. "The normal dependencies of aging." In R. A. Kalish, ed., *The Dependencies of Old People.* (Occasional Papers in Gerontology, vol. 6.) Ann Arbor, Michigan and Wayne State University, Detroit: Institute of Gerontology, 1969.

Blenkner, M. "Social work and family relationships in later life with some thoughts on filial maturity." In E. Shanas and G. E. Streib. eds., *Social Structure and the Family.* Englewood Cliffs, New Jersey: Prentice-Hall, 1965.

Bloom, B. L. "Definition aspect of the crisis concept." *Journal of Consulting*

Psychology, American Psychological Association, 27, No. 6 (1963), pp. 498–502.

Bloom, M., "Interviewing the ill aged." The Gerontologist, 2(4) (1971), pp. 294–299.

Bloom, M. Configurations of Human Behavior. New York: Macmillan Publishing Co., 1984.

Boszormenyi-Nagy, I., and G. Spark. Invisible Loyalties. New York: Harper and Row, 1973.

Bowen, M. "Aging: A symposium." The Georgetown Medical Bulletin, 30, No. 3 (1971), pp. 4–27.

Brink, T. L. Geriatric Psychotherapy. New York: Human Services Press, 1979.

Brody, E., "The aging family." The Gerontologist, No. 6 (1966), pp. 201–206.

Brody, E. "Aged parents and aging children." In P. Ragan, ed., Aging Parents. Los Angeles, California: University of Southern California Press, 1979.

Brody, E. "Women in the middle and family help to older people." The Gerontologist, 21 (1981), pp. 471–480.

Brody, E. "Parent care as a normative family stress." Donald P. Kent Memorial Lecture presented at the 37th Annual Scientific Meeting of the Gerontological Society of America. San Antonio, Texas, November 18, 1984.

Brody, E., Mental and Physical Health Practices of Older People. New York: Springer Publishing Company, 1985.

Brody et al. "Planning for the Long-Term Support/Care System: The Array of Services to be Considered." Region III Center for Health Planning, 7 Benjamin Franklin Parkway, Philadelphia, Pennsylvania, June 1979.

Brody, E.; S.W. Poulshock; and C. Masciocchi. "The family caring unit: A major consideration in the long-term support system." The Gerontologist, 18 (1978), pp. 556–561.

Bromley, D.B. "Approaches to the study of personality changes in adult life and old age." In A. D. Isaacs and F. Post, eds., Studies in Geriatric Psychiatry. Rochester, New York: 1978.

Buckley, W. Sociology and Modern Systems Theory. Englewood Cliffs, New Jersey: Prentice Hall, 1967.

Burgess, W. "The family in a changing society." American Journal of Sociology, III (May 1948).

Burnside, I.M. (ed.) Working with the Elderly. Group Process and Techniques. North Scituate, Massachusetts: Duxbury Press, 1978.

Butler, R.N. "The life review: An interpretation of reminiscence in the aged." Psychiatry, 26 (1963), pp. 65–76.

Butler, R.N. "Directions in psychiatric treatment of the elderly: Role of perspectives of the life cycle." Gerontologist, 9, No. 2 (1969), pp. 134–138.

Butler, R.N. "Toward a psychiatry of the life-cycle: Implications of sociopsychologic studies of the aging process for the psychotherapeutic situation." In A. Simon and L. Epstein, eds., Aging in Modern Society. Washington, D.C.: The American Psychiatric Association, 1968, pp. 233–248.

Butler, R.N. Why Survive? Being Old in America. New York: Harper and Row, 1975.

Butler, R.N., and M. Lewis. Aging and Mental Health, Positive Psychological Approaches. St. Louis, Missouri: C. V. Mosby Co., 1973.

Butler, R.N., and M. Lewis. Sex After Sixty. A Guide for Men and Women for their Later Years. New York: Harper & Row, 1976.

Cain, L. "The growing importance of legal age in determining the status of the elderly." The Gerontologist, 14 (1974), pp. 167–174.

Carr, A.C. "Bereavement as a relative experience." In B. Schoenberg et al., eds., Bereavement: Its Psychosocial Aspect. New York: Columbia University Press, 1975.

Carter, E.A., and M. McGoldrick. "The family life cycle and family therapy." In E. Carter and M. McGoldrick, eds., The Family Life Cycle: A Framework for Family Therapy. New York: Gardner Press, Inc., 1980.

Cartwright, Dorwin P., and Alvin F. Zander (eds.). Group Dynamics: Research and Theory. New York: Harper and Row, 1960.

Center for Studies of the Mental Health of the Aging. "Research Update on Alzheimer's Disease—1984." Rockville, Maryland: U.S. Department HHS–NIMH, 1984.

Clark, N., and W. Rakowski. "Family caregivers of older adults: Improving helping skills." The Gerontologist, 23, No. 6 (1983), pp. 637–642.

Coe, R.M. "Professional perspectives on the aged." The Gerontologist, 7 (1967), pp. 114–119.

Cohen, G.D. "Mental health services and the elderly: needs and options." In S. Steury and M. L. Blank, eds. Readings in Therapy with Older People. Rockville, Maryland: National Institute of Mental Health, U.S. Department of HEW, No. (ADM 77–409), 1977.

Cohen, G.D. Fact Sheet: Depression in the Elderly. Rockville, MD: U.S. Department of HEW, NIMH, 1980.(a)

Cohen, G.D. Fact Sheet: Senile Dementia (Alzheimer's Disease). Rockville, MD: U.S. Department HEW-NIMH, 1980. (b)

Cohen, G.D. "The mental health professional and the Alzheimer patient." Hospital and Community Psychiatry, 35 (February 1985), pp. 115–122.

Cohen, P.M. "A group approach for working with families of the elderly." The Gerontologist, 23, No. 3 (1983), pp. 248–250.

Cohler, B. "Autonomy and interdependence in the family of adulthood: A psychological perspective." The Gerontologist, 23 (1983), pp. 33–39.

Collins, G. "First portrait of the very old: Not so frail." The New York Times, Thursday, January 3, 1985.

Comfort, A. "Sexuality in later life." In J. E. Birren and R. B. Sloane, eds., Handbook of Mental Health. Englewood Cliffs, New Jersey: Prentice-Hall, Inc., 1980.

Cook, A.S. Contemporary Perspectives on Adult Development and Aging. New York: MacMillan, 1983.

Corby, N., and R. Solnick. "Psychosocial and physiological influences on sexuality in the older adult." In J. E. Birren and R. B. Sloane, eds., Handbook of Mental Health. Englewood Cliffs, New Jersey: Prentice-Hall, Inc., 1980.

Cottrell, S. "Interpersonal interaction and the development of the self." In A. Goslin, ed., Handbook of Socialization Theory and Research. Chicago, Illinois: Rand McNally College Publishing Co., 1969.

Craik, F.I.M. "Age differences in human memory." In J. E. Birren and K. W. Schaie, eds., Handbook of the Psychology of Aging. New York: Van Nostrand Reinhold, 1977.

Crandall, R.C. Gerontology—A Behavioral Science Approach. Reading, Massachusetts: Addison-Wesley, 1980.

Crook, T. "Geriatric psychopharmacology update." Rockville, Maryland: Center for Studies of the Mental Health of the Aging, NIMH, 1983, pp. 6–8. Reprint from Tomorrow's Pharmacist 4, 1 (January 18, 1982).

Crook, T. "Antidementia Drugs." NCDEU Updates, Vol. 19. Rockville, Maryland: Center for Studies of the Mental Health of the Aging, NIMH, 1983, pp. 69–71.

Daatland, S.O. "Care systems." *Aging and Society*, 3 (March 1983), pp. 1–21.

Deasy, L. *Persons and Positions*. Washington D.C.: The Catholic University of America Press, Inc., 1969.

Dell, P., and H. Goolishian. "Order through fluctuation, and evolutionary epistemology for human systems." Paper presented at the Annual Scientific Meeting of the A. K. Rice Institute, Houston, Texas, March 1979.

Dickstein, L.S., and S.J. Blatt. "Death concern, futurity and anticipation." *Journal of Consulting Psychology*, 30, No. 1 (1966), pp. 11–17.

Diggory, J.C., and D.Z. Rothman. "Values destroyed by death." *Journal of Abnormal and Social Psychology*, 63 (1961), pp. 205–210.

Donaldson, P.J. "Denying death: A note regarding some ambiguities in the current discussion." *Omega*, 3, No. 4 (1972), pp. 285–290.

Dowd, J., and V.L. Bengtson. "Aging in minority populations: An examination of the double jeopardy hypothesis." *Journal of Gerontology*, 33, No. 3 (1978), pp. 427–436.

Duke University Center for the Study of Aging. *Multidimensional Functional Assessment: The OARS Methodology*, 2nd ed. Durham, North Carolina: Duke University, 1978.

Ebersole, P.E. "Establishing reminiscing groups." In I. M. Burnside, ed., *Working with the Elderly: Group Process and Techniques*. North Scituate, Massachusetts: Duxbury Press, 1978, p. 233.

Eckstein, R., and R.S. Wallerstein. *The Teaching and Learning of Psychotherapy*, 2nd ed. New York: International University Press, 1972.

Eisdorfer, C. "Dementias: A challenge for bio-psycho-social study and intervention." Paper presented (on Tape 1-122A) at the Conference on Aging and the Dementias, Rockefeller University, New York, October 24, 1984. (Available through Conference Copy Incorporated, 1671 East 16th Street, Brooklyn, New York 11229.)

Elwell, F., and A. Maltbie-Crannell. "The impact of role loss upon coping resources and life satisfaction of the elderly." *Journal of Gerontology*, 36 (March 1981), pp. 223–232.

Erikson, E. *Childhood and Society*. New York: Norton, 1950.

Erikson, E. *Insight and Responsibility*, 2nd ed. New York: Norton, 1964.

Eyde, D.R., and J. Rich. *Psychological Distress in Aging: A Family management Model*. Rockville, Maryland: Aspen Publications, 1983.

Federal Council on Aging, *Public Policy and the Frail Elderly*. Washington D.C.: U.S. Department Health Education Welfare Office of Human Development Services, December, 1978.

Feifel, H., and A.B. Branscomb. "Who's afraid of death?" *Journal of Abnormal Psychology*, 81, No. 3 (1973), pp. 283–288.

Feldman, F.L. and F.H. Scherg, *Family Social Welfare*. New York: Atherton, 1967.

Ferreira, A.J., and W.D. Winter. "Family interaction and decision making." *Archives General Psychiatry*, 13 (1965), pp. 213–233.

Finkel, S.I.; E. Stein; N. Miller; I. Cameron; S. Hontela; and C. Eisdorfer. "Special perspectives on treatment planning for the elderly." In American Psychiatric Association, *Treatment Planning in Psychiatry*, Washington, D.C.: APA, 1982, pp. 379–433.

Fischer, J. *Effective Casework Practice: An Eclectic Approach*. New York: McGraw-Hill, 1978.

Fiske, M. "Tasks and crisis of the second half of life: The interrelationship of commitment, coping and adaptation." In J.E. Birren and R.B. Sloane, eds., *Handbook of Mental Health and Aging*. Englewood Cliffs, New Jersey: Prentice-Hall, Inc., 1980.

Fleming, J., and T. Benedek. *Psychoanalytic Supervision*. New York: Grune and Stratton, 1966.

Freed, A.O. "The family agency and the kinship system of the elderly." *Social Casework*, 56 (December 1975), pp. 579–586.

Freud, S. "Thoughts for the time on war and death: Our attitudes toward death." *Collected Papers*, Vol. 4. London: Hogarth Press, 1925, pp. 304–317.

Freud, S. "Group psychology and the analysis of the ego." In *The Standard Edition of the Complete Psychological Works of Sigmund Freud*, Vol. 18. London: Hogarth Press, 1953, pp. 69–143.

Freud, S. *Introductory Lectures on Psychoanalysis*. New York: Norton, 1920 (rev. ed. 1966).

Freudenberger, H.J. "Staff burn-out." *Journal of Social Issues*, 30 (1974), pp. 159–165.

Gafford, L.S., and V. Gates. "Genograms, ECO-maps, and structured outlines: Clients and students working together on psychosocial assessments." Presented at the 29th Annual Program Meeting of the Council of Social Work Education, March 14, 1983.

Gaitz, C., and P. Baer. "Diagnostic assessment of the elderly: A multi-functional model." *The Gerontologist*, Part I (Spring 1970), pp. 47–52.

Garfinkel, R. "The reluctant therapist." *The Gerontologist*, 15, No. 2 (1975), pp. 136–137.

Garrett, A. "Historical survey of the evolution of casework." In C. Kasius, ed., *Principles and Techniques of Casework*. New York: Family Service Association of America, 1950, pp. 393–411.

Germain, C.B. (ed.). *Social Work Practice: People and Environments*. New York: Columbia University Press, 1979.

Giddings, F.H. *Theory of Socialization*. London: The Macmillan Company, 1897.

Glenwick, D., and S. Whitbourne. "Beyond despair and disengagement: A transactional model of personality development in later life." In M. Bloom, ed., *Life Span Development*. New York: MacMillan, 1980.

Gluck, N.R.; E. Dannefer; and K. Milea. "Women in families." In M. McGoldrick and E. A. Carter, eds., *The Family Life Cycle: A Framework for Family Therapy*. New York: Gardner Press, 1980.

Goldenberg, I., and H. Goldenberg. *Family Therapy: An Overview*. Monterey, California: Wadsworth Press, 1980.

Goldfarb, A.I. "Group therapy with the old and aged." In H. I. Kaplan and B. J. Sadock, eds., *Comprehensive Group Psychotherapy*. Baltimore, Maryland: Williams & Wilkins Co., 1971.

Goldfarb, A.I. "Psychiatry in geriatrics." Reprinted in S. Steury and M.L. Blank, eds., *Readings in Psychotherapy with Older People*. Washington, D.C.: U.S. Department of HEW-NIMH, 1977, pp. 73–181.

Goldfarb, A.I. and J. Sheps. "Psychotherapy of the aged." *Psychosomatic Medicine* 16, No. 3 (May–June 1954). (Reprinted in S. Steury and M.L. Blank, eds., *Readings in Psychotherapy with Older People*. Washington, D.C.: U.S. Department of HEW-NIMH, 1977, pp. 182–192.)

Goldfarb, A.I., and H. Turner. "Psychotherapy of the aged: II. Utilization and effectiveness of 'brief' therapy." *American Journal of Psychiatry*, 109, No. 12 (1953), pp. 245–251.

Goldstein, H. *Social Work Practice: A Unitary Approach.* Columbia, South Carolina: University of South Carolina Press, 1973.

Gordon, E. *Living with an Elderly Parent. The Effects on the Family.* A literature review. Jerusalem: Research Department, The Ministry of Labour and Social Affairs, 1981.

Gouldner, A.W. "Norm of reciprocity." *American Sociological Review*, 25 (June 1960), pp. 161–178.

Granick, S. "Psychologic assessment technology for geriatric practice." *Journal of the American Geriatric Society*, 31, No. 12 (1983), pp. 728–742.

Green, J. *Cultural Awareness in the Human Services.* Englewood Cliffs, New Jersey: Prentice-Hall, 1982.

Greene, R. "Life Review and the Use of Photographs in Family Therapy." National Association of Social Workers Professional Symposium, San Diego, California, 1977.

Greene, R., "Bubba and Zehdah—Part of the Family Tree or Out on a Limb?" Grossingers, New York, Conference on Jewish Communal Workers, May 1978.

Greene, R. "Families and the nursing home social worker." *Social Work in Health Care*, 1, No. 3 (Spring 1982), pp. 57–67. (a)

Greene, R. "Life review: A technique for clarifying family roles in adulthood." *The Clinical Gerontologist*, 2 (Winter 1982), pp. 59–67. (b)

Greene, R. "Step on a crack, break an old man's back: Learning assignments for social work students in the field of aging." *Journal of Geriatrics and Gerontology Education*, 1983.

Greene, R. "Ageism, death anxiety and the caseworker." *Journal of Social Service Research*, 7, No. 1 (Fall 1984). (a)

Greene, R. "The use of long-term care resources in an ethnic community." *The Gerontologist*, 24 (October 1984), p. 307. (b)

Greene, R. "Cross-cultural communications with diverse ethnic and minority elderly." *Continuing Education for Gerontological Careers*, Washington, D.C.: Council on Social Work Education, 1985. (a)

Greene, R. "Managing countertransference in social work with the aged." *Journal of Gerontological Social Work*, 1985. (b)

Greene, R.; E. Fleshner; G. Kraft; and M. Rafner. "Managing countertransference issues in therapy with the aged." *The Gerontologist*, Special Issue, 24 (October 1984), p. 307.

Gross, N.C.; S. Ward; and W. McEachern. *Explorations in Role Analysis: Studies of the School Superintendency Role.* New York: Wiley, 1967.

Group for the Advancement of Psychiatry. *The Field of Family Therapy*, VII, 78 (March 1970).

Guerin, P.J., and E.G. Pendagast. "The evaluation of family system and genogram." In P. J. Guerin, ed., *Family Therapy and Practice.* New York: Gardner, 1976.

Gurland, B.J. "The assessment of the mental health status of older adults." In J. E. Birren and R. B. Sloane, eds., *Handbook of Mental Health and Aging.* Englewood Cliffs, New Jersey: Prentice-Hall, Inc., 1980.

Gurland, B.; J. Copeland; L. Sharpe; M. Kelleher; J. Kuriansky; and E. Simon. "Assessment of the older person in the community." *International Journal of Aging and Human Development*, 8, No. 1 (1977–78), pp. 1–8.

Gurland, B; J. Kuriansky; L. Sharpe; R. Simon; P. Stiller; and P. Birkett. "The comprehensive assessment and referral evaluation (CARE): Rationale, development and reliability." *International Journal of Aging and Human Development*, 8, No. 1 (1977–78), pp. 9–42.

Guyton, A.C. *Basic Human Physiology: Normal Function and Mechanisms of Disease*. Philadelphia, Pennsylvania: Saunders, 1977.

Haley, J. "A review of the family therapy field." In J. Haley, ed., *Changing Families*. New York: Grune and Stratton, 1971.

Haley, J. "Family therapy." In C. Sager and H. S. Kaplan, eds., *Progress in Group and Family Therapy*. New York: Brunner/Mazel Publishers, 1972.

Haley, J., and L. Hoffman, *Techniques of Family Therapy*. New York: Basic Books, Inc. 1967.

Hall, A.D., and R.E. Fagen. "Definition of system." In W. Buckley, ed., *Modern Systems Research for the Behavioral Scientist*. Chicago, Illinois: Aldine, 1968.

Hamilton, G. *Theory and Practice of Social Casework*. New York: Columbia University Press, 1951.

Hartford, M.E. "The use of group methods for work with the aged." In J. E. Birren and R. B. Sloane, eds., *Handbook of Mental Health and Aging*. Englewood Cliffs, New Jersey: Prentice-Hall, 1980, pp. 806–826.

Hartford, M., and R. Parsons. "Groups with relatives of dependent older adults." *The Gerontologist*, 22, No. 4 (August 1982), pp. 394–398.

Hartman, A., and J. Laird. *Family-Centered Social Work Practice*. New York: The Free Press, 1983.

Hartmann, H. *Ego Psychology and the Problem of Adaptation*. New York: Columbia University Press, 1974.

Havens, B., and E. Thompson. *Agency Needs Assessment Schedule*. Winnipeg, Canada: Department of Health and Community Services, Province of Manitoba, 1976.

Havighurst, R.J. *Development Tasks and Education*. New York: David McKay Co., Inc., 1972.

Havighurst, R.J. *Human Development and Education*. New York: Longman, 1948.

Havighurst, R.J. "History of developmental psychology: Socialization and personality development through the life span." In P. B. Baltes and K. W. Schaie, eds., *Life-Span Developmental Psychology*. New York: Academic Press, 1973.

Hendricks, J., and C.D. Hendricks. *Aging in Mass Society*. Cambridge, Massachusetts: Winthrop, 1977.

Herman, S. "Somatoform Disorders." In A.D. Whanger and A. C. Myers, eds., *Mental Health Assessment and Therapeutic Intervention with Older Adults*. Rockville, Maryland: Aspen, 1984.

Herr, J., and J. Weakland. *Counseling Elders and Their Families*. New York: Springer, 1979.

Hess, R. and G. Handel. *Family Worlds*. Chicago: University of Chicago Press, 1959.

Heyman, K., and H. Polansky. "Social casework and community services for the aged." In E. W. Busse and E. Pfeiffer, eds., *Behavior and Adaptation in Late Life*. Boston: Massachusetts: Little, Brown, 1977.

Hill, R. "Generic features of families under stress." In H. J. Parad, ed., *Crisis Intervention: Selected Readings*. New York: Family Service Association of America, 1965.

Hoelter, J.W. "Multidimensional treatment of fear of death." *Journal of Consulting and Clinical Psychology*, 47, No. 5 (1979), pp. 996–999.

Hollis, F. "The psycho-social approach to the practice of casework." In R. Roberts and R. Nee, eds., *Theories of Social Casework*. Chicago, Illinois: University of Chicago Press, 1970.

Hollis, F., *Casework: A Psycho-Social Therapy*. New York: Random House, 1964 (Rev. ed., 1972).

Hollis, F. "Social casework: The psychosocial approach." In J.B. Turner, ed.-in-chief, 17th Issue, *The Encyclopedia of Social Work*. Washington, D.C.: NASW, 1977, pp. 1300–1308.

Holzberg, C.S. "Ethnicity and aging: Anthropological perspectives on more than just the minority elderly." *The Gerontologist*, 22, No. 3 (1982), pp. 240–257.

Huttman, E.D. *Social Services for the Elderly*. New York: The Free Press, 1985.

Ingersoll, B., and L. Goodman. "History comes alive: Facilitating reminiscence in a group of institutionalized elderly." *Journal of Gerontological Social Work*, 2, No. 4 (Summer 1980), pp. 305–320.

Iowa Gerontology Model Project. *A Training Manual on the Components of a Community-Based Long-Term Care System for the Elderly*. Davenport, Iowa: The University of Iowa, 1982.

Jackson, D.; J. Riskin; and V. Satir. "A method of analysis of a family interview." In D. Jackson, ed., *Communication, Family and Marriage*, Palo Alto, California: Science and Behavior Books, Inc., 1970. Vol. 1.

Jackson, J.J. "The blacklands of gerontology." *Aging and Human Development*, 2 (1971), pp. 156–172.

Jahoda, M. "Criteria for positive mental health." In W.S. Sahakian, ed., *Psychopathology Today*. Itasca, Illinois: F. E. Peacock, 1979, pp. 23–28.

James, W. *The Principles of Psychology*. New York: Holt, 1890.

Janchill, M.P. "Systems concepts in casework theory and practice." *Social Casework*, 15, No. 2 (February 1969).

Jewish Family and Children's Service of Baltimore. *Getting the Best from the Rest. An Experiential Handbook for Senior Adult Groups*. Baltimore, Maryland: Jewish Family and Children's Service of Baltimore, 1978.

Johnson, C.L., and D. Catalano. "Childless elderly and their family supports." *The Gerontologist*, 21, No. 6, (1981), pp. 610–618.

Journal of American Medical Association. "Attempts to vanquish Alzheimer's disease intensify, take new paths." *Medical News*, 251, No. 14 (April 13, 1984), pp. 1805–1814.

Jung, C.G. *Man and His Symbols*. London: Aldus Books, 1964.

Kadushin, A. *The Social Work Interview*. New York: Columbia University Press, 1972.

Kadushin, A. *Supervision in Social Work*. New York: Columbia University Press, 1976.

Kahn, R.L., Goldfarb, I. Pollack, M. "The evaluation of geriatric patients following treatment." In P. H. Hoch and J. Zubin, eds., *Evaluation of Psychiatric Treatment*. New York: Grune and Stratton, 1964.

Kalish, R.A. *Late Adulthood: Perspectives on Human Development*. Monterey, California: Brooks/Cole Publishing Co., 1982.

Kane, R.L., and R.A. Kane. "Alternatives to institutional care of the elderly: Beyond the dichotomy." *The Gerontologist*, 20, No. 3 (1980), pp. 249–259.

Kane, R.L., and R.A. Kane *Assessing the Elderly: A Practical Guide to Management*. Lexington, Massachusetts: D.C. Heath, 1981.

Kantor, D., and W. Lehr. *Inside the Family*. San Francisco, Washington, London: Jossey-Bass Publications, 1975.

Kapust, L.R. "Living with dementia: The ongoing funeral." *Social Work in Health Care*, 7, No. 4 (Summer 1982), pp. 79–91.

Kastenbaum, R. *Growing Old*. New York: Harper & Row, 1979.

Kastenbaum, R., and P.T. Costa. "Psychological perspectives on death." *Annual Review of Psychology*, 28 (1977), pp. 225–249.

Kastenbaum, R.; V. Derbin; P. Sabatini; and S. Artt. "'The ages of me': Toward personal and interpersonal definitions of functional aging." *International Journal of Aging and Human Development*, 3 (1972), pp. 197–212.

Katz, S. "Assessing self-maintenance: Activities of daily living, mobility, and instrumental activities of daily living." *Journal of the American Geriatric Society*, 31, No. 12 (1983), pp. 721–727.

Keesing, F.M. *Cultural Anthropology*. New York: Rinehart and Co., Inc. 1958.

Keller, J.F., and G.A. Hughston. *Counseling the Elderly*. New York: Harper and Row, 1981.

Kidwell, I.J., and A. Booth. "Social distance and intergenerational relations." *The Gerontologist* (1977), pp. 412–420.

Kilty, K.M., and A. Feld. "Attitudes toward aging and toward the needs of older people." *Journal of Gerontology*, 31, No. 5 (1976), pp. 586–594.

Kimmel, D.C. "Life history interviews of aging gay men." *International Journal of Aging and Human Development*, 10 (1979–1980), pp. 239–248.

Kluckhohn, C. "Values and value orientations." In Talcott Parsons and Edward A. Shils, eds., *Toward Theory of Action*. Cambridge, Massachusetts: Harvard University Press, 1951.

Kogan, N. "Attitudes toward old people: The development of a scale and an examination of correlates." *Journal of Abnormal and Social Psychology*, 62 (1961), pp. 44–54.

Kogan, R. *Personality Theory*. Englewood Cliffs, New Jersey: Prentice-Hall, Inc., 1976.

Konopka, G. *Social Group Work: A Helping Process*. Englewood Cliffs, New Jersey: Prentice-Hall, 1963.

Kübler-Ross, E. "What is it like to be dying?" *American Journal of Nursing*, 71, No. 1 (1971), pp. 54–61.

Lang, N. "Some defining characteristics of the social work group: Unique social form." In S. L. Abels and P. Abels, eds., *Social Work with Groups Proceedings 1979 Symposium*. Louisville, Kentucky: Committee for the Advancement of Social Work with Groups, 1981, pp. 18–50.

Langs, R. *The Technique of Psychoanalytic Psychotherapy*. New York: Jason Aronson, 1974, Vol. II.

Larson, E.; B.V. Reifler; C. Comfield; and G. Cohen. "Evaluating elderly outpatients with symptoms of dementia." *Hospital and Community Psychiatry*, 35 (May 1984), pp. 425–428.

Lawton, M.P.; M. Moss; M. Fulcomer; and M.A. Kleban. "A research and service-oriented multilevel assessment instrument." *Journal of Gerontology*, 37, 1 (1982), pp. 91–99.

Lederer, W.J., and D. Jackson. *The Mirage of Marriage*. New York: Norton, 1968.

Lerea, L.E., and B.F. Li Mauro. "Grief among healthcare workers: A comparative study." *Journal of Gerontology*, 37, No. 5 (1982), pp. 604–608.

Lester, D. "Re-examination of Middleton's data: Sex differences in death attitudes." *Psychological Reports*, 27 (1970), p. 516(a).

Levande, D. "Family theory as a necessary component of family therapy." *Social Casework*, 57 (May 1976), pp. 291–295.

Likert, R. *New Patterns of Management.* New York: McGraw Hill, 1961.

Likert, R. *The Human Organization, Its Management and Value.* New York: McGraw Hill, 1965.

Linton, R. *The Study of Man.* New York: Appleton-Century Craft, 1936.

Little, V.C. "Assessing the needs of the elderly: State of the art." *International Journal of Aging and Human Development*, 11 (1980), pp. 65–76.

Livingston, P.B., and C.N. Zimet. "Death anxiety, authoritarianism and choice of speciality in medical students." *The Journal of Nervous and Mental Disease*, 140, No. 3 (1965), pp. 222–229.

Livson, N. "Developmental dimensions of personality: A life-span formulation." In P. B. Baltes and K. W. Schaie, eds., *Life-Span Developmental Psychology.* New York: Academic Press, 1973.

Long, I. "Human sexuality and aging." *Social Casework*, 5, No. 4 (April 1976), p. 239.

Lowenthal, M., and C. Haven. "Interaction and adaptation: Intimacy as a critical variable." *American Sociological Review*, 33, No. 1 (February 1968), pp. 139–147.

Lowy, L. *Social Work with the Aging: The Challenge and Promise of the Later Years.* New York: Harper and Row 1979.

Lowy, L. "Social group work with vulnerable older persons: A theoretical perspective." *Social Work with Groups*, 5, No. 2 (1983), pp. 21–32.

Lowy, L. *Social Work with the Aging.* New York: Longman, Inc., 1985.

McAdoo, H. *Black Families.* Beverly Hills, California. Sage, 1981.

Mace, N.L., and P.V. Rabins. *The 36-Hour Day.* Baltimore, Maryland: Johns Hopkins University Press, 1981.

McTavish, D.G. "Perceptions of old people: A review of research methodologies and findings." *The Gerontologist* (Winter 1971), Part II, pp. 90–108.

Maddi, S. *Personality Theories.* Homewood, Illinois: Dorsey Press, 1972.

Marcus, L. "Communication concepts and principles." In F. J. Turner, ed., *Social Work Treatment.* New York: The Free Press, 1974, pp. 372–399.

Maslach, C. "Burned-out." *Human Behavior* (September 1976), pp. 16–22.

Mattason, M.A. "Organic mental disorders." In A. D. Whanger and A.C. Myers, eds., *Mental Health Assessment and Therapeutic Interventions with Older Adults*, Rockville, Maryland: Aspen, 1984, pp. 41–60.

Merton, R.K. *Social Theory and Social Structure.* Glencoe, Illinois: The Free Press, 1957.

Mindel, C., and R. Wright. "Satisfaction in multigenerational households." *Journal of Gerontology*, 37 (1982), pp. 483–489.

Minuchin, S. *Families and Family Therapy.* Cambridge, Massachusetts: Harvard University Press, 1974.

Moriwaki, S., and F. Kobata. "Ethnic minority aging." In D. Woodruff and J. Buren, eds., *Aging. Scientific Perspectives and Social Issues.* Monterey, California: Brooks/Cole Publishing Co., 1975.

Munson, C.E. (ed.). *Social Work Supervision: Classic Statements and Critical Issues.* New York: The Free Press, 1979.

Mutschler, P. "Factors affecting choice of and perseveration in social work with the aged." *The Gerontologist*, 11 (1971), pp. 231–241.

National Association of Social Workers. *NASW Standards and Guidelines for Social Work Case Management for the Functionally Impaired.* Silver Spring, Maryland: NASW, 1984.

National Association of Social Workers. *Encyclopedia of Social Work*. Washington D.C.: NASW, 1977.

National Institute on Aging and National Institute of Mental Health. *The Older Woman: Continuities and Discontinuities*. Workshop Report. Washington, D.C.: U.S. Department of Health, Education and Welfare, 1978.

National Urban League. *Double Jeopardy, the Older Negro in America Today*. New York: National Urban League, 1964.

Nelson, L.D., and C.C. Nelson. "A factor analytic inquiry into the multidimensionality of death anxiety." *Omega*, 6, No. 2 (1975), pp. 171–178.

Neugarten, B. (ed.). *Middle Age and Aging*. Chicago, Illinois: University of Chicago Press, 1968.

Neugarten, B. "Personality and aging." In J. E. Birren and K. W. Schaie, eds., *The Psychology of Aging*. New York: Van Nostrand Reinhold Co., 1977.

Neugarten, B., and N. Datan. "Sociological perspectives on the life cycle." In P. B. Baltes and K. W. Schaie, eds., *Life-Span Developmental Psychology*. New York: Academic Press, 1973.

Neugarten, B; J. Moore; and J. Lowe. "Age norms, age constraints and adult socialization." In B. Neugarten, ed., *Middle Age and Aging*. Chicago, Illinois: University of Chicago Press, 1968.

Newman, B., and P. Newman. *Development Through Life: A Psychosocial Approach*. Revised ed. Homewood, Illinois: The Dorsey Press, 1979.

Northen, H. *Clinical Social Work*. New York: Columbia University Press, 1982.

Nuessel, F. "The language of ageism." *The Gerontologist*, 22 (1982), pp. 273–276.

Nydegger, C. "Family ties of the aged in cross-cultural perspective." *The Gerontologist*, 23 (1983), pp. 26–32.

Office of the Assistant Secretary for Planning and Evaluation, Department of Health and Human Services. *Alzheimer's Disease. A Report to Congress*. Washington, D.C.: U.S. Government Printing Office, February 1985.

Otten, A. "The oldest old." *The Wall Street Journal*. Monday, July 30, 1984, Vol. CCIV, No. 20, White Oak, Maryland, p. 1.

Palmore, E. "Facts on aging: A short quiz." *The Gerontologist*, 17 (1977), pp. 315–320.

Palmore, E. "Facts on aging quiz: A review of findings." *The Gerontologist*, 20 (1980), pp. 669–672.

Parsons, T. *The Social System*. New York: The Free Press, 1951.

Patterson, R.D. "Grief and depression in old people." In S. Steury and M.L. Blank, eds., *Readings in Psychotherapy with Older People*. Rockville, Maryland: U.S. Department of HEW, NIMH, 1977.

Peck, R. "Psychological developments in the second half of life." In B. Neugarten, ed., *Middle Age and Aging*. Chicago, Illinois: University of Chicago Press, 1968.

Perlman, H. H. *Social Casework. A Problem-Solving Process*. Chicago, Illinois: University of Chicago Press, 1957.

Perlman, H. H. *Persona: Social Role and Personality*. Chicago, Illinois: University of Chicago Press, 1968.

Perlman, H. H. *Persona*. Chicago, Illinois: The University of Chicago Press, 1974.

Pfeiffer, E. "Psychopathology and social pathology." In J. E. Birren and K. W. Schaie, eds., *Handbook of Psychology of Aging*. New York: Van Nostrand Reinhold Co., 1977.

Pincus, A. "Toward a developmental view of aging for social work." *Social Work*, 12 (July 1967), pp. 33–41.

Posner, W. "Basic issues in casework with older people." *Social Casework*, 42, Nos. 5–6 (1961), pp. 234–239.

Pratt, H. "*I Remember. . . .*" Alexandria, Virginia: Mental Health Association, 1981.

Prisuta, R. "Gender/ethnicity differences in self-reported social indicators among the elderly." Special Issue, *The Gerontologist*, 24 (October 1984), p. 261.

Rappaport, R. "Normal crisis, family structure and mental health." *Family Process*, 2, No. 1 (1963), pp. 68–80.

Reedy, M.N. "Personality and aging." In D. S. Woodruff and J. E. Birren, eds., *Aging: Scientific Perspectives and Social Issues*. Monterey, California: Brooks/Cole Publishing Company, 1975.

Reynolds, B. "Can social work be interpreted to a community as a basic approach to human problems?" *The Family*, 13 (1933), pp. 336–342.

Rhodes, S.L. "A developmental approach to the life cycle of the family." In M. Bloom, ed., *Life Span Development*. New York: Macmillan, 1980. [Originally in *Social Casework*, 58 (May 1977), pp. 301–311, Family Service Association of America.]

Richmond, M. *Social Diagnosis*. New York: Russell Sage Foundation, 1917.

Richmond, M. *What is Social Casework? An Introductory Description*. New York: Russell Sage Foundation, 1922.

Riley, M.H.; A. Foner; B. Hess; and M. Toby. "Socialization for the middle and later years." In D. A. Goslin, ed., *Handbook of Socialization, Theory and Research*. Chicago, Illinois: Rand McNally College Publishing Co., 1969.

Riskin, J. "Methodology for studying family interaction." In D. Jackson, ed., *Communication, Family and Marriage*, Palo Alto, California: Science and Behavior Books, Inc., 1968, Vol. 1 pp. 251–260.

Robinson, B. "Validation of a caregiver strain index." *Journal of Gerontology*, 38, No. 3 (1983), pp. 344–348.

Robinson, B., and N. Thurner. "Taking care of the aged parents: A family cycle transition." *The Gerontologist*, 19, No. 6 (1979), pp. 586–593.

Rodgers, R.H. "Three facets of family dynamics." In C. E. Munson, ed., *Social Work with Families, Theory and Practice*. New York: The Free Press, 1980.

Rogers, C., and B. Stevens. *Person to Person: The Problem of Being Human*. New York: Pocket Books, 1967.

Rogers, C.R. " The necessary and sufficient condition of therapeutic personality change." *Journal of Consulting Psychology*, 21 (1957), pp. 95–103.

Rogers, C.R. *The Therapeutic Relationship and Its Impact*. Madison, Wisconsin: University of Wisconsin Press, 1967.

Rommeweit, R. *Social Norms and Roles*. Minneapolis, Minnesota: University of Minnesota Press, 1955, as discussed by Dorwin P. Cartwright and Alvin F. Zander, eds., in *Group Dynamics: Research and Theory*. New York: Harper and Row, 1960.

Ross, H. *How to Develop a Neighborhood Family*. Miami, Florida: University of Miami, 1978.

Rossman, I. "Comprehensive functional assessment." *Journal of the American Geriatric Society*, 31, No. 12 (December 1983), pp. 763–765.

Rubenstein, L. "The clinical effectiveness of multidimensional geriatric assessment." *Journal of the American Geriatric Society*, 31, No. 12 (1983), pp. 758–762.

Sarbin, T.R. "Notes on the transformation of social identity." In L. M. Roberts, S. Greenfield, and H. Miller, eds., *Comprehensive Mental Health*. Madison, Wisconsin: University of Wisconsin Press, 1968.

Satir, V. *People Making*. Palo Alto, California: Science and Behavior Books, Inc., 1972.

Schaie, K. W., and J. P. Schaie. "Clinical assessment and aging." In J. E. Birren and K. W. Schaie, eds., *Handbook of the Psychology of Aging*. New York: Van Nostrand Reinhold Co., 1977.

Schell, R., and E. Hall. *Developmental Psychology Today*. New York: Random House, 1979.

Schmidt, M. "Interviewing the old old." *The Gerontologist* 15, No. 6 (1975), pp. 544–553.

Schonfield, D. "Who is stereotyping whom and why?" *The Gerontologist*, 22 (1982), pp. 267–272.

Schwartz, D. "Helping the worker with countertransference." *Social Work*, (1978), pp. 204–209.

Seltzer, M., and R. Atchley. "The concept of old: Changing attitudes and sterotypes." *The Gerontologist*, 1 (1971), pp. 226–230.

Shanas, E. "Family responsibility and the health of older people." *Journal of Gerontology*, 15 (1960), pp. 408–411.

Shanas, E. "The family as a social support system in old age." *The Gerontologist*, 19 (1979), pp. 169–174.

Sheffield, E.A. *The Social Case History*. New York: Russell Sage Foundation, 1924.

Sherman, S.N. "Family services: Family treatment." In *Encyclopedia of Social Work*. Washington, D.C.: Encyclopedia of Social Work, 1977, pp. 435–440.

Sherman, S.N. "Family therapy." In F. J. Turner, ed., *Social Work Treatment: Interlocking Theoretical Approaches*. New York: The Free Press, 1974, pp. 457–494.

Shibutani, T. *Society and Personality*. Englewood Cliffs, New Jersey: Prentice-Hall, Inc., 1961.

Shulman, L. *The Skills of Helping Individuals and Groups*. Itasca, Illinois: Peacock Publishers, Inc., 1979.

Silverstone, B., and A. Burack-Weiss. "The social work function in nursing homes and home care." *Journal of Gerontological Social Work*, 5, No. 1/2 (Fall/Winter, 1982), pp. 7–33.

Silverstone, B., and A. Burack-Weiss. *Social Work Practice with the Frail Elderly and their Families*. Springfield, Illinois: Charles C. Thomas, 1983.

Simon, R. "Family life cycle issues in the therapy system." In E. A Carter and M. McGoldrick, eds., *The Family Life Cycle: A Framework for Family Therapy*. New York: Gardner Press, 1980.

Solomon, M. "A developmental conceptual premise for family therapy." *Family Process*, 12 (1973), pp. 179–188.

Soniat, B. "Aging Minority Content in Direct Service Curriculum." Paper presented at the Council on Social Work Education, New York, March 1982.

Soyer, D. "Reverie on working with the aged." *Social Casework*, 50, No. 5 (1960), pp. 291–294.

Spark, G. "Grandparents and intergenerational family therapy." *Family Process*, 13 (June 1974), pp. 225–237.

Spark. G., and E. Brody. "The aged are family members." In C. Sager and H. Kaplan eds., *Progress in Group and Family Therapy*. New York: Brunner Mazel Publishers, 1972, pp. 712–725.

Spiegel, J.P. "The resolution of role conflict within the family." In N. W. Bell and E. F. Vogel, eds., *Modern Introduction to the Family*. New York: The Free Press, 1968, rev. ed.

Stagner, R. *Psychology of Personality*. New York: McGraw-Hill Book Co., Inc., 1965.

Stamm, I. "Family therapy." In F. Hollis, eds., *Casework: A Psycho-social Therapy*. New York: Random House, 1972.

Stanfeld, S. "Conceptions of role and ego in contemporary psychology." In J. Rohrer and M. Sherif, eds., *Social Psychology at Crossroads*. New York: Harper Bros., 1961.

Stern, K.; J.M. Smith; and M. Frank. "Mechanism of transference and countertransference in psychotherapeutic and social work with the aged." *Journal of Gerontology*, 8 (1953), pp 328–332.

Strean, H.S. "Role theory, role models and casework: Review of the literature and practice applications." *Social Work*, 12, No. 2 (April 1967), pp. 77–88.

Strean, H.S. "The application of role theory to social casework." In H. S. Strean, ed., *Social Casework Theories in Action*." Metuchen, New Jersey: Scarecrow Press, 1971.

Sumner, A.C. "The psychology of aging." In L. Navran and J. Becker, eds., *Preparatory Course for the National and State Licensing Examinations in Psychology*. Berkeley, California: Association for Advanced Training in the Behavioral Sciences, 1982.

Sussman, M. "Relationships of adult children with their parents in the United States." In E. Shanas and G. Streib, eds., *Social Structure and the Family: Generational Relationships*, Englewood Cliffs, New Jersey: Prentice-Hall, Inc., 1965, pp. 62–92.

Sussman, M.B., and L. Burchinal. "Kin family network: Unheralded structure in current conceptualizations of family functioning." *Marriage and Family Living*, 24 (1962), pp. 231–240.

Szasz, T. "Repudiation of the medical model." In W. S. Sahakian, ed., *Psychopathology Today*. Itasca, Illinois: F. E. Peacock Publishers, Inc., 1979, pp. 42–49.

Taeuber, C.M. *America in Transition: An Aging Society*. Washington, D.C.: U.S. Department of Commerce, Bureau of the Census, Current Population Reports, Special Studies Series, P-23, No. 128, September 1983.

Tager, R.M. "Physical assessment." In S. H. Zarit, ed., *Aging and Mental Disorders*. New York: The Free Press, 1980.

Taulbee, L.R. " Reality orientation: A therapeutic group activity for elderly persons." In I. M. Burnside, ed., *Working with the Elderly: Group Process and Techniques*. North Scituate, Massachusetts: Duxbury Press, 1978.

Taylor, E.B. *Primitive Cultures*. New York: Brentano, 1924.

Temerlin, M. "The inability to distinguish normality from abnormality." In W. S. Sahakian, ed., *Psychopathology Today*. Itasca, Illinois: F. E. Peacock Publishers, Inc., 1979, pp. 23–28.

Terkelson, G. "Toward a theory of the family cycle." In E. A. Carter and M. McGoldrick, eds., *The Family Life Cycle: A Framework for Family Therapy*. New York: Gardner Press, 1980.

Thomas H. "Personality and adjustment to aging." In J. E. Birren and H. B. Sloane, eds., Handbook of Mental Health and Aging. Englewood Cliffs, New Jersey: Prentice-Hall, 1980.

Thorson, J. A. " Variations in death anxiety related to college students' sex, major field of study, and certain personality traits." Psychological Reports, 40 (1977), pp. 857–858.

Tibbits, C. "Can we invalidate negative stereotypes of aging?" The Gerontologist, 19 (1979), pp. 10–20.

Torren, N. Social Work: The Case of a Semiprofession. Beverly Hills, California: Sage Publications, 1972.

Towle, C. Common Human Needs. Washington, D.C.: U.S. Government Printing Office, 1945.

Treas, J. "Family support systems for the aged: Some social and demographic considerations." The Gerontologist, 17 (1977), pp. 486–491.

Troll, L.E. "The family of later life: A decade review." Marriage and Family Living, 33 (1971), pp. 263–290.

Turner, F. Social Work Treatment. New York: The Free Press, 1974.

Turner, H. "Use of the relationship in casework treatment of aged clients." Social Casework, 42, Nos. 5–6 (1961), pp. 245–251.

Turner, R. H. "Roletaking, role standpoint and reference group behavior." In J. Biddle and J. Thomas, eds., Role Theory Concepts and Research. New York: Wiley, 1961.

U.S. Department HEW Office of Human Development Services, Federal Council on Aging. Public Policy and the Frail Elderly. Washington, D.C., December 1978.

U.S. Senate Special Committee on Aging and American Association of Retired Persons. Aging America. Trends and Projections. Washington, D.C. 1984.

Walsh, F. "The family in later life." In E. A. Carter and M. McGoldrick, eds., The Family Life Cycle: A Framework for Family Therapy. New York: Gardner Press, Inc., 1980.

Ward, R. The Aging Experience: An Introduction to Social Gerontology. New York: Lippincott, 1979. (a)

Ward, R. "The never married in later life." Journal of Gerontology, 34, 6, (November 1979), pp. 861–869 (b)

Wascow, M., and M. Loeb. "Sexuality in nursing homes." In R. L. Solnick, ed., Sexuality and Aging. Los Angeles, California: The University of Southern California Press, 1978.

Wasser, E. "The sense of commitment in serving older persons." Social Casework, 45, No. 8 (1964), pp. 443–449.

Weg, R.B. "Changing physiology of aging: Normal and pathological." In D. S. Woodruff and J. E. Birren, eds., Aging—Scientific Perspectives and Social Issues. Monterey, California: Brooks/Cole, 1975.

Weinstein, S.E. "Senior Medical Student Attitudes Toward Death and Dying." Unpublished Doctoral dissertation, University of Maryland, 1978.

Weisman, A. On Dying and Denying. New York: Behavioral Publications, 1972.

Weisman, S., and R. Shusterman. "Remembering, reminiscing and life reviewing in an activity program for the elderly." Concern (December–January 1977), pp. 22–26.

Whanger, A.D., and A.C. Myers. Mental Health Assessment and Therapeutic Intervention with Older Adults. Rockville, Maryland: Aspen, 1984.

White House Conference on Aging. Report of the Technical Committee on

Family Social Services and other Support Systems. Washington, D.C.: Department of Health and Human Services, 1981.

White, W. *A Systems Response to Staff Burn Out.* Rockville, Maryland: HCS, Inc., 1978.

Wilensky, H.L. *Intellectuals in Labor Unions: Organizational Pressures of Professional Roles.* Glencoe, Illinois: The Free Press, 1956.

Wilensky, H., and J. Barmack. "Interests of doctoral students in clinical psychology in work with older adults." *Journal of Gerontology,* 21 (1966), pp. 410–414.

Wilson, B. and N. Moffat. "Running a memory group." In B. A. Wilson and N. Moffat, eds., *Clinical Management of Memory Problems.* Rockville, Maryland: Aspen Systems Corporation, 1984.

Wolff, K. "Personality type and reaction toward aging and death." *Geriatrics,* 21 (1966), pp. 189–192.

Wynne, L. "Some guidelines for exploratory conjoint family therapy." In Jay Haley, ed., *Changing Families.* New York: Grune & Stratton, 1971.

Zarit, S. *Aging and Mental Disorders.* New York: The Free Press, 1980.

Zarit, S. "Group and family intervention." In S. Zarit, ed., *Aging and Mental Disorders.* New York: The Free Press, 1980.

Zarit. S.; K. Reever; and J. Bach-Peterson. "Relatives of the impaired elderly: Correlates of feelings of burden." *The Gerontologist,* 20, No. 6 (1980), pp. 649–655.

Facts on Aging—A Short Quiz[a]

T[†] F 1. The majority of old people (past age 65) are senile (i.e., defective memory, disoriented, or demented).

T F 2. All five senses tend to decline in old age.

T F 3. Most old people have no interest in, or capacity for, sexual relations.

T F 4. Lung capacity tends to decline in old age.

T F 5. The majority of old people feel miserable most of the time.

T F 6. Physical strength tends to decline in old age.

T F 7. At least one tenth of the aged are living in long-term care institutions (i.e., nursing homes, mental hospitals, homes for the aged).

T F 8. Aged drivers have fewer accidents per person than drivers under 65.

T F 9. Most older workers cannot work as effectively as younger workers.

T F 10. About 80% of the aged are healthy enough to carry out their normal activities.

T F 11. Most old people are set in their ways and unable to change.

T F 12. Old people usually take longer to learn something new.

T F 13. It is almost impossible for most old people to learn new things.

T F 14. The reaction time of most old people tends to be slower than the reaction time of younger people.

T F 15. In general, most old people are pretty much alike.

T F 16. The majority of old people are seldom bored.

T F 17. The majority of old people are socially isolated and lonely.

T F 18. Older workers have fewer accidents than younger workers.

T F 19. Over 15% of the U.S. population is now age 65 or over.

T F 20. Most medical practitioners tend to give low priority to the aged.

T F 21. The majority of older people have incomes below the poverty level (as defined by the federal government).

T F 22. The majority of old people are working or would like to have some kind of work to do (including housework and volunteer work).

T F 23. People tend to become more religious as they age.

T F 24. The majority of old people are seldom irritated or angry.

T F 25. The health and socioeconomic status of older people (compared to younger people) in the year 2000 will probably be about the same as now.

---

[a]E. Palmore, "Facts on Aging: A Short Quiz," *The Gerontologist*, 17 (1977), pp. 315–320.

[b]Even-numbered statements are true; odd-numbered statements are false.

[†]Circle "T" for True, "F" for False.

Appendix B
Nathan Kogan's "Old People" Scale[a,b]

	1	2	3	4	5	6
1. It would probably be better if most old people lived in residential units with people of their own age.	___	___	___	___	___	___
2. It would probably be better if most old people lived in residential units that also housed younger people.	___	___	___	___	___	___
3. There is something different about most old people; it's hard to figure out what makes them tick.	___	___	___	___	___	___
4. Most old people are really no different from anybody else; they're as easy to understand as younger people.	___	___	___	___	___	___
5. Most old people get set in their ways and are unable to change.	___	___	___	___	___	___
6. Most old people are capable of new adjustments when the situation demands it.	___	___	___	___	___	___
7. Most old people would prefer to quit work as soon as pensions or their children can support them.	___	___	___	___	___	___
8. Most old people would prefer to continue working just as long as they possibly can rather than be dependent on anybody.	___	___	___	___	___	___
9. Most old people tend to let their homes become shabby and unattractive.	___	___	___	___	___	___
10. Most old people can generally be counted on to maintain a clean, attractive home.	___	___	___	___	___	___

	1	2	3	4	5	6

11. It is foolish to claim that wisdom comes with old age. ___ ___ ___ ___ ___ ___

12. People grow wiser with the coming of old age. ___ ___ ___ ___ ___ ___

13. Old people have too much power in business and politics. ___ ___ ___ ___ ___ ___

14. Old people should have more power in business and politics. ___ ___ ___ ___ ___ ___

15. Most old people make one feel ill at ease. ___ ___ ___ ___ ___ ___

16. Most old people are very relaxing to be with. ___ ___ ___ ___ ___ ___

17. Most old people bore others by their insistence on talking about the "good old days." ___ ___ ___ ___ ___ ___

18. One of the most interesting and entertaining qualities of most old people is their accounts of their past experiences. ___ ___ ___ ___ ___ ___

19. Most old people spend too much time prying into the affairs of others and giving unsought advice. ___ ___ ___ ___ ___ ___

20. Most old people tend to keep to themselves and give advice only when asked. ___ ___ ___ ___ ___ ___

21. If old people expect to be liked, their first step is to try to get rid of their irritating faults. ___ ___ ___ ___ ___ ___

22. When you think about it, old people have the same faults as anybody else. ___ ___ ___ ___ ___ ___

23. In order to maintain a nice residential neighborhood, it would be best if too many old people did not live in it. ___ ___ ___ ___ ___ ___

	1	2	3	4	5	6
24. You can count on finding a nice residential neighborhood when there is a sizable number of old people living in it.	____	____	____	____	____	____
25. There are a few exceptions, but in general most old people are pretty much alike.	____	____	____	____	____	____
26. It is evident that most old people are very different from one another.	____	____	____	____	____	____
27. Most old people should be more concerned with their personal appearance; they're too untidy.	____	____	____	____	____	____
28. Most old people seem to be quite clean and neat in their personal appearance.	____	____	____	____	____	____
29. Most old people are irritable, grouchy, and unpleasant.	____	____	____	____	____	____
30. Most old people are cheerful, agreeable, and good humored.	____	____	____	____	____	____
31. Most old people are constantly complaining about the behavior of the younger generation.	____	____	____	____	____	____
32. One seldom hears old people complaining about the behavior of the younger generation.	____	____	____	____	____	____
33. Most old people make excessive demands for love and reassurance.	____	____	____	____	____	____
34. Most old people need no more love and reassurance than anyone else.	____	____	____	____	____	____

[a]Matched pairs of statements: Odd numbers, negative; even numbers, positive; compare positive/negative mean scores.

[b]N. Kogan, "Attitudes Toward Old People: The Development of a Scale and an Examination of Correlates," *Journal of Abnormal and Social Psychology*, 62 (1961), pp. 44–54.

Appendix C
Supervisor's Checklist for Supervisory Conference[a]

Conditions for Supervisory Conference
1. Am I punctual for the supervisory conference?
2. Do I accept telephone calls or allow other distractions?
3. Am I supportive of the worker?

The conference
1. Did I prepare for the conference? For example, did I read the process recording or listen to worker's tape?
2. Did I plan teaching objectives for this conference?
3. Did I clarify the terms used during the discussion, such as what was meant by "neglect," "ambivalence," etc.?
4. Did I adequately reconstruct the case situation with the worker?
5. Did I offer alternative ways to deal with the client situation?
6. Did I consider the learning style in the use of learning resources, such as role play, role reversal, mirroring techniques, observation of experienced worker, etc.?
7. Did I help the worker express how he or she felt about the client situation, the agency, or any policies?
8. Did I act defensively in any discussion related to agency policy?
9. Was I ready to assume my responsibility, or my mediating role, in handling an administrative issue brought by the worker?
10. Did I seek feedback from the worker about our supervisory transactions?
11. Did I evaluate what was gained through the conference and review worker's progress up to this point?
12. If the worker is displaying learning problems, have I clearly stated these and have they been adequately discussed so that the worker understands his or her status?
13. Did we begin to plan during the conference the focus of our next conference and our mutual responsibilities for preparing?

General considerations
1. Do I assume my responsibility in meeting at least weekly with the worker?
2. Do I view these supervisory conferences as the worker's entitlement?
3. Am I aware of my ethical responsibilities in terms of providing adequate administrative, teaching, and supportive help to the worker?
4. Do I recognize the responsibility of the supervisor and administrator to help workers avoid burnout?

---

[a]Reproduced with permission from Sister M. J. Vincentia, The Catholic University of America, Washington, D.C.

Appendix D
Practitioner's Checklist for Supervisory Conference[a]

Conditions for supervisory conference

1. Am I punctual for the supervisory conference?
2. Do I accept calls or allow other distractions?
3. Am I responsive to the supervisor?

The conference

1. Did I prepare for the conference? For example, did I prepare (process) a recording, a tape, or a paragraph of interview dialogue?
2. Did I plan learning objectives for this conference?
3. Did I raise terms for clarification during discussion?
4. Did I adequately reconstruct the case situation for the supervisor?
5. Did I seek alternative ways of handling the client situation?
6. Was I open to participate in various learning resources?
7. Did I try to express how I felt about the client situation, the agency, or any policies?
8. Was I inappropriately aggressive about agency policy?
9. Was I ready to assume my responsibility in handling any administrative issues brought by the supervisor?
10. Did I seek/give feedback from the supervisor about our supervisory transactions?
11. Did we evaluate what was gained through the conference and review my progress up to this point?
12. Have I dealt "squarely" with learning problems?
13. Did we begin to plan for our next conference with mutual responsibility?

[a]Modified with permission from preceding Supervisor's Checklist, Appendix C.

Subject Index

A